BANKING ON FLEXIBILITY

For Maureen, Pat, Carole and Darrow

Banking on Flexibility

A comparison of flexible employment in retail banking in Britain and France

JACQUELINE O'REILLY

Avebury

Aldershot · Brookfield USA · Hong Kong · Singapore · Sydney

Published by
Avebury
Ashgate Publishing Limited
Gower House
Croft Road
Aldershot
Hants GU11 3HR
England

Ashgate Publishing Company
Old Post Road
Brookfield
Vermont 05036
USA

British Library Cataloguing in Publication Data

O'Reilly, Jacqueline
  Banking on Flexibility: Comparison of
  Flexible Employment in
  Retail Banking in Britain and
  France
  I. Title
  331. 11913321

ISBN 1-85628-549-9

Typeset at
Wissenschaftszentrum Berlin
Reichpietschufer 50
Berlin D-10785
Germany

Printed and bound by Athenæum Press Ltd.,
Gateshead, Tyne & Wear.

Contents

Figures and tables

Abbreviations

AFB	Association Française des Banques
ANPE	Agence Nationale Pour l'Emploi
ASTMS	Association of Scientific, Technical and Managerial Staff
BACS	Bankers Automated Clearing System
BGSU	Barclays Group Staff Union
BIFU	Banking, Insurance and Finance Union
BOG	Bank Officers Guild
CFDT	Confédération Française Démocratique du Travail
CFTC	Confédération Française des Travailleurs Chrétiens
CGC	Confédération Générale des Cadres
CGT	Confédération Générale du Travail
CHAPS	Clearing House Automated Processing System
CNP	Commission National Partaire
CNPF	Conseil National du Patronat Français
CWIP	Clerical Work Improvement Programme
DOT	Dictionary of Occupational Titles
FO	Force Ouvrière
FTC	Fixed-term contract
FTE	Full-time equivalent
INSEE	Institut National de la Statistique et des Etudes Economique
LFS	Labour Force Survey
MSF	Management, Science and Finance union
NUBE	National Union of Bank Employees
TUC	Trades Union Congress
WIRS	Workplace Industrial Relations Survey

Acknowledgements

A great many people have helped me in the process of conducting the research and writing this book. Without all of their support this task would never have been possible. First, I must thank Duncan Gallie for supervising the research for my D.Phil at Nuffield College, Oxford. His thoughtful and meticulous criticisms have attempted to teach me how to master and sharpen the arguments, although I still have a long way yet to go. Whilst in France I benefited from the support and supervision of Odile Benoit-Guilbot, who together with Henri Mendras kindly welcomed me at the Observatoire Sociologie du Changement in Paris. I would also like to thank the following people who have read and commented on my written work at various stages: Rosemary Crompton, Colin Crouch, Colette Fagan, Alan Felstead, Jay Gershuny, John Goldthorpe, Abigail Gregory, Linda Hantrais, Anthony Heath, John MacInnes, Patrick McGovern, Susan McRae, Nigel Meager, Sigrid Quack, Jill Rubery, Günther Schmid, Andrew Scott, Arndt Sorge, May Tam, Nina Wakeford, and Richard Whitley. The staff at Nuffield College, who work so hard to make it such a comfortable place to study, especially Ann Bowes and Elaine Herman. And, in particular I want to thank Chris Dagleish in the library for the friendship and help he has given me over the years. Thanks also goes to Charles Harvey at Royal Holloway College, London University, for giving me the time and encouragement to finish this work. I have to thank Andrew Cox and Jack Hayward, for encouraging me to go on to study for a doctorate in the first place. In Paris "Le Bande du Quatre" opened my eyes to the vast and rich terrain of French sociology. I am particularly grateful for the insights into French society provided in their methodological approach of "faire du terrain". I would like to thank Marco Oberti, Patrick LeGalès, Jean-Vincent Phrisch, Jean-Hugh, Joelle Basso, and Martine Fontnoy for helping me translate my questionnaire, and for the fun we had together while I was in France.

This research would never have been possible without the help and co-operation of the women employees, and the managers of the banks who patiently answered my questions, and encouraged me in my research. I would especially like to thank Mr R. Davies in Britain, and Madame E. Goujard in France. I would also like to thank the trade unionists who helped me with this research: Pierre Gendre at Force Ouvrière, Alain Bonnet at CFDT, Roger Almeras and Joslyn Potavin at the CGT, Jo Stuart, Jon Robinson and Bernadette Fisher at BIFU and Iain Maclean and Steven Weeks at BGSU.

I am grateful to The Leverhulme Trust for providing me with a scholarship which allowed me to spend 18 months in France. I would particularly like to thank Miss Bennett for her efficient administration. Financial support was also provided by the ESRC, the Peter Kirk Studentship, the Zaharoff Scholarship and Nuffield College. A grant from The Nuffield Foundation allowed me to up-date this work on a research visit to Paris. A grant from the DAAD also allowed me to spend time writing at the WZB in Berlin in 1993.

I want to thank my Mum and Dad, Maureen and Pat, for their love and support. This book is dedicated to them because they have always believed in the value of education. Without pushing me, they have always supported me to do what I wanted. By their own example they showed me that the things which seem so distant and unobtainable can sometimes be achieved with determination, hard work and most of all the support of the ones you love. I want to thank Carole, my sister and closest friend, for keeping me sane over the years, through her sceptical criticism of academia and the fun we have shared together, supporting each other in our different projects. And, especially for Carole as she puts into practice what I only try and theorise about. My thanks to them extends beyond this dedication. Finally, and most of all, I want to thank Darrow. He has been very important in encouraging and reassuring me through the difficulties and successes. Sharing his love, enthusiasm, and sense of humour have made the time spent writing this book a real pleasure.

Finally I must accept responsibility for the interpretation

and results that are presented in these pages. One of the problems of re-writing a thesis has been the realisation of how much more I need to understand and include in my analysis. Nevertheless, the time comes when I have to draw a halt, and hope that I will be able to pick up and continue on the themes that I have only just started to begin to understand. I hope that these limitations do not cause too much frustration for the reader, and I hope you will find something of interest in these pages. For those who are embarking on a similar project, I wish you good luck, until the day arrives when you are also writing your acknowledgements; eventually everybody arrives, at their own pace, the most important thing is to enjoy what you are doing.

Jacqueline O'Reilly,
June 1994, WZB Berlin.

Introduction

1. Introduction

Discussion on restructuring, flexibility, multiskilling and atypical workers were found peppered through studies of industrial organisation during the 1980s and early parts of the 1990s. Concern with these ideas reflected an acknowledgement of changing paradigms in industrial organisation. At the heart of these debates has been a concern over the extent to which these changes have actually occurred. Has there been a universal move "in search of flexibility" (Boyer 1986; Atkinson & Meager 1986); or, have these changes only occurred in a piece-meal and *ad hoc* manner, if at all? (Pollert 1991; Gilbert et al. 1992; Hunter et al. 1993). Disputes over the extent of a universal change have drawn on evidence from selective case studies, or from national data sets in attempts to grapple with these issues. Unfortunately, systematic, comparative and empirical studies of these changes have been thin on the ground (exceptions to this are for example Rodgers and Rodgers 1989; Gregory 1989; OECD 1986). The aim of the research presented here is to redress this imbalance. This book seeks to examine the debates on labour flexibility from a cross-national comparative perspective. This examines employment practices both at the national level, and in the light of a detailed empirical study of the retail banking sector in Britain and France.

Contemporary concerns with labour flexibility have their roots in earlier debates in labour market theory. Neo-classical theorists attributed labour market differentials to the results of individuals investment in their 'human capital'. This was based on the assumption that pay reflected skills, and that personal

1

investment in training could improve an individual's labour market position. Doeringer and Piore in their classic work *"Internal Labor Markets and Manpower Analysis"* (1971) argued that firms constructed internal labour markets in order to achieve a particular type of worker. This approach shifted the emphasis away from individuals to the role of employers in structuring labour market opportunities. Later developments in dual labour market theory developed a diverse range of explanations for the differing employment status between workers. Initially the debates were concerned with identifying divisions in the size of companies, and their use of advanced technology. These factors were used to develop structural explanations for the divisions found in the labour market. Later revisions to these theories included the role of trade unions (Rubery 1978), the distinctions created by legal regulation (Berger & Piore 1980; Michon 1981), and managerial control strategies (Edwards 1979; Gordon, Edwards & Reich 1982) as agents of segmentation.

The interest in flexibility has widened and re-orientated the terms of these debates. On one hand, research has focused on the macro implications of increasing labour flexibility. On the other hand, greater attention has also been given to practices of employers within their firms. The work of Lui (1990) has marked a further turn in the literature by emphasising the affect of supply side preferences for flexible working patterns on the type of policies employers can effectively utilise. Hodson and Kaufman (1982) have argued that a more fruitful discussion of developments in the labour market can be developed from a perspective which emphasises the resources and vulnerability of the actors involved, rather than the static and structural approach of early theorists.

This book seeks to draw on these earlier debates and contemporary discussions in order to understand if, how and why employers have sought to develop labour flexibility. It is argued here that we need to go beyond one sided explanations focused solely on employers actions. A broader perspective, which situates employers behaviour within a social context, needs to be adopted. To show the relevance of this approach to the flexibility debates, which have largely focused on single country studies, this book explores the processes which affect labour market outcomes, and the opportunities and constraints which shape the way employers develop their policies from a comparative perspective. It examines the commercial, organisational and technological pressures that have emerged in the retail banking sector in recent years. It also looks at how patterns of female labour supply are constructed and how they vary in the two countries. It examines the affect of the industrial relations system, the system of education and training, and the role of government intervention to show how these factors shape the arena in which employers make decisions. This approach does not reduce effects to deterministic explanations, i.e. technology, or to the action of only one set of actors, i.e. employers. As a result, it can better account for the variety of strategies adopted by the different actors involved. This is particularly helpful when making cross-national comparisons. It allows us to account for the interaction of different structural constraints and the varied way in which these are managed and adapted by the social actors in each country.

2. Outline of the book

This book aims to examine theoretical issues raised by the flexibility debates by means of an empirical study of the retail banking sector in Britain and France. The questions this book seeks to address are the following. Have the banks in each country been developing flexible employment strategies? Are these practices similar? And, how does the different economic, social and institutional context in each country affect the way employers utilise labour?

Part One outlines the context of these discussions. Chapter 1 examines the theoretical and methodological issues pertaining to comparative cross-national research. It also outlines the research design and methodology adopted to address these questions. Chapter 2 situates this study in the context of earlier and contemporary theoretical debates concerning firms, labour markets and labour flexibility. Chapter 3 compares the organisational structure of the retail banking sector in each country. This examines how changing product markets, automation and organisational restructuring vary between the two countries, and how these changes have implications for the way employers identify their labour requirements.

Part Two examines flexibility in practice. Chapter 4 analyses the development of multi-skilling and functional flexibility. This identifies where employers have been looking to develop this policy and how employees have experienced change.

Is the use of functional flexibility related to a conscious policy on the part of employers to provide training and up-skilling, and has this development occurred in a similar way in both countries? Chapter 5 looks specifically at the use of temporary work as a method of using external workers. Chapter 6 examines and compares the rationales surrounding the use of subcontracting. Chapter 7 analyses the use of part-time work. What kinds of flexibility do these different contracts offer employers? What are the reasons employers resort to these contracts, and are they the same in each country?

Part Three sets these findings in a broader societal perspective. As these debates have focused exclusively on employers' behaviour, this section attempts to redress this bias. Chapter 8 will fill an important gap in the literature on part-time work and flexibility by examining the extent to which employers' policies are constrained by women's work preferences, at the same time how employers have been able to exploit requests for reduced working time in plans for organisational restructuring. This will examine the attitudes, qualifications and domestic situation of a comparable group of women employees in each country. Chapter 9 looks at the distinctive characteristics of industrial relations and labour regulation in each country. This analysis will examine how this impinges on the type of labour flexibility employers can successfully implement. Chapter 10 aims to synthesise these findings from the empirical study within a theoretical framework which can take account for the differentiated use of labour flexibility in each country. It is argued in this book that employers behaviour needs to be situated in a specific societal context, so as to avoid simplistic dichotomisation of employers rationales. Employers' labour strategy is negotiated and legitimised in relation to a wider group of social actors who have largely been ignored in previous debates. The existence of variability needs to be incorporated into any explanatory model and this can be done by recognising the resources and vulnerabilities of different actors, and how this affects the choices they make and their potential to formulate a strategy. At the same time we also need to understand the social construction of opportunities and constraints for all the social actors. The central argument developed in the chapters to follow rests on the claim that employers policies cannot be fully understood and explained without taking account of the social context in which they have been created.

1 Approaches to cross-national employment research

1. Introduction

A revived interest in cross-national comparative research has been stimulated in recent years by unexpected and radical economic and social changes. Few societies have been immune to these developments. Within Europe attempts to integrate and expand the European Union have generated intense political debates and conflicts. In central and eastern Europe the collapse of communist regimes has posed significant challenges for the future economic and political development of these regions. Further, competition from the Far East has continued to undermine Western capacity to adapt to changing markets, technology and working practices. Changes have also occurred in the nature of accepted social relations between men, women, families and different ethnic groups. Knowledge of these changes has been accelerated by technologically improved communications, travel and access to disposable income and leisure. These developments have fed into a general curiosity to understand the differences or similarities in the way we and others live.

Academic research has not been immune to these changes. The increasing number of books and journals with an international and comparative aspect has been a noticeable growth sector of the "intellectual industry". Despite the interest in "things foreign", thorough discussions of the theoretical and methodological issues involved in comparative research are often sadly neglected. The tendency has been for researchers to rush out and find a foreign collaborator, in order to apply for research funding. The attractions of comparative research should extend beyond the pleasures of flying visits to "exotic" foreign capitals, and encountering strangers who fulfil, or refute, our preconceived national assumptions and biases. For those concerned with serious academic research the key questions are: why do we want to conduct comparative research? Where, and how, do we begin to analyse neighbouring or distant societies? And, finally, how does this analysis inform theory?

Although contemporary developments have stimulated a revived interest in cross-national research, this is not a new field.[1]

> The use of systematic observation across societies as a basis for generalizing about human behaviour is as old as Herodotus (ca. 495-424 B.C.) and as new as data banks. (Warwick and Osherson 1973:3).

There are a variety of reasons why researchers embark on comparative projects. These can include simple curiosity, or a sense of affinity to a particular foreign culture; concern for the competitive success, or failure, of their own country in comparison to others; or concerns about inequality and possible social policy solutions. Two major factors which have stimulated an interest in this area have come from "managerial", and theoretical concerns.

Managerial motives for conducting cross-national research have been concerned with identifying "best practice". This can be seen from the recent fashion for Japanese working practices like Just-In-Time (JIT) and Total Quality Management (TQM). Subsequent attempts have been made to adopt and adapt these practices in Western organisations, with varying degrees of success (Ouchi 1981; Oliver and Wilkinson 1988; Garrahan and Stewart 1992; Pollert 1991). In social policy, concerns to identify "best practice" have also encouraged the use of cross-national comparisons. For example, several studies have been conducted on the effects of welfare benefits or child care provision in Scandinavia, the US, UK, France and other countries (Moss 1990; Morris 1990; Barrère-Maurisson et al. 1989; Schmid et al.1992; Reissert 1993; Bradshaw et al. 1993; Dex et al. 1993).

Empirical cross-national research has highlighted theoretical weaknesses in generalisations applied and exported to "foreign" cultures. Warwick and Osherson (1973) argue that,

> Relationships once assumed to be universal have been

6

shattered on the proving ground of the non-Western world. As a result there is now a more cautious and less grandiose attitude in theory construction, and a renewed quest for explanations that will stand the test of varying socio-cultural conditions. (1973:6)

The understandings developed from cross-national comparisons can be used to augment theory formulation. Nowak (1989) argues that the current crisis in social theory can be informed and improved by adopting such an inductive and exploratory approach to comparative research. One of the major values of such research is that it can challenge implicit assumptions that our own national system of organisation is the best, or only, way to organise. We can also recognise that the varied experience of industrialisation has had long-term influences on contemporary industrial organisation. These differences can lead us to raise questions about the causes and effects of different types of social structure and social action. This extends concern beyond the academic community, so that managerial and social science motives need not be exclusive.

Although both sets of motives can often inform each other, it is also important to recognise that the central focus of interest from each perspective varies. Managerial perspectives tend to seek normative and prescriptive solutions, whilst social science approaches are more interested in analytical methods and theoretical implications. However, each perspective can be mutually informative. Social science can inform managers why there are no "quick fix" solutions, whilst managerial concerns can, and are, focusing research agendas on pertinent contemporary issues.

The aim of this chapter is to take us on an exploration of the theories and methods pertaining to comparative research in industrial and organisational sociology, and theories related to management practice. First, it analyses the different theoretical approaches which have been used in cross-national studies. Second, it critically discusses the various research methods available to researchers. Finally, an outline is given of the rationale and framework of the research presented here; the theoretical implications developed throughout this book are discussed in more detail in chapter 10. This theoretical framework emerged during the process of conducting this research. It is intended that this should provide, not only a tool for conducting research in the future, but also as a conceptual framework which can allow us to account for the similarities and differences observed in the employment practices of different countries.

2. Theoretical approaches to comparative research

Cross-national research has been influenced by broader developments and debates in the field of social, political and economic thought. Comparative research was of interest to nineteenth and early twentieth century writers like Marx, Durkheim and Weber, who, according to Warwick and Osherson (1973:4-5), were influenced by classical evolutionist research. The concept of evolutionism when applied to social development suggested that societies pass through a similar series of universal and historical stages, as they become more 'civilised'. Despite coming from different political positions, these universalist theorists shared a similar set of basic underlying assumptions about the trajectory of human development.

However, the unilinear model of social evolution was challenged by anthropological research. Malinowski's functional analysis of single societies suggested that these societies were unique coherent entities. This implies that a society needs to be understood in its entirety. Such an approach is opposed to isolating particular characteristics, and comparing them across societies.[2] Instead greater emphasis is given to showing the relationship and development between different aspects of the society.

These differences of approach have underpinned disputes about universal and particular trends in social development. These conflicting traditions run deep and persist. Today debates in cross-national research are divided between those who emphasise differences and divergence, in contrast to those who focus on similarities and convergence. Writers who emphasise difference tend to take more account of the impact of culture. Those who stress universal trends often underplay cultural differences.

The concept of culture as a significant explanatory variable is a key concern in cross-national comparative research. However, this idea has received quite diverse theoretical treatment. Hill (1973) points out that the problems in comparative research stem from, the current status of the comparativist's major independent variable: cultural or societal heterogeneity. Clearly, the variable is N-dimensional, and comparative sociologists have not as yet agreed on the size of N, let alone on the conceptual nature of the dimensions that define N-space. (Hill 1973:459)

One of the problems in trying to conceptualise, and operationalise culture for empirical research is, as Casassus-Montero (1989) points out: *"Où faut-il chercher pour trouver l'explication des différences?"* Any analysis incorporating the impact of culture would need to include a comparison of the norms and values of a specific "culture"(Hofstede 1980), and/or the mechanisms or institutions transmitting these values, for example the family, the state, the education and training system, or the trade unions (Dore 1973; Gallie 1978 & 1983; Maurice et al 1982; Whitley 1991a and b). The implications this has for comparative, empirical research are potentially overwhelming (Grimshaw 1973:9; Tayeb 1988:42-3). Nevertheless, important contributions to the field of cross-national research have sought to grapple with these problems both at an intellectual and empirical level in relation to the theoretical framework they have developed and in terms of their research design, as will be seen in the following review of key examples of cross-national research.

2.1 Universal theories of convergence

Universal theories, although coming from different political perspectives, share a similar underlying theme: they assume a universal dynamic. The main contribution of these differing schools of thought to comparative research has been to argue that there are common, universally identifiable, pressures and trends working across all industrialised societies. Some of these early theories have been modified to accommodate empirical evidence which refuted the predicted universal pattern. Nevertheless, at the core of these theories is the assumption that generalisations can be made on the universal level applicable to all countries. Although, as Kerr (1983) points out, there are several universal theories on the issue of convergence, here we will focus on Marxism, Industrialism and Contingency theory because of their immediate concern with employment related issues.

2.1.1 From a Marxist perspective, the dynamic of capitalist society has been the relentless pursuit of private profits. This has entailed the exploitation and tendency to deskill workers through the introduction of technology, in order to extract surplus value from labour (Braverman 1974). The inherent class struggle between capitalists and workers either to reduce, or protect, wage rates and skill levels would be resolved in the ultimate socialist and then communist society. Marx, on the basis of his research of the Industrial Revolution in England argued that capitalism would develop as a universal phenomenon (Morgan 1990:195).[3] Such a perspective is predicated on the belief that although ruling elites may respond to the universal contradictions and pressures of capitalism in different ways, essentially their motivations are the same. Nevertheless, within Marxism a variety of approaches and interpretations have emerged (Schecter 1994). This is partly due to attempts to explain why societies have not developed in the way Marx prescribed, and the present state of Eastern and Central Europe bear empirical evidence to the weak predicatory claims of these theories.

Lane (1989:26-7) argues that Marxist concerns with capitalism as an international system has led them to make "grand sweep" generalisations. This has meant a relative neglect of "meso-level peculiarities",

> This methodological shortcoming of a narrowly Marxist analyses may be attributed to the fact that the actor and his/her perception and manipulation of organisational relations tends to disappear from sight. (Lane 1989:27)

Maurice et al. (1986:205-9) make a similar point when they criticise Marxist approaches for being "reductionist". Whilst developments in Marxist thought have allowed for a degree of autonomy amongst actors, ultimately productive relations are,

> determined by the forms of capital or its contradictions - that is in our view, by historical or national contingencies affecting the way the capitalist mode of production operates and reproduces itself. (Maurice et al. 1986:208)

Instead, Maurice et al. argue that capital can be influenced by other social and historical factors, not determined by capitalism alone. These factors affect the forms capitalist production takes.

Maurice et al. argue for the development of *"useful ways of thinking about the ways in which education and labor organisation influence wages."* (1986:208)

Nevertheless, some of the strengths which can be drawn from a Marxist approach are the emphasis on the concept of struggle and change. Societies and the social relations within them are dynamic, not static. The comparative work of Sisson (1987), although not essentially Marxist, is a good example of how a perspective of historical conflicts and compromises between elites and organised labour can be used to understand the varied traditions in contemporary industrial relations. The importance of acknowledging conflict and contradiction is also made by Sorge and Warner (1986) and Sorge (1994:3). Sorge argues for the development of a dialectical theory in the comparative study of employment relations and organisations.

> The notion of dialectical theory used to raise the hair of so-called positivist scholars, who considered it a misguided endeavour to tolerate confusion and arbitrariness, things which were thought of as unscientific. ... By trying to do full justice to real-world events, dialectical theory therefore displays an inherent tension between the ambition to reduce contradictions and the recognition that this has clear limits.(Sorge 1994:3)

Thus whilst Marxist approaches have tended to focus on universal generalisations concerning the determinants of capitalist organisation, recognition of conflicting interests and change are useful aspects which can be borrowed from these theories.

2.1.2 Industrialism presents a more conservative perspective on contemporary social development. This approach argues that technological innovation and increasing wealth lead to the universal adoption of similar working practices. The level of technological sophistication was seen as a determining factor shaping the characteristics of organisations. It was assumed that technological progress would occur along a single trajectory of development. These assumptions can be seen in the early work of Haribson et al. (1955). In their study of a steel plant in the US and W. Germany they identified several differences in the characteristics of the employees and in the organisation of work itself.[4] The authors acknowledged the influence of social

11

differences, for example in the education and training provided in each society. However, they argued that these differences would be minimised if both plants used similar technology. This conclusion was popularised in the later work of Haribson in collaboration with Kerr et al. (1960) *"Industrialism and Industrial Man"*.

Kerr (1983) states that one of the aims of this earlier collaborative work was to challenge the ideology that capitalist and communist societies were polar opposites. The theory of industrialism argues that there is an inherent logic to industrialism, regardless of the political context. *"Much of what happens to management and labour is the same regardless of auspices."* (Kerr 1983:18). Industrialism requires: a skilled and mobile workforce; large-scale production in large cities, together with political consensus for government intervention; a professional elite of managers; workforce participation in the benefits of industrialism and political acceptance of this system. This system is regulated by a web of rules (Kerr et al. 1960:33-46). Despite caveats to recognise the persistence of diversity, the tenor of evangelical universalism rings through,

> The empire of industrialism will embrace the whole world; and such similarities as it decrees will penetrate the outermost points of its sphere of influence, and its sphere comes to be universal. Not one, however, but several roads lead into this new and ultimate empire. (Kerr et al. 1960:46)

The key assumption in this work is that industrial societies present similar problems which can be resolved by similar solutions. As societies progress the differences, rooted in traditional practices and relationships would disappear. Productive technology acts as an intrinsic imperative forcing all societies in the direction of industrialism.

However, Lane (1989:22) argues that this perspective *"discounts the powerful impact of history."* Like Marxism, the industrialism approach assumes societies will cross a historical "threshold" before entering a new form of industrial order. But, as we hear frequently in the post-perestrokia period, attempts of former Eastern Bloc countries to cross this "threshold" are constrained by the historical and political baggage from their former experiences.

2.1.3 Contingency theory has developed to counter some of the weaknesses of industrialism. However, it too is intellectually rooted in the same implicit assumption of the unilinearity of industrial development. Contingency theory, unlike industrialism, is more limited in its scope: it has sought only to account for differences in business structures, rather than in whole societies. The central concern of this approach has been with the differences in organisational design and practices in relation to contingent factors like organisational size, the environment (Lawrence and Lorsch 1967), or the type of technology used (Woodward 1965 and 1970). The central plank of this theory rested on the argument that under a given set of conditions, or contingencies, it was possible to identify optimal organisational behaviour and structural solutions because external contingencies were potentially malleable.

The Aston School in Britain developed contingency theory in comparative research (Hickson et al. 1979). They explained the differences in organisations in relation to their "task environment" i.e. organisational size, the technology used, and dependency relations. Residual factors which could not be explained by these variables were accounted for in terms of culture. Culture was given to mean where a specific society was situated on a scale of being socially progressive. Culture was reduced to a single external variable, without being integrated into the analysis of other variables (See McMillan et al. 1973 for the first exposition of these theories, and Roberts 1970 for early criticisms of this approach). Lane (1989:24) argues that the success of this approach was due to the consistency of *some* results derived from standardised surveys in several countries.

However, as Tayeb (1988) and Lane (1989) both point out, this approach is very formalistic, focusing solely on organisational structures. Contingency theory is based on the premise that organisational success requires the optimal fit of an organisation's structure to its environment. However, Tayeb (1988:22-4) argues that this perspective raises several problems. There are inconsistencies in empirical findings and methodological weaknesses; the theory also suffers from an inherent reductionism and "theoretical ambiguity". For example, how does one isolate the organisational characteristics and structures which account for success? Also, it is not clear that managers are always capable of consciously adapting the structure of their organisation to achieve efficient and effective performance (see also the discussion on managerial strategy in chapter two).

This emphasis on formal structures neglects the influence of human action and informal relations (Sorge 1994). What is of interest is not necessarily the formal structures in themselves, but rather the way they are understood and interpreted by the people who occupy these spaces in different countries (Lane 1989:25; Hofstede 1980). Through their behaviour and values these people embody cultural differences.

> Contingency theorists see an approach from culture as complementary to their own in as far as they suggest that an explanation from culture might explain the varying magnitude of correlation coefficients i.e. of the mathematical value calculated for the relationship between a contingent factor and a structural property of an organisation. (Lane 1989:24)

However, intellectually this approach is rooted in the paradigm which assumes a unitary logic of action under a given set of circumstances. Contingencies in two or more organisations are examined and compared in isolation, without analysing the relationship between other phenomena (Tayeb 1988:23). Cultural approaches make more effort to analyze the relationship between different phenomena in the same context, in an attempt to identify the affect of culture on organisations. The difference between these two approaches reflects the deep run divisions in social science discussed earlier, between universalists and cultural relativists.

Contemporary developments in contingency theory, although less academic in style, can be seen in the populist work of Peters and Waterman (1982), and Peters (1992). They attempt to identify and prescribe recipes to achieve excellent companies. Unfortunately, some of the companies they awarded the laurels of excellence were seen floundering shortly after publication and public accolade. Even Peters (1992) admits the limitations of his earlier work,

> With the exaltation of IBM and more than one nod to GM, we implicitly endorsed the humongous American technocratic enterprise in general - the institutions that economist John Kenneth Galbraith and business historian Alfred Chandler had not so long before declared almost perfect instruments for achieving America's economic

manifest destiny. (Peters 1992:xxxi)

Peters excuses their previous misjudgments because they were the intellectual "off-spring" of Galbraith and Chandler. In admitting this, Peters unconsciously acknowledges the deep rooted influence of American culture on his own thinking. However, the effect of cultural specificity is not fully developed in his recent work. Despite recognition of global diversity, his prescription for *Liberation Management*' has a distinctively American tone: "Yo Fashion!", frenzy, speed, and, spider plant organisations! Despite much enthusiastic entreaty, American prescriptions may well be inappropriate, both at home and abroad because they lack a deep rooted sociological understanding of the cultural context in which organisations work.[5]

Overall, the contribution of these theories to comparative employment research has been to argue that it is possible to identify universal pressures or imperatives. These encourage successful organisations, under similar conditions, to adopt analogous practices. Despite the public success of many of these theories, in practice they have been found inadequate. Even if organisations experience comparable pressures it cannot be assumed that they will adopt identical strategies to deal with these. Change is frequently mediated by specific institutions and values which shape the national culture. In Marxism, Industrialism and Contingency theory the concept of culture is relegated to the periphery. The motors of change are universal: class dynamics, technological imperatives, or markets. However, these universal theories have been challenged by attempts to give greater weight to the role of culture. We will now turn to review some of these theories and their contribution to comparative research.

2.2 Cultural approaches

Approaches giving greater emphasis to the importance of culture have not been able to agree on how the concept of culture should be integrated in their theoretical and empirical framework (see Lammers and Hickson 1979; Maurice et al. 1986:Appendix; d'Iribarne 1991; Maurice 1992). Defining culture, as Hill (1973) points out, is a contentious issue. What is culture, and where do we begin to dissect it? Unless the concept is clearly specified, it can become a 'black box' into which all un-explained differences are allocated, willy nilly. Child and Tayeb (1982-3) argue that culture should be conceived as a substantively distinct field, separate from other social areas. Sorge (1982-3) on the other hand proposes that culture mediates action at every level: the institutions of society are organised according to specific cultural values.

There is a considerable literature on organisational and national cultures which would be impossible to critically summarise in the context of this chapter. Therefore, we propose to examine some of the key texts in this section according to whether they belong to an ideational or institutional approach with regard to their use of the concept of culture; studies which cross these distinctions are also discussed.

2.2.1 An ideational approach interprets culture as the practices and beliefs, or values of individuals within a given system. One of the best known examples of this approach is the work of Hofstede's "Culture's Consequences" (1980). In earlier work he argued that culture was,

> .. the complex of intangibles, assumed to be anchored in people's minds, which we need to explain tangible and recurrent differences in collective behaviour. (Hofstede 1979:98)

Culture, for Hofstede, is about the *"collective mental programming"* shared by a group, a tribe, a minority, or a nation.

In his seminal work Hofstede attempted to operationalise his concept of culture in the context of a survey of employees from 54 different countries. For Hofstede the aggregate personality traits of individuals in a particular country was equivalent to a national culture, or mind set.

> The dimensions of national culture are best understood by comparison with the dimensions of personality we use when we describe individuals' behaviour (1980a:475)

He sought to measure differences in attitudes to work along four dimensions: power distance, uncertainty avoidance, individualism-collectivism and masculinity-femininity. From a survey questionnaire of employees, all working for the same multinational, later identified as IBM, Hofstede tried to hold constant the influence of corporate culture. The results of these surveys indicated that the United States, for example, had a the highest individualist ranking, a relatively low power distance score, a higher acceptance of uncertainty, and a higher masculinity score. Countries like Singapore and Hong Kong had a high score on the power distance variable, compared to countries like Finland or Sweden. On the basis of these scores Hofstede attempts to link them to known research which suggests that certain types of leadership or management practice will be accepted in some countries and not in others. One of the major implications of Hofstede's findings is to argue that institutional transfer, or the transfer of managerial practices, from one country to another has to take into consideration the mind set of the people in a different culture.

However, some of the problems with Hofstede's work arise from his reduction of national cultures to aggregated personality traits based on four dimensions. For example, if respondents agreed with a series of statements like "Big and fast are beautiful" (Hofstede 1980a:480) they were considered to show more masculine traits. It is over simplistic to reduce the cultural identity of a society to an aggregate standardised score based on individual responses. Also within our own societies we know that conflicting identities exist between different sub-cultures and ethnic groups, which is not accounted for in Hofstede's schema. Further, Hofstede's approach allows little room for an analysis of historical change. He states that national cultures do not change very fast, if at all (Hofstede 1980). Finally, Hofstede's claims that these attitudes make certain forms of management style more acceptable than others is unsystematically drawn from other research rather than being obtained from his own findings.

One of the problems with an ideational approach is the overemphasis given to the attitudes and values of aggregate numbers of individuals. An ideational approach can only explain behaviour after the event. This approach takes little account of how values change over time. Values on their own are not enough to understand different working and organisational practices; values need to be rooted into the social and economic structure of a given society. An approach which gives more importance to the role of institutions is required (Berger and Luckmann 1971:72). Sorge and Warner (1986:41) argue that institutions represent the "*typified and habitualised patterns of reciprocal social action*". They also argue that an institutional approach is more fruitful for cross-national comparisons because it captures the dialectic between universal economic rationales and the particularism of institutional constraints. In more recent work Sorge (1994) has argued that a combination of ideational and institutional approaches is required, in order to account for psychological as well as societal factors. But, before we assess this we will now turn to examine the contribution of institutional approaches to cross-national research.

2.2.2 Institutional approaches give culture a more materialist underpinning: value differences are embedded in the social and economic institutions which support the continuation of traditional values and practices. For example, such an approach would argue that the economic success of Germany is not attributable to individual Germans having a strong "work ethic", being "disciplined" and hard working. In fact Germans work comparatively fewer hours than many other industrial countries (Sorge 1994; Financial Times 10/5/94) Instead, an institutional approach would emphasise the influence of the comprehensive education and vocational training system which has created a highly skilled workforce (Prais & Wagner 1983; Steedman & Hawkins 1993; Lane 1989 chp3); this has been complemented by a consultative industrial relations system (Sisson 1987), and long term financial support from banking institutions and the local state (Zysman 1983; Cox 1986; Soskice 1993; Vitols 1993). In Japan comparable institutions like MITI, company unions, and consultative practices through quality circles have been seen as a key to Japanese success (Whitehill 1991). Again the emphasis is on institutions that support industrial organisation, rather than on the attributes of individuals.

The institutional approach is illustrated in the work of Maurice, Sellier and Silvestre (1986). They have argued that we cannot examine separate aspects of a given system without locating it in its specific societal context. They have argued that there is a strong relationship between the organisation of work at the micro level of the firm and national institutions at the macro level. Their work examines the relationship between the educational system, the structure of business, and the sphere of industrial relations. They argue that skill attainment, for example, is affected by the relationship between the educational system and the workplace hierarchy. Each dimension has a degree of autonomy but also forms part of an interdependent structure. They argue that,

... there are common features shared by firms in a particular country though they use different types of technology. ... the explanation of these similarities lies not in the effects of some sort of invisible hand or teleological principle but rather in the systematic structure of social factors influencing both the formation of the actors and the development of the industrial work system, factors that are at once the result of specific social relations and the cause of those relations. (Maurice et al. 1986: 78-9)

Commonality is attributable to belonging to a particular country, where social relations and the institutions which govern them have, historically, developed symbiotically. Social behaviour takes place within the context of particular institutions in a given society. The behaviour of social actors (groups or individuals) is influenced by these institutions, but it is also modified by the behaviour of these actors. Their approach is widely known as the "societal effect".

In their research of French and German manufacturing they found that German managers possessed a higher degree of technical skill, and were expected to perform a broader range of tasks compared to equivalent managers in France. French organisations also had more levels of management than German firms. They sought to explain these differences in relation to the structure of 1) the educational and vocational training system 2) the nature of business organisation & 3) the differences in the industrial relations organisation & structure. Their work is important in linking the micro and macro levels of industrial organisation within a society.

Although Maurice et al. offer a fresh perspective for conducting comparative research, they have been criticised for the functionalist nature of their explanations, although they would deny this (1982:374). Rose (1985) has argued that their approach allows only a limited role for individual action; it also fails to incorporate an analysis of how change comes about. Lane (1989:36) questions the nature of causality in the systems they outline: does the syndrome they set out determine the organisation of work, or is it a case of "mutual adaption" between business organisations and other institutions in society? Maurice et al. argue that by putting the education system at the centre of their analysis they can focus on the relations between skill attainment and the organisation of workplace hierarchy. However, their analysis takes limited account of the gendered

19

construction of skill (Maurani & Nicole 1989; Walby 1989; Cockburn 1981). In seeking to bring down the bastions of Marxist laws of economics, and the work on convergence and technological determinism, they admit that they have given greater weight to the differences they found, which is inherent in their methodological perspective (Maurice et al 1982:263).

A more recent institutional approach has been developed by Whitley (1992a & b) who advocates a Business Systems perspective. He focuses on the characteristics of the business system in terms of the nature of the firm, the way the market is organised, and the authoritative coordination and control systems. His emphasis is on recognising how these characteristics are shaped by background social institutions, i.e. kinship trust, loyalty and authority relations, as well as by proximate social institutions including business relations with the state, financial system, education and training system, unions, and other professional organisations. Whitley uses this approach to account for the differences in firm organisation in Asia and Europe.

However, one of the problems with Whitley's approach is that whilst it draws attention to the way institutions are shaped, and how this is linked to the historical development of the society under observation, his analysis leaves little room for change. This is because of his emphasis on the historical legacy of institutions and social relations. We can clearly see the institutions of a particular society, but we have little sense of the people occupying these. The weight of history also make it difficult to identify the nature of conflict between major social actors, thus generating a rather static model of industrial organisation.

Overall, the strength of institutional approaches to comparative research has been to give a distinct material basis to the nature of cross-national differences in work organisation. However, this has on occasion been at the expense of loosing sight of the role of local actors and heterogeneity within nation state societies.

2.2.3 Intermediary approaches which cross the boundaries of the ideational and institutional schools can be seen in the work of Dore (1973) and Gallie (1978). Dore in "*British Factory, Japanese Factory*" (1973) compares organisational practices and the values of employees at English Electric in the UK and Hitachi in Japan. Dore opposes the argument that Japanese distinctiveness was a product of industrial "backwardness" (1973:375). Instead, he argues that the distinctiveness of the Japanese system developed from: a) the creation of new institutions to suit their cultural disposition; b) the selective adoption of foreign models; and c) an unconscious evolution and continuity of existing pre-industrial institutions (Dore 1973:376). However, what is more significant to Dore is not the existence of "*institutional inertia*", but rather why certain choices were consciously made by Japanese industrialists which, accumulatively, have created the Japanese system (1973:401). Dore argues that the disposition to make certain kinds of choices was influenced by the "*modified Confucian world-view*" which assumed original virtue rather than original sin (1973:401) This predisposed Japanese industrialists to see benevolence as efficient. The ideological context made them more willing to make certain choices rather than others. Second, it shaped their objectives; for example, leadership in Japan required a moral force as well as a purely material one. And third, ideology affected different objectives: the ideological emphasis on honour and respect led them to give greater weight to these factors than was the case amongst other industrialists.

Essentially Dore's argument for the difference between British and Japanese firms was based on the impact of i) Confucian ideology and ii) the late development of Japanese industrialisation. The choices made by early British industrialists in the mid-nineteenth century were very different to those posed to Japanese industrialists in the early half of the twentieth century. Late development meant that late comers benefit, not only from advances in technology, but also from "*social technology*", for example, education, personnel management techniques and "ideologies" of increased democratisation. Dore argues that egalitarian democratic ideologies which developed in advanced industrialised societies, "*can have independent life and force of their own when diffused to societies just beginning industrialisation.*" (Dore 1973:12). He argues that the need to handle complex technology and organisations, and the need to meet demands for status equality does not create imperatives requiring identical institutional solutions. Instead, he argues, diversity will persist. This is because of a) the varied pre-industrial history; b) the diversity of other imperatives like war and revolution, the ideology of the elite group, the role of state intervention, as well as the social and racial composition of the country; and c) the experience of industrialisation (Dore 1973:419) These factors account for the persistence of differences between Japanese and British firms. Although Dore emphasises the affect of Confucian ideology on management decision making, he also gives equal weight to how history has shaped the parameters of these decisions. Unlike Hofstede he assess the significance of values and attitudes from a historical and case-study approach. This has the advantage of linking attitudes to the historical evolution of social institutions. Dore, like Gallie (1978), criticises the simplistic determinism of arguments based on technological imperatives.

Gallie (1978) is interested in examining contingency theory and Marxist arguments on the deterministic affect of technology on a) the social integration of workers in the capitalist enterprise, b) on the structure of managerial power, and c) on the nature of trade unionism (1978:36). He asks whether the use of advanced technology leads to the integration or alienation of workers. This research question is examined empirically within the context of a comparative study of four oil refineries in Britain and France. Gallie argues that a comparative approach to these questions can allow him to include "*the influences of societal differences in culture and social structure.*" (1978:37). He is interested not only in identifying the similarities and differences in the structure of work organisation in each country, but also in how the attitudes and aspirations of workers in these plants compare. In this way his work straddles the ideational and institutional approaches to comparative research.

In terms of social integration Gallie found that French workers were more discontent with their wages and the salary structure than the British workforce. The conflict which arose over 'manning' levels created greater friction in the French plant than in the British one. Although there were disputes over how work should be organised, Gallie argues that the relationships between the British management and workers was more 'co-operative' than in France, where this relationship was seen as more 'exploitative' by the French workforce. The British workers were more content with the system of negotiating with managers. French workers felt consultations were superficial, symbolising their exclusion from participation in decision making within the firm. By drawing on large scale survey research Gallie seeks to generalise this to the national level (1978:146-8). French workers were not only more discontent with existing power structures but they also had much higher aspirations of what they wanted to achieve in terms of control of the enterprise. Gallie argues that,

Although market economies involve similar objective conflicts of interest between employers and employed, these contradictions appear to have different implications for the workers' perception of the firm in different societies..... The effects of institutional structure are not, then, mechanical, but are conditional upon certain cultural contexts. (1978:206)

Gallie attempts to identify the variables which links the way workers aspirations and experience are formed within given institutional structures. He argues that were the "*value of equality has more salience*", but where participation is blocked, this creates greater tension between management and workers: "*it is the interaction of cultural values and institutional structures that is crucial.*" (1978:210)

In his explanations for these differences he focuses on the structure of managerial power and the nature of trade unionism in each country. French management was more paternalistic, compared to the 'semi-constitutional' strategy of British management. French managers were more active in reminding the work force of their discretionary powers whereas British managers played down their potential powers. In France the legitimacy of managerial authority was low. French management retained a tighter degree of control than British managers. The organisation of the unions in each country differed significantly. This affected the way union demands were formulated, and the role they saw for themselves in the firm and society in general. In France, union membership was comparatively low and fragmented. The French unions were highly politicised, so that their demands were linked to a broader long term strategy to bring about societal change and mobilise the workforce to this goal. In Britain union density was much higher. This gave them a greater potential to coerce management. Gallie argues that they had a more representative role: the unions negotiated on a narrower range of issues which emerged from shop floor grievances. Gallie argues that there was little evidence that union structures, both within the plants and at the national level, would converge; instead he argues that their distinctiveness would persist.

In conclusion Gallie argues that technology per se has negligible influence on the integration of workers in a capitalist enterprise. He argues that social interaction at the work place is determined by the patterns of culture and social structure within a given society (1978:295).

> The crucial mediating variables, we would suggest, are factors like the managerial ideology, the typical structure of power in social institutions, and the ideology and mode of action of the trade union movement characteristic of the specific society. (1978:318)

Thus, Gallie draws on comparative empirical evidence to counter the universalist thesis of technological determinism in workplace organisation. His approach clearly seeks to show the relationship between societal structures and institutions and the attitudes of the people who populate these spaces in relation to their working environment. In a later book he attempts to identify the historical factors which have shaped these institutions in each society (Gallie 1983).

By reviewing previous cross-national studies we have seen that approaches which have emphasised the importance of culture in understanding cross-national differences in work organisation have given differing weight to the role of individual and social values as well as institutional effects. A purely ideational approach fails to fully recognise social heterogeneity within a single society. It tends towards a post-hoc account for national differences without accounting for how these differences came about. An institutional approach on the other hand is more successful at identifying the material and historical basis for particular societal characteristics. However, the tendency to emphasise historical origins can create a rather static conception of social arrangements, with little account given to the role of actors in shaping and interpreting these. The intermediate approaches are more successful in this respect. They manage to identify both the historical constraints and perceptions of contemporary actors in their accounts for societal differences. They also recognise how conflict and change emerge through changing alliances of elites and organised labour. Before we go on to see how these approaches have influenced the work presented here, we need to spend time examining the different methods available to see how these affect the theoretical framework developed.

3. Methodological issues

Walton (1973:173) has argued that comparative research suffers from a lack of distinctive and systematic strategies at the empirical level. Methodological questions concerning appropriate and feasible research design have been a key issue of concern. To what extent do the research methods used in cross-national research differ substantively from work conducted in only one country? Grimshaw (1973) argues that,

> while the problems involved are no different in kind from those involved in domestic research, they are of such great magnitude as to constitute an almost qualitative difference for comparative, as compared to non-comparative, research. (1973:4)

Whether comparative work requires a unique methodological approach, or whether it is merely an extension of existing methods, duplicated in several countries, has been one of the key issues of debate (Warwick & Osherson 1973; Smelser 1973; Przeworski & Teune 1973; Myrdal 1973; Nißen & Peschar 1982; Armer and Grimshaw 1973; Armer and Marsh 1982). In this section we will critically review the quantitative and qualitative methods available to cross-national researchers.

A traditional, if somewhat misleading, debate has persisted in the social sciences regarding the use of quantitative or qualitative research methods. To a large extent these debates revolve around epistemological issues. The extreme version of these two positions could be summarised as follows. A quantitative perspective sees the social sciences as capable of generating laws comparable to the natural sciences. Such an approach is also known as nomothetic theory: *"meaning a non-contradictory body of statements which are empirically proven."* (Sorge 1994:2). One can know and observe the world through scientific and systematic observation. Measures of sociological phenomena can be rationally constructed and empirically applied to generate data, and verification of results can be tested through repeat experimentation.

Alternatively, a qualitative perspective emphasises the specific historical and systemic conditions in which a given phenomenon occurs. This is also known as a idiographic approach: *"the study of particular cases (e.g. persons, social groups, works of art)"* (Bullock and Stallybrass 1982:299). An extreme version of such an analysis would emphasises that the world only exists as a social construction in people's minds. Such an approach draws on anthropological research to show how different societies conceptualise and construct time and space through rites which are accorded particular significance. For those outside this society these rites may appear illogical or meaningless, because outsiders do not share the same value systems and therefore cannot understand the meanings of particular phenomena. Therefore the role of the social researcher is to interpret the meaning and significance of various rites and symbols associated with a particular group.

Although this debate between qualitative and quantitative methods has generated a sometimes fierce polemic amongst researchers, in fact this stark either/or choice is somewhat misleading. A thorough research design will need to develop a variety of tools and draw on a vast array of available material, which can be used to cross verify the conclusions developed. For example, in employment research this can mean combining data from secondary analysis, labour force or attitude surveys with case study material from organisations and information on the institutional regulatory framework, data from labour law, collective agreements, tax and social security regulations. Different sources of data can be mutually enriching (Marsden 1986; Gallie 1978; Walton 1973). However, the choice of research methodology is often determined by the research questions, the preferences and skills of the researcher, the amount of time, the availability of resources, and the degree of access provided to required respondents. We will now turn to examine in more detail the leverage offered by specific research methods for cross-national comparative research on employment.

3.1 Large scale surveys

At the national and sectoral level large scale surveys can allow us to identify aggregate trends in the different forms of employment, for example in the case of part-time or temporary work (Hakim 1991; ILO 1989). Such data can be used to measure change over time *within* countries, although we need to be more cautious when making direct international comparisons. Such data can also allow us to compare the distribution of workers by industry, sex or age, as these measures are reasonably reliable and less influenced by the concepts and methods of collection (ILO 1989). Large scale data is useful in identifying the trends according to broadly defined categories, but it cannot usually pick out the causal explanations for these developments, unless combined with a multivariate, theoretically informed use of secondary analysis. One off surveys on their own provide a static snap-shot picture of the current situation; longitudinal or panel surveys attempt to compensate for these weaknesses. Even though it is claimed that regressions, multivariate analysis and increasingly sophisticated statistical correlation tests can identify significance between variables, their distance from the subject may lead to misleading findings. Such approaches require an *a priori* rigorous theoretical underpinning and reliable data.

Dale and Glover (1989) cite three major difficulties in making comparisons using this type of aggregate national labour force survey data. First, there are conceptual difficulties which affect who is included in the data, for example whether unpaid family workers are included or excluded. These discrepancies are related to *"the historical and ideological backgrounds which affect the meaning of concepts concerned with employment"* (Dale & Glover 1989). Second, there are substantive differences, for example, the existence of conscription, or the legal age of entering and leaving the labour force. Third, measurement difficulties in employment may not be declared and may vary in significance between countries, which thus affect the comparison (Dale and Glover 1989 and 1990; Beechey 1989; Walton 1973). Beechey (1989) also cautions against the use of international comparisons using nationally produced labour force statistics. She argues that activity rates are not created in a neutral way, they are essentially social constructions (Beechey 1989: 370), and therefore we cannot assume that we can make direct comparisons from available data. Women's unemployment is a particularly good example of this problem.[6] The use of temporary work, subcontracting and self-employment are also examples of where it is notoriously difficult to formulate distinct and comparable categories (Casey 1988; Meager 1993). These criticisms point out the potential hazards involved in cross national comparisons using officially published labour force data.

Alternatively, to compensate for the general categories used in national labour force surveys a researcher, or more appropriately a research team, can conduct a cross-national survey with a specifically designed questionnaire. This has been the approach adopted by Hofstede (1980) and the Aston school (Hickson et al. 1979). This has been one of the most popular methods used in comparative research. Child and Loveridge

(1990) point out that,

> Surveys, particularly when conducted through postal
> questionnaires, permit a much greater coverage of locations
> and speedier analysis of results for the same resource
> outlay than do the more laborious methods associated with
> case studies such as intensive interviewing, documentary
> analysis and observation. (Child and Loveridge 1990:64)

Survey research can be comparatively cheap and quick, and
researchers often feel more confident about making
generalisations from nationally representative data.

Although such a method allows researchers to obtain a
large number of responses, there are significant problems of
relying solely on questionnaire survey data. For example, it is
not always clear that the responses collected mean the same
thing in different countries. Obtaining equivalence of meaning
is a key issue in comparative research (Przeworski & Teune
1973; Loetsch 1982; Nießen 1982; Peschar 1982). Walton argues
that,

> Distinctive comparative strategies should involve, beyond
> doing the same thing in a variety of locations, taking
> precautions to ensure that the units studied and the
> subsequent results are meaningfully comparable. (Walton
> 1973:178)

Armer (1973) also emphasises the importance of comparing
equivalent units with culturally appropriate concepts. This may
not necessarily lead to exact comparisons; Nießen (1982) and
Schmid (1992) discuss the importance of obtaining "functional
equivalence". Maurice, Sellier and Silvestre (1982:367) make a
similar point. They argue that it is rare to find identical objects
of comparison, citing the example of the differences between the
French foreman and the German "Meister". As a consequence,
Armer (1973) advocates "purposive sampling" where
units/groups are chosen in relation to the specific research
interests. These groups are chosen on the basis of their
significance and the feasibility of access. The problem with
surveys is that they are not always sensitive to these problems
and differences.

Equivalence of meaning applies not only to the objects
studied, but also, in survey work, to the "*labels attached to pre-*

structured scales" (Child and Loveridge 1990:64). Ethnocentricity is a common criticism made against comparative survey research. This means that concepts are often developed from the perspective of one culture, and therefore are not always applicable abroad. The use of pre-coded questionnaires, which reduce responses into a pre-defined category, do not allow for unanticipated rationales. The use of open-ended questions coded up after the interview can reduce this effect. Child and Loveridge (1990) also point out that there is a tendency to dump all the "un-explained" differences into a black box concept of culture, without specifying how national culture is understood and analysed.

Overall, labour force surveys, or cross-national team generated questionnaires have the advantage of obtaining extensive coverage comparatively quickly and cheaply. However, this is often at the expense of neglecting indepth information and diverse rationales that can only be identified through more qualitative case study research. Knowing whether the datat is really comparing like with like is one of the major problems when using large scale surveys.

3.2 Comparative case-study analysis

Studies which have given greater weight to cultural specificity have tended to adopt a combination of case-study methods (Dore 1973; Gallie 1978; Maurice et al. 1982); although Hofstede (1980) is an exception to this. Case-study methods have often been seen as *"soft, subjective and speculative"* compared to using quantitative methods and large scale surveys which are *"hard, objective and rigorous"* (Burgess 1984). However, they are by no means incompatible. The term case study, as Platt (1988) has pointed out, has been used to refer to a diverse set of research practices. The unit of analysis for case studies can vary quite significantly from an individual, to a group, an organisation, a polity, or a nation, all of which can be considered as separate cases. The uniqueness of a case study approach is that the distinctiveness of the case is retained, even where several cases are used or compared, *"the number of cases falling into a given category is not treated as of significance"* (Platt 1988:2). What is important is identifying the variables which enter into a particular case.

A case study method essentially involves selective interviewing, collecting documentary evidence, historical sources and observational analysis,

> In detective-like fashion, comparative case studies probe here and there, assembling as many pieces of information as are available into a general picture. (Walton 1973:175).

The comparison of different sources of data can give the findings greater validity. By focusing on a small scale, researchers interested in employment issues can probe the dynamics of change. Data can be collected from organisational documentation, archives and the accounts of a variety of long serving employees or members. Thus a picture of change over time within an organisation can be more convincingly re-constructed and verified through the data collection process itself. This method can also identify opposing rationales and conflict, rather than assume a unitary logic on organisations and actors. Child and Loveridge (1990) argue that this method provides,

> sufficient depth and sensitivity to specific variations and underlying processes, rather than to offer a report on the latest developments. (Child and Loveridge 1990:64)

Further, this method can allow for unanticipated explanatory variables to be introduced through the research process.

An approach to cross-national case-study research which has been adopted by Campinos-Dubernet et al. (1988), in France, has advocated a sectoral analysis on the basis that this is a relatively homogeneous arena in which companies confront each other (Casassus-Montero 1989:159). This is similar to the approach adopted independently by Child and Loveridge (1990). The sector is a "sub-social sphere" where national characteristics are observable, but it is also subject to specific product and labour market conditions. One of the advantages of adopting this perspective is to disaggregate the trends which are identified at the national level. However, there are problems in trying to generalise to the national level on the basis of sectoral studies. For example, many of the characteristics attributed to the British system of industrial relations are based on studies of the manufacturing sector, and these characteristics do not always apply to other sectors of the economy (Räsänen & Whipp 1992).

Small scale data collection makes it difficult, although not impossible, to generalise findings (Platt 1988:17). In order that "quirks" or prejudices held by the researcher are avoided, elements of control need to be built into the research design. But, as Walton (1973) and Burgess (1984) both point out the procedures employed are usually incompletely disclosed, unsystematic and difficult to replicate; and, the selection of cases can also makes it difficult to control for all relevant variables. However, by linking small scale comparative questionnaires to results obtained from large scale national surveys can allow a researcher to test the reliability of their data, as well as supplementing national studies with a comparative perspective.

Overall, case-studies cannot claim the same extent of coverage, compared to surveys, and they are relatively laborious and time consuming to conduct. However, the basis of their representativeness relies on the specificity of the sample and the key research question. This method has the advantage, not only of collecting information directly related to the specific research questions, but which is also sensitive to cultural differences.

Ideally a combination of methods is required to enable researchers to identify general structural characteristics and relate these to the level of actors perceptions and behaviour. This can allow researchers to move between the general and the specific, to see how social structures affect actors and how actors interpret and interact in given structural conditions. In this way methodological tools and a comprehensive research design can be used directly to address the theoretical discussion of the relationship between structure and agency, which are discussed in more detail in chapter 2.

Thus, we have seen that there are various quantitative and qualitative methods which can be used to conduct comparative research. The sensitivity of these methods to the concept of differences in cross-national research vary depending on how the concept of culture is integrated into the research design. Whilst case study methods have been more popular with approaches emphasising societal differences, Hofstede (1980) has used large scale surveys to examine cultural differences. We need to be aware of how the methods used may lead to over-emphasising the similarities or differences in the results obtained from different countries.

4. Conclusions

In this chapter we have critically examined a variety of

theoretical and methodological debates related to the field of cross-national research on employment. This chapter has had three main aims. First, it has sought to introduce the reader to some of the debates on the distinctiveness and rationales for conducting comparative research. The importance of such research is becoming ever more apparent both within Europe, in its broadest sense, and because of the growing interest in the economic and social development of Japan and the newly industrialising countries. This interest emerges from concerns about how we understand developments in foreign countries and relate them to changes within our own society.

Second, this chapter has sought to critically outline the various theoretical approaches to comparative research. We have seen how universal and culturalist studies vary significantly in their treatment of differences and similarities. Universalists tend to ignore the concept of culture, or at best acknowledge it as a marginal phenomena or additional variable. Culturalists, on the other hand, have sought to integrate the concept of culture into their analysis at a socio-economic and institutional level as well as at the psychological level of the individual.

Third, this chapter has sought to critically review the strengths and weakness of various quantitative and qualitative methods used in comparative studies. On one hand, the use of secondary analysis and large scale surveys has been a very popular method. This is partly due to the potential to generalise findings based on nationally representative survey samples. This method has proved useful in identifying general trends and changes in employment relations over time within particular countries. Additionally, it is a comparatively cheap method, compared to case-study analysis. However, as discussed in greater detail earlier, such an approach can be problematic when extended to international comparisons. It is not always clear that the phenomenon being measured are strictly comparable; further, results obtained from correlations need to be interpreted in the context of a rigorous theoretical framework which can claim to identify causality. On the other hand, more qualitative case-study methods have had greater flexibility in identifying unanticipated rationales and causes. By focusing on the process of change they can also identify conflict between different actors under scrutiny, and are more sensitive to cultural specificity. However, a case-study approach can be very labour intensive. And, it is not always easy to generalise from the specific results obtained.

It has been argued in this chapter that the weaknesses of various methodological approaches should not lead to their outright rejection. Instead, a research design which can incorporate a range of tools has the advantage of analysing change at various levels. This has been the aim of the research presented in this book. Where relevant, quantitative data from labour force surveys has been used to identify the extent and nature of various forms of employment like part-time and temporary work. However, this research has also sought to complement such data by drawing on case-study evidence from employers, employees and trade unionists active in the banking sector in Britain and France. This research involved interviewing senior personnel managers from the major banks in each country, in order to review general employment trends in this sector. One bank in each country was selected for more detailed analysis, although other banks were also visited. Research in the case-study banks involved conducting semi-structured interviews with branch managers, departmental managers and supervisors from the branch networks and clearing operations in each country. Employee attitudes and experiences were elicited with a questionnaire including pre-coded and open ended questions. A total of 126 part-time and full-time female employees, working in comparable jobs, were interviewed from the two countries. Observational methods were employed in various visits to branches and administrative operations in several banks. Supplementary interviews and archival research was conducted with representatives of the major trade unions active in the banking sector in each country. Additional material was collected from secondary sources. The French research was conducted over a period of 18 months while based at the Observatoire Sociologie du Changement (CNRS), in Paris. The British data was collected while studying at Nuffield College, Oxford, from banks in the south of England and north London. The aim of this research design was to identify and compare the rationales and behaviour of various actors in the employment relationship.[7]

This research design sought to link generalisable data available at the national level with more particular data from the sectoral and company level. In this way different methodological tools provided access to various levels of analysis. It was also possible to identify where particular developments at the case-study level were related to generalised trends at the national level. One major theme running through this chapter has been that methodological and theoretical frameworks are not distinct: the method chosen often reflects the theoretical biases of the researcher, this affects the results obtained and the way they are interpreted. Thus researchers should seek to develop methods which are sensitive to identifying both similarities and differences.

In the process of doing this research it became clear that employers in the banking sector in each country were seeking to achieve flexibility thorough a range of different measures. It also became clear from the employee questionnaires that women's expectations of paid employment differed in each country; and further, that the trade unions had quite distinct, and sometimes incompatible, strategies. As these differences emerged the societal approach of Maurice et al. (1982) became very influential in helping interpret the results as they were being analysed. However, there were also problems with this approach. While providing a coherent assessment of the inter-dependence of a societal system, this approach suffers from a limited conception of change and conflict by actors within different spheres. Also, there was a complete lack of any gendered analysis. Rubery (1993) has called for an integrated approach to understanding the nature of national production regimes. By this she means that in order to understand how the industrial sector of paid employment is structured, we need to have a fuller and more integrated analysis of how social reproduction is organised. She argues that the two are inter-related, and that they vary between countries (Rubery 1988). An approach which has helped synthesise both the comparative and gender aspects of this research has been the work of Connell in (1987). His ideas are discussed in more detail in chapter 8. He distinguishes between distinct 'gender regimes' including the home, paid employment social regulation and peer groups. These regimes exist within an overarching 'gender order' which shape the relations between men and women in a given society. These concepts permitted an interpretation of the data from both a comparative and gendered perspective. This approach could account for variations in the 'gender order' in different countries. It could also help understand how the nature of social reproduction influenced the organisation of economic production in the sector studied. It is argued in this book that such a perspective can contribute towards developing a more integrated approach between economic production and social reproduction, as advocated by Rubery. Further, it suggests where friction can arise and change ensue. In this way these three writers have shaped the way this research has been interpreted and the framework of analysis which is developed throughout this book, and ultimately synthesised in chapter 10. But before we start comparing British and French societies we need first to examine the theoretical debates which this empirical research sought to address.

Notes

1. Herodotus' compared the different customs and social relations between the Greeks and Egyptians; Thucydides was interested in the different ways Spartans and Athenians secured control from their allies; and Aristotle's comparison of 158 political constitutions was one of the earliest studies in comparative government.

2. However, these studies rarely tended to be systematically cross-national or comparative, and were more often an analysis of a single society.

3. Glenn Morgan cites Capital vol 1, p8 (London: Lawrence and Wishart 1970)

4. For example, more graduates were employed in the American plant; the work experience and craft knowledge of the German foremen and supervisors was much higher than amongst their American equivalents.

5. Even Peters recognises this (1992:756). He acknowledges the resistance to his ideas from middle managers who would loose their jobs, and from government organisations.

6. In Britain official statistics only count people who are receiving unemployment benefit as unemployed. It excludes those who are ineligible to claim benefit, those who are discouraged from registering, although they may be looking for work, and those registered on government training schemes. In France the definition of unemployment is much closer to that of the ILO. Benefits and unemployment are defined separately. To be counted as unemployed you have to be looking for a job, be free to take a job and have no other professional activity at the time. This inevitably effects the conception of the active labour force in each country.

7. It would also have been helpful to follow up a small sub-set of matched female employees from each country, in order to obtain a more detailed understanding about their domestic relations. However, this was beyond the scope of this project.

2 Labour markets, firms and flexibility

1. Introduction

A growing concern with changes in labour market patterns has developed in recent years. This has been due to a number of factors: rising levels of unemployment, a mismatching of skills and firm needs, a fall in comparative competitiveness, as well as concern with labour market inequalities. Firms and governments have been faced with trying to manage these dilemmas. Labour market "rigidities" have been criticised with a demand for greater flexibility in wages, job demarcation and working hours.

A variety of academic perspectives have been used to examine contemporary developments in Western labour markets. These studies range from neo-classical economics, dual and segmented labour market theory, to regulation theory and theories concerned with labour flexibility. This chapter sets out to critically examine the main contributions of these theories concerned with labour markets, firms and flexibility. In doing so it seeks to assess their relevance to comparative research and theories of women's labour market participation. In this way this review is intended to establish the theoretical context in which this empirical study has been conducted.

2. Human capital and dual labour market theory

Orthodox economic thought has argued that wage differentials are due to differing levels of productivity, workers' preferences, or monopolies preventing an equalisation of wages (Dex

1988a:83). However, these factors do not fully account for wage inequalities between men and women. Human capital theory developed as a response to this critique. Swedberg and Granovetter (1992:1-3), although critical of this approach, argue that the work of Becker marked a significant change within economic thought. This was because political and sociological topics were now considered suitable for analysis using economic models. Becker (1975) argued that the decision of an individual to invest in obtaining skills and work experience affected their long term acquisition of human capital. According to this theory individuals assess the value of investing in education in terms of future market rewards. Women are less likely to invest in their human capital because their work trajectories are interrupted by childrearing and a loss of earnings. The focus of human capital theory is based on the actions of 'rational' actors.

However, this approach has been widely criticised. Human capital theorists assume a direct correlation between pay and qualifications. They also imply that human behaviour is primarily affected by economic incentives. The empirical evidence to support this is weak (Nolan 1983:299; Dex 1988a:285; Rubery 1988a:253). It reduces industrial production to a simple method of combining various technological and economic factors, with capital and labour, to produce outputs (Osterman 1984:5). This completely ignores the importance of social aspects in the employment relationship. Rubery, herself and economist, argues that,

> The so-called strengths of neo-classical theory have been its generality and its ability to predict equilibrium outcomes. The development of models of multiple equilibria based on information costs, bargaining strategies, and non-transferability of factors detract from these characteristics and pull it in the opposite direction towards historical, institutional and contingent explanations of market outcomes (Rubery 1988a:253)

The focus on supply side factors and the actions of atomised individuals denies any active role for firms, employers and discriminatory practices.

Dual labour market theory developed as a critique of neo-classical accounts of labour market inequalities. This approach gave greater importance to the role of social processes. Dual labour market theorists have argued that it is not the actions of employees which determines job allocation and pay, but rather it is the actions of employers who structure employment opportunities in the way they divide up the labour market to suit their own labour requirements. Models of a dual labour market have been developed in the work of Edwards (1979; and Gordon, Edwards & Reich 1982) and Piore (Doeringer and Piore 1971; Berger and Piore 1980; Piore and Sabel 1984); although they differ quite radically in the explanations for these divisions. Edwards (1979) establishes three central categories to describe the labour market: independent primary, subordinate primary and the secondary sector. These are broadly similar to those defined by Piore (1980).[1] According to Edwards, skilled, white collar jobs are found in the independent primary sector. Low status, unionized jobs are characteristic of the subordinate primary sector; and, low paid, precarious jobs are found in the secondary sector.

Employees' labour market status is linked to company size and the use of technology. Large companies organised on a bureaucratic basis and using advanced technology, employ independent primary workers. Large companies using standardised mass production technology employ sub-ordinate primary workers. Small, labour intensive companies use secondary sector labour. Edwards distinguishes between the sectors in terms of the historical development of technology. Gordon et al. (1982) elaborate on this theme by identifying three distinct historical periods in the evolution of labour markets. The 1820s to 1890s represented the initial proletarianization with an overall increase in the number of wage earners, although this was not accompanied by a transformation of the labour process at this stage. The second period from the 1870s to the Second World War saw an increased mechanisation of the labour process and a homogenisation of labour. The third stage of segmentation, which developed after the 1930s, allowed corporations to control increasingly militant trade unions by institutionalising them, and segmenting the labour market.

According to this approach the characteristics of employees in each sector are distinctive. The traditional working class are found in the subordinate primary sector. Over 70% of those belonging to the independent primary labour market are white males (Edwards 1979). Employment in the secondary sector was performed by blacks from the urban 'ghetto' who were confined to this sector (Doeringer and Piore 1971). As the theory has developed the secondary sector has also come to encompass women, immigrants, young people and the working poor. However, one of the problems with the concept of secondary sector is that it has become a catch all category for everything the primary sector is not.

Although Piore (Berger and Piore 1980) identifies similar categories to those of Edwards he gives greater emphasis to "skill" requirements and the learning process, rather than forms of managerial control. Secondary sector jobs involve a narrower range of diverse and irregular tasks (Berger and Piore 1980:70). Stricter supervision is a result of employing lower skilled workers. Control is a secondary concern, skill levels are key. Primary jobs in the lower tier involve a broader range of tasks. This requires an extrinsic understanding of the job and concrete learning, symbolised by on-the-job training (Berger and Piore 1980:20). Internal labour markets become a means to maximise on the training given to these staff. Jobs in the upper tier of the primary sector involve a wide range of tasks and a broad conceptualisation of the work process. This is obtained through abstract learning (Berger and Piore 1980). These workers have greater geographical and institutional mobility than those in the lower tier.

Internal labour markets refute the neo-classical idea of an open competitive labour market. Primary sector employment is characterised by internal labour markets which offer job security, the prospects of career advancement and preferential wages and conditions. Doeringer and Piore (1971) argued that internal labour markets were developed in large, oligopolist, capital intensive companies. Their use of advanced technology required skilled workers who were obtained through on-the-job training. A commitment to permanent employment helped reduce turnover and maximised on training costs. Members of internal labour markets were protected from the vagaries of the open competitive market by formal administrative rules governing the allocation of labour and determining wages. These internal labour markets also encourage co-operation from the workers with the incentives of promotion, job and wage security.

Internal labour markets can be imposed by management or demanded by the unions (Doeringer and Piore 1971:13; Osterman 1984). They can be understood as a mechanism to resolve potential conflicts of interest between employers and workers: both parties benefit but for different reasons. Such practices can impose rigidities on management as workers seek to protect their own self-interest. Internal labour markets are

40

less likely to develop in small firms because of their more precarious market position. Wages in these smaller companies are generally lower and turnover is high; in general working conditions are poor, with little chance for career advancement.

The key feature then of dual labour market theory has been to argue that the labour market is not an open and competitive market where wages and jobs are allocated on the basis of skills and market demands. Instead, greater emphasis has been given to showing how the labour market is structured by firms, into advantaged and disadvantaged sectors. A variety of explanations have developed within dual, and subsequently segmented labour market theory to account for these divisions; these explanations have focused on the importance of managerial control, the effects of company size and market stability, legal regulation and union organisation, as well as the different behavioural characteristics of primary and secondary sector workers. We will examine each of these explanations in turn before going on to assess the emergence of current debates on labour market flexibility.

2.1 Managerial control

Explanations in terms of managerial control have been most notably developed by Edwards (1979) and Gordon, Edwards and Reich (1982). The core of their argument is that employers need to control the workforce to maximise profits. The means of control have developed historically in relation to the changing composition of labour-capital relations. Small, traditional, labour intensive companies need to exercise strict supervisory control over their work force who are characterised as secondary sector workers. The growth of automation increased the size of the work force, and technical methods of control are used to manage the growing role of unions. At a later stage bureaucratised systems of control developed in large organisations as a means to reduce the role of trade unions and the costs of direct supervisory control. The process of managerial control has created segments in the labour market and this is seen as a means of dividing the working class into class fractions, so as to undermine the potential of collective class action.[2]

However, this approach has received considerable criticism. Their is a poor conceptualisation of the role of the state (Nolan and Edwards 1984). The emphasis on managerial control as the key explanatory factor for labour market divisions over-simplifies managerial strategy: *"the many ways of gaining compliance are reduced to a few straightforward rules"* (Nolan and Edwards 1984:214). To reduce employers motives to methods of control over simplifies the complexity of class struggle. Hodson and Kaufman (1982) advocate a perspective which conceptualises labour market structures in terms of resources and vulnerabilities.

> The insight that economic structure is created and manipulated by the capitalist class is valuable but only tells one side of the story. Such economic structures are created in interaction with labor. And, capital structure, once in place, creates resources and vulnerabilities for workers in their struggles at the workplace." (Hodson and Kaufman 1982:735-6)

Hodson and Kaufman move away from a control determined analysis. They take account of the relative power of different actors, and how this interaction structures labour market outcomes. The relevance of such a critique can be seen once we look beyond the US. By basing their argument solely on the US experience, Gordon et al. (1982) assume a unilinear pattern of industrial development. However, as Dore (1973) has shown for Japan, there are different patterns of industrialisation. The comparative work of Sisson (1987) also furthers this point in his comparison of collective bargaining patterns in Europe, Japan and the US. He points out that strength of organisation and the nature of conflict between employers and organised labour has varied between countries, which has in turn affected the nature of these conflicts. Such variation puts into question the arbitrary historical periodisation of Gordon et al. (1982). Moreover the simplistic typology of employers used by Gordon et al. ignores the diverse range of labour strategies used within the same firm to distinguish between employees with advantageous positions and those in less secure jobs.

2.2 Company size and market stability

The early literature on dual labour markets draws tight parallels between company size and the structure of the labour market. The theory claims that a small group of core firms and industries can dominate the market because of the extensive resources they commanded, whilst smaller companies remained isolated at the periphery (Averitt 1968). Baron & Bielby (1984), although critical of the simplicity of this theory, sum up the characteristics of these early theories as follows,

> Relative to periphery firms, centre organisations are larger, more complex, differentiated, technologically sophisticated, diversified, concerned with long term goals, varied in their skill mix, reliant on management (versus technology) in dictating internal arrangements, globally oriented, and less restricted in obtaining finance and other crucial resources. (Baron & Bielby 1984:456)

Large firms are insulated from the competitive pressure experienced by smaller firms, so that they can offer preferential terms of employment to secure the skilled staff they require.

Edwards argues that the tendency to find small firms in a competitive industry and large firms in a monopoly industry is an enduring characteristic. Small companies which operate in a monopoly industry, or large companies in a competitive industry, *"are in fact transitional situations"* (Edwards 1979:83). Edwards (1979:vii) argues that there is a continuous trend towards the growth of large companies. Company mergers make available the resources to invest in advanced technology which leads to benefits in economies of scale. Market power is the key factor distinguishing between large and small companies: smaller companies are more vulnerable to market insecurity. Nevertheless the existence of small companies is perennial.

Company size as an explanatory variable remains important in the later developments of dualist theory. A revised version of the dual economy paradigm continues to hold sway in the thinking of writers like Piore and Sabel (1984). however, the small firm was no longer seen as an anachronism: it became functional to larger companies. As the period of post-war prosperity began to falter, large firms have farmed out the increasing unstable aspects of production to these smaller units (Kumazawa and Yamada 1989). Self-limiting product market policies have become a means for large companies to protect their investments. Companies, like Du Pont and Benetton, who divide up the market into sectors of stable and unstable demand, leave smaller companies to produce for short term peaks in demand. Piore cites Arthur Moxham of Du Pont who comments on the relationship between fluctuating demand and the company's market share,

If we control only 60% of it all (the market) and make that 60% cheaper than others, when slack times came, we could still keep our capital employed to the full... (Berger and Piore 1980:67).

The central objective in mass production has been to obtain high volume sales. However, in the mid-1980s Piore argued that market fragmentation encouraged a policy of self-limitation. This was for some time successful for large companies like IBM (Piore and Sabel 1985:204). However, they have been vulnerable to continual encroachment of their market share by companies from Japan and the newly industrialised countries. The assumption of a direct parallelism between a dual economy and the structure of the labour market has become outdated, with the advent of increased economic uncertainty. Large as well as small firms have become increasingly vulnerable to competitive pressures and economic instability, for example in the steel sector, retailing and insurance (Hodson and Kaufman 1982:733), as well as in electronics and the car industry. Apart from company size and vulnerability to instability, distinctions need to be made relating to the type of product sold. It is necessary to distinguish between the products made in terms of their quality and the delivery process. Fluctuations in demand can have differing effects for banks and supermarkets compared to companies selling cars or computers.

2.3 Legal regulation and union organisation

Institutional differentiation distinguishes between large and small firms in core and secondary sectors (Berger & Piore 1980:32). However, Piore argues that these distinctions are "found" rather than "made". Piore is sceptical of conspiratorial theories which suggest that the institutional framework responds directly to the needs of capitalism, although he recognises that these legal exceptions served to protect traditional interests of small and medium sized companies in countries like Italy and France (Berger & Piore 1980:49). These differences reinforce labour market segmentation. Piore cites examples, drawn from Italy, where restrictions on making redundancies are not applied to companies of less than 10 employees; the right for trade unions to organise is restricted to plants of 16+ employees (Berger and Piore 1980:32). Small companies not only evade these restrictions but also pay lower wages; and for example in

Italy the informal economy is completely outside any form of regulation. In France employment in small companies is notoriously poorly protected: a *'délégué du personnel'* operates in companies of over 10 employees, and a *'comité d'entreprise'* requires 50+ employees for it to be established. In Britain too, limited employment protection creates divisions between different types of workers according to the number of hours they work (Morton 1987; Deakin and Mückenberger 1992:139-140).

Workers who are found in the secondary sector belong to what Piore calls "pre-industrial" classes, and in periods of unemployment can fall back on their *"traditional economic activities"* (Berger & Piore 1980 loc.cit). However, as Murray (1983) points out, in practice it is not clear that this is what happens. The main point is that legal regulation can serve to create distinctions between different types of workers in the labour market. Higher levels of protection and job security can be related to the size of the employing firm, as in France or Italy, or to the number of hours worked and continuity of employment, as in Britain.

Linked to the role of regulation, Rubery (1978) has pointed out that the actions of trade unions has created and sustained differential forms of labour market segmentation. Piore argues (Berger and Piore 1980) that the gains made by trade unions in France, Italy and America in the late 1960s came from a desire for security. A similar point is also made by an OECD study on flexibility,

> Workers have a natural desire to exercise control over the work which they do, they seek to build a fence around their work against that of other workers (OECD 1986:119).

This is particularly true for traditions of workers control in manufacturing, rather than in the service sector. Trade union achievements, made in periods of growth, limit employers' capacity to adapt the work force to fluctuations in the business cycle. Piore argues that the rights gained by these workers operate within a distinct legal regime.

Whilst unions have been instrumental in institutionalising their gains in the post war period, little attention has been given to the influence of gender in this process. The work of Cockburn (1981) is an exception. She convincingly shows how male dominated unions in the printing industry in Britain actively operated to exclude women. Recognition of the affects of gender needs to be more fully integrated into these theories to explain why, for example part-time work is dominated by women. One effect of these developments has been to create a secondary labour market for female workers, although the forms of segmentation and degrees of segregation vary between countries (Rubery and Fagan 1992). The key point is that the role of legal regulation and union organisation have created distinct forms of labour market segmentation.

2.4 Behavioural differences between primary and secondary sector employees

The concept of internal labour markets, which is meant to distinguish between primary and secondary workers, has become an issue of debate. The prevalence of internal labour markets, even in firms which have other "primary sector" characteristics is not always evident (Gallie 1988:17; MacInnes 1987). The conceptual development of internal labour markets relies heavily on studies conducted in blue-collar manufacturing in the USA. This also raises questions as to the extent that they can be directly applied to other sectors and countries. Osterman (1984) argues that greater attention needs to be given to the diversity of internal labour markets especially in white collar jobs. Manwaring (1984) contends that instead of talking about distinct, dichotomous markets which are either open in the case of secondary markets, or closed in the case of core sectors, we should talk about degrees of closure. The experience of internal or extended internal labour markets varies considerably between regions and industries, diminishing the validity of a strictly dualist model as a generalised phenomenon. The work of Manwaring (1984) suggests that secondary labour market may be more structured than early theorists envisaged, and that employment in this sector is not completely separate from primary sector employment. This may be seen in the use of part-time and temporary work as an intermediary stage between core work and non-participation in paid employment. Such criticisms raise serious problems for the simple dual model of labour markets.

Distinctions between primary and secondary workers also exist in terms of different behavioural characteristics: unreliable workers with low job commitment are found in precarious employment, compared to employees with a stronger work ethic in the primary sector. This also includes the general category of women, whose primary interests, according to Piore, lie outside the paid labour market. Doeringer and Piore (1971) claim that compared to the "*average American*", members of the secondary labour market have lower educational levels, higher unemployment, more part-time work, and less job experience.

> Discrimination, the quality of work available to the disadvantaged, and the style of life in low-income neighbourhoods are major causal factors which may overshadow problems of inadequate education and skill. (1971:183).

The life style of secondary sector workers does not encourage them to develop working patterns to conform to the requirements of the primary labour market:

> Primary employment, in contrast, requires the individual to abandon street life and to conform to an ethical code which is not recognised on the street.(1971:176).

However, as the secondary sector has come to include the young, diverse ethnic groups, immigrants and women this is not particularly illuminating in understanding the diverse characteristics of members of the secondary sector and their orientation to work. The arguments of Doeringer and Piore (1971) are essentially based on the requirements of advanced technology for high skilled staff and these are matched to labour force characteristics and behaviour patterns. These are essentially structuralist explanations and do not offer an explanation for how people arrive in a particular category. They also offer no explanation for how people can move from between categories. The assumption is that people are confined to a given sector.

Although precarious employment is one of the key characteristics associated with secondary employment, it is not clear where these boundaries are drawn. For example, Doeringer and Piore (1971) show in the Appendix to Chapter 8 of Internal Labor Markets and Manpower Analysis how adult women in the Boston area had longer job tenure than men, how "*non-white adults can be expected to have 15 weeks more job tenure than whites*", and that recent immigrants to the Boston area were found by employers to be more reliable (1971:187). All of these groups, however, should be found in a more precarious position by virtue of their unstable employment characteristics. This raises questions about how we define secure and precarious employment over time and between different countries (Mosley and Kruppe 1992).

The difficulty of incorporating change into the dual market paradigm is also seen with the issue of mobility and confinement: are secondary sector employees confined to these types of employment as Doeringer and Piore (1971:167) suggest? One of the problems with this theory is its failure to explain the mechanisms through which labour is allocated to these sectors: to what extent is it self-selecting or, is there no alternative to accepting precarious work? An extensive debate has grown around this issue in relation to part-time work. To what extent does it represent a form of "chosen" working time or, is it the only option available for women to combine paid work and domestic responsibilities? (Maruani and Nicole 1988b and 1989; Beechey and Perkins 1987; Gregory 1987a and 1987b; Hurstfield 1978) With regard to mobility between sectors, young people often enter the labour market on temporary work contracts, which employers use as a form of extended selection, before deciding whether or not to offer permanent employment. The problem of mobility and change are not fully accounted for in these earlier debates. Nevertheless these questions have become of increasing interest to subsequent theoretical developments.

3. From segmentation to flexibility

The debate has moved on from a simple explanation of persistent labour market differentiation to ask how these boundaries have been created and adapted in relation to changing product market and labour market conditions,

> The issue became not the explanation of the persistence of stable differences in employment rewards between sectors and organizations, but the analysis of how boundaries between primary-type and secondary-type employment were being redrawn as employers responded to changing product and labour market conditions by developing new employment strategies. (Rubery 1988:256).

The changing terms of the debate are a reflection of the changing economic environment. It has become increasingly more difficult for employers to divide up the product market into stable and unstable sectors, product demand has become increasingly fragmented, and the costs for fixed permanent employees have increased (Berger and Piore 1980; Piore and Sabel 1984; Boyer 1986). It has been argued that these developments have encouraged firms to look for greater flexibility.

The term flexibility has become so popular in ordinary discussions that its use as a conceptual tool has been considerably weakened. Flexibility has been used to describe developments like multiskilling and the adaptability of work force skills; the mobility of workers and the increase in precarious forms of employment; as well as wage flexibility, the impact of legislative protection and tax thresholds on firm's employment practices.

On one hand, interest in these developments has encouraged a reassessment at the level of macro regulation, as represented in the work of Boyer (1988). On the other hand, academic research on labour market segmentation has moved its attention away from the labour market in general, to focus on developments within firms at the micro level. This research has sought to understand how employers divide up stable and precarious forms of employment within their companies. We will first look at the work of Boyer, before going on to examine firm based research.

Boyer (1988) argues that there have been strong, universal pressures on all Western economies following the economic crises of the mid 1970s; the oil crisis and the separation of the dollar from the gold standard sent shock waves through these economies. Fordist systems of accumulation and regulation have been unable to continue managing aggregate demand and production. Boyer's claim is based on the premise that,

> ...the gradual transformation of social relations leads in time to a change in the laws governing the operation of particular economic systems. ... the success of regulation is gauged by its ability to guide and channel the process of capital accumulation, and to contain the imbalances that this tends to generate. (Boyer 1988:8)

One response to these changes has been "*The search for labour market flexibility*". Despite common general trends, nationally specific solutions have been developed.

.... strategies to increase flexibility vary from one country to another and follow different paths, depending on the history of industrial relations, industrial specialisation, and the country's position in world markets. Beyond the universal 'pursuit of rigidity', there are particular components (wages, working time, or levels of employment) and particular groups (the young, foreign workers, women) who have borne the burden of the adjustment implied by the crisis. (Boyer 1988:221)

His central argument is that western societies face a structural crisis. This has shaken the system of accumulation, which undermincs the mode of regulation between production and social demands.

The strengths of his approach are that it identifies an active and diverse role for the state and key institutions in shaping wage/labour relations. He recognises that different countries have historically developed various methods of regulation. These legacies affect the capacity of societies to respond to the challenges he documents. However, there are some problems with his argument, in particular with the concept of a universal Fordist system of regulation (Gilbert et al. 1992; Clarke 1992; Pollert 1990). Whilst he acknowledges the difference between Fordist production practices and Keynesian economics, he asserts that the two are symbiotically linked. However, when we look at specific societies it is hard to reconcile the diversity of industrial organisation and economic regulation with a general concept of a Fordist form of production and regulation. In outlining the challenges that face European economies Boyer acknowledges a range of potential macro-economic options and their implications. However, these tend to be framed as exclusive alternatives, in a somewhat stylised bleak or sanguine scenario. Further, whilst recognising the vast amalgam of flexible practices he rarely goes beyond a macro level analysis. He recognises that we need to know more about how these developments are operating at the local level, for example within firms and through the actions of employers.

A number of studies have looked into the development of flexible working practices at the firm level (Atkinson and Meager 1986; Meurs 1987; Maruani and Nicole 1988b; Brunhes 1989; Elgar and Fairbrother 1990; Pollert 1991; Penn 1992; Hunter and MacInnes 1992; Hunter et al. 1993). These firm level studies have focused on specific employment contracts like part-time work, self employment, temporary work, job sharing, the use of trainees and short term contracts. These "non-standard" contracts are usually discussed in terms of secondary sector employment, or precarious forms of work. The concept of numerical flexibility has become a popular way to refer to the type of flexibility these contracts offer employers. In contrast, the development of multiskilled workers has concentrated on core, permanent employees in the primary labour market. These workers provide employers with task, or functional flexibility. The focus of many of these studies has been on employment status. With the exception of part-time work, less attention has been given to the specific social characteristics of the workers who make up the flexible work force, or the types of control operated by various employers. To some extent the focus on the firm level and the diversity of contractual arrangements used by employers represents a healthy break from the structuralist arguments of early dual labour market theorists. Nolan (1983) and Rubery (1988) suggest that such an approach can, potentially, identify the possibility of choices open to employers to use different forms of flexibility. This can allow greater leverage in accounting for variety. Before we examine these implications for cross-national research let us first examine in more detail the concepts that have been developed in relation to flexible employment.

3.1 Functional flexibility

Functional flexibility is found amongst core sector employees, in contrast to numerical flexibility provided by the secondary sector. Functional flexibility has also been referred to as multiskilling and polyvalence. It is essentially concerned with adapting staff, and the tasks they perform, to meet changing product market demands (Atkinson and Meager 1986:38). Functional flexibility is concerned with breaking down the traditional demarcation between skills and creating Japanese styled "mechatronics" (OECD 1986:122). This combines traditional craft skills with information technology skills. This is key to the development of flexible specialisation (Piore and Sabel 1984). However, this concept has relied heavily on studies of the manufacturing sector (Kern and Schumann 1989).

 In contrast to the arguments of deskilling put forward by Braverman (1974), advocates of flexibility argue that technological change can encourage the development of functional flexibility. Market uncertainty can also be a causal factor in the development of this policy. Atkinson and Meager (1986) claim that there are two approaches a company can take to developing this strategy, although they take the concept of strategy for granted. Either a company can adopt a piecemeal extension of job descriptions, or they can take on the principle whole-heartedly by dispensing with specific tasks and job descriptions.

> Instead, workers are divided into groups distinguished by competence or skill level and their deployment is "as required" constrained by that competence and skill. (Atkinson and Meager 1986:39).

Functional flexibility reduces traditional forms of workers' control based on job specific skills. This allows companies greater freedom to change the terms of employment contract to their own advantage, leaving a worker with little basis on which to control their conditions.

Functional flexibility has had the most success in Japan, where worker identity is more closely tied to the company, compared to the more conflictual industrial relations traditions in Britain and France. Obstacles to functional flexibility have been attributed to the ingrained spirit of Taylorism, where tasks are parcelled up into distinct jobs and are separate from supervisory tasks (OECD 1986:119). Entrenched working practices and pay differentials have been considered an obstacle to introducing this form of flexibility (Atkinson and Meager 1986:41). Different groups of workers and unions have sometimes been hostile to such changes. On the management side, opposition to functional flexibility has been based on a belief that the costs involved, in terms of training and increasing salaries to create multiskilled craftsmen, would exceed the benefits. Where there no consensus exists between different companies, this policy has suffered from fear of a free-rider problem: rival firms could avoid the expense of training, whilst being able to offer more competitive salaries to poach higher skilled staff from other companies.

One of the major criticisms of the concept of functional flexibility has focused on the broad range of practices that it attempts to account for. The model implicitly assumes that an expansion of tasks is equivalent to increasing workers skills. However, critics have argued that this confuses work intensification with up-skilling. Pollert (1987:14) questions the claims that these are new strategies, and argues that functional flexibility is merely the renaming of traditional productivity enhancing measures, associated with rationalisation and job enlargement in the 1970s. Thus one of the unresolved issues to emerge from these debates has been with whether or not the development of functional flexibility has led to an increase in the skills and qualifications of employees. This question is examined in greater detail in chapter 4 of this book.

3.2 Numerical flexibility

The concept of numerical flexibility explains how employers match workers to work load fluctuations. They can do this in either of two ways: they can bring in "additional workers", with the assumption that they can get rid of them when work levels are low; or, employers can use their existing workers to re-organise working time to cover these fluctuations, (Atkinson & Meager 1986:14). A wide range of employment contracts can be used to achieve numerical flexibility: these included temporary work, part-time work, permanent staff working overtime and/or an alteration of shift patterns and flexible working time. Numerically flexible workers can have the advantage of reducing overtime costs, and meeting trade union demands for a reduction in working time for full-time, permanent employees. Temporary staff can also be used, without employers entailing any subsequent commitment to them, to meet the benefits gained by permanent staff. For example numerically flexible workers provide cover for permanent staff on sick leave, holidays or maternity leave. Atkinson and Meager (1986) claim that whilst it was easy enough to re-schedule shift patterns, the use of arrangements like intermittent contracts[3] meant re-scheduling entire blocks of time; work force opposition to such a flexible measure was seen as potentially hostile[4]. Nevertheless this will be a key issue for the future (Schömann and Kruppe 1993).

However, one of the problems with the concept of numerical flexibility is again the diverse range of employment contracts which are subsumed under the one category. This has resulted in an exaggeration of the size and growth of peripheral employment (Meager 1986; Hakim 1987; Gallie and White 1991; Casey 1988). Numerical flexibility has also been criticised for not making a sufficient distinction between existing staff and additional workers who provide numerical flexibility. If numerical flexibility is essentially about using additional workers and dispensing with them, i.e. they have little job security, characteristic of secondary forms of employment, is it appropriate to argue that permanent employees working overtime, or permanent part-timers, (i.e. existing workers) offer the same type of flexibility as temporary workers (additional workers)? The question revolves around the concept of job security which is not fully brought out in the analysis, and confuses the nature of flexibility that is offered by these different forms of employment contract. Employers' criteria for using these forms of employment are reduced to a simple motivation of matching staff to work load levels. These issues are examined in relation to motivations for using temporary staff in chapter 5, and part-time work in chapter 7.

3.3 Flexible inter-firm relations

The issue of developing more flexible relations between firms has received considerable attention not only in the work on flexible specialisation but also in studies of subcontracting. Piore and Sabel (1984) argue that the potential development of flexible specialisation is generating positive new forms of co-operation and competition between firms. Atkinson and Meager (1986) use the concept of distancing to discuss the substitution of traditional employment contracts by purely commercial ones. They argue,

> Why attempt to be more flexible to deal with these pressures (greater competition, market pressures, volatility, uncertainty) if its easier to pay some one else to deal with them? (Atkinson & Meager 1986:54).

Distancing covers a gamut of contracts including subcontracting, in-store concessions, franchising, self employment, homeworking and networking. However the extent of some of these developments has been limited, for example with regard to networking it has only had a limited impact in a handful of multinational companies working in the computer field (Huws 1984; Upton 1984).

Pollert (1987:15) argues that the motivation to subcontract may come about from the desire to reduce inventories and costs rather than an active project to introduce flexibility itself.

Nevertheless Piore and Sabel (1984:214-220) recognise that cost pressures have been one of the stimulus to develop flexibility in the first place. The implication that employers world wide are seeking to improve inter-firm relations is questioned in the work of Nishiguchi's (1989). His comparison of subcontracting and supplier relations in Japan, the US and Europe suggests that the nature and motivation to develop these relations vary between different countries. This highlights the problem of attributing management with a coherent managerial strategy, when this may be tangential to other aims (Rubery 1988:271). This issue is examined in more detail in chapter 6.

The various models of flexibility share many of the conceptual problems raised by dual labour market theory. Many of these arise from the dichotomised models that they employ. The key concepts of functional and numerical flexibility have been criticised for conflating diverse elements under generalised catch-all categories. They suffer from the problems of comparing heterogeneous groups, allocated on the basis of functional or numerical flexibility, to the primary or secondary labour market respectively. What is needed in these debates is a reassessment of the extent and nature of the flexibility firms are attempting develop. Further, many of the advocates of flexibility argue that these developments represent a new and radical strategy on the part of management.

3.4 Problems of strategic analysis

Although the idea of "strategy" is fundamental to these debates, it has often been treated as unproblematic. Crow (1989) points out that, although the concept of strategy has received extensive popularity in the vocabulary of various social researchers, the theoretical underpinning of the concept have been neglected. When we talk about managerial strategy, for example, how is this different from saying "this is what managers do"? The term strategy has to refer to a choice, and this implies exercising power. However, we have to specify who we are attributing with "strategic" action, and at what level strategy is formulated and implemented (Silverman 1987; Bernoux 1985:125-156).

Crow points out that in a wide range of social science research the capacity to act strategically has been attributed to individuals, groups, households, and organisations. However trying to identify strategies in practice has been a fraught exercise (Knights & Morgan 1990). In its simplest form a strategy has to have an identifiable aim, which can be achieved by a range of different methods. The subject has to be aware of the alternatives open to them, so that we can say they have a strategy. However this simple definition is not so easy to identify in the real world, especially when unconscious behaviour can also be referred to as strategic (Crow 1989:7; cf: Edwards & Ribbens 1991). Theoretically the concept of strategy attributes the actor with a degree of rationality and access to information which in reality is not always apparent.

Purcell and Sisson (1983) have shown how managerial strategies are often incremental and contradictory. They argue that the post-war growth of large companies and conglomerates, with a multidivisional organisation and a specialised and fragmented managerial elite, makes it even more difficult to attribute managers with coherent strategic planning. Purcell and Sisson attempt to identify a generalised strategy which can claim to be characteristic of British employers, but what they find is a diversity of contradictory developments between different sectors. Child (1985) is resistant to the use of a strict definition of strategy which restricts analysis to cases where one can identify coherent policy rationales. Such an approach assumes that a direct line from policy to implementation can be identified (Child 1985:109). Instead, Child argues that the chain from formulation to implementation is subject to obtaining the co-operation of lower level managers and workers, whose influence may bring about unintended consequences. Child advocates a perspective which takes account of the possibility of variation and emphasises the "contextual factors" that can explain such variation. Recognising these problems however does not mean it is completely hopeless to conduct research in terms of strategy (Morris 1985), but we have to be cautious "who" we impute with a strategy.

Hodson and Kaufman (1984) avoid the term strategy altogether. They give greater emphasis to the nature of power relations between different actors according to their resources and vulnerabilities. This situates the discussion of strategy in a context where we can begin to unravel the often complex rationality and motivations of actors. Too often actors are attributed with simplistic motivations. Instead, these actors should be seen as active subjects capable of formulating and re-formulating their own rationales. Employees, for example, are often seen as the victims of employers policies without any recognition of the choices that are available to them in relation to paid employment. Strategy has to be seen in terms of a process of interaction, and in doing so it can highlight the complexities of the "contextual factors" within which actors operate.

In order to understand why employers might seek to use numerical or functional flexibility we need to have a broader appreciation of the economic and social context within which these strategies are developed. Gallie and White (1991) have argued that employers policies need to be analysed in relation to structural factors like the type of industry, its size and labour market location. Contextual considerations also need to be included, related to product market strategy and competitive pressures. We also need to take account of the role of trade unions, labour regulation and the attitudes and preferences of employees to understand the nature of the resources or constraints these impose on employers' ability to develop particular types of flexibility. To what extent can employers act in a unilateral way? How do they legitimise their decisions and gain support to implement them? The relevance of these questions are particularly highlighted when it comes to cross-national research and women's employment.

4. Conclusions

This chapter set out to examine theories which have been concerned with explaining how employers make decision about labour allocation, the type of contracts they use and the type of people they employ for various jobs within their organisations. From this review we can draw out three key issues concerning multi-skilling, precarious employment and the capacity for employers to act strategically.

First, the literature on dual and segmented labour markets argues that firms develop job or company specific skills through internal labour markets. The flexibility literature has developed this idea with the concept of functional flexibility. However, it is not clear where the requirement to perform a wider range of tasks is linked with an improvement in the training and skills of these employees. One of the areas of contention has been over whether changing organisational strategies have encouraged deskilling or an increase in skills or core sector employees. This issue is examined more closely in chapter 4.

The second major issue relates to the use of secondary

sector labour. Part-time and temporary work are seen as examples of the growth in non-standard employment. These type of contracts are meant to offer employers numerical flexibility in the sense that numbers employed can be varied according to work load fluctuations. However, concern has arisen with regard to the precarious nature of these jobs. This implies that we need to establish to what extent these contracts provide employers with numerical flexibility and whether this type of flexibility is the same in both countries. Further, the issue of exclusion or confinement to a secondary or peripheral sector needs to be addressed. These issues are examine in chapters 5,6 and 7.

Third, the question of employers' capacity requires further examination. What is the nature of the constraints and resources available to employers to develop flexible forms of employment? Employers' behaviour has been the key focus of much of the literature on dual and segmented labour market theory and in the flexibility debates. However, subsequent critiques of this research have suggested that greater attention needs to be given not only to the commercial constraints imposed on employers, but also to the role of trade unions, labour regulation and the characteristics of available forms of labour. These factors are examined in chapters 8 and 9. It is argued here that these factors set the parameters within which employers can develop flexibility. Further, these parameters vary between countries, which implies that employers will seek to develop different types of flexible labour according to the limitations and resources available within the specific societal context in which they find themselves. This is the main argument developed through the empirical work presented in this book, and synthesised in chapter 10. But before we go on to examine this we need to have a closer understanding of the characteristics of the banking sector which is presented in chapter 3.

Notes

1. Piore labels the categories upper and lower tier primary sectors and the secondary sector.

2. Edwards (1979) does, however, allow for some deviation between different job types and control systems. *"It should be clear that the relationship between types of control and*

labor market segments is not perfect or exhaustive. Anomalies appear and, more importantly, development occurs such that any static typology can never adequately capture all the transitional and developmental situations." (1979:178-9)

3. This is where employees are contracted to work a specified number of hours over a year or a season. Companies like Christian Dior, in France, have been successful in introducing this form of contract when faced with the unexpected demand for their new perfume "Poison", a rapid increase in production was required to meet this demand (Autrand 1988).

4. See Gregory (1987) for case study evidence of this in French supermarket attempts to organize a fixed late evening shift. Eventually employers had to compromise to staff demands for a rotating shift.

3 The banking sector

1. Introduction

The traditional stereotyped image of a bank employee has been characterised by the bowler-hat, pin-striped suit and stiff collar of the male clerk, possessed with a certain sense of status and self importance. Working for a bank is commonly perceived of as having a "good" job, because the banks have offered secure, white collar employment, and the possibility of internal career progression. However, the "white-blouse revolution"[1] heralded the large scale entry of women into this sector, at the same time employment status declined. More recently the announcements in the newspapers of massive redundancies suggest that the banks are no longer the protected bastions of all that was safe and secure in the "good old days". What has happened? Why have these changes come about?

This book examines whether these changes correspond to the claims that the banks in Britain and France are looking for similar types of labour flexibility as discussed in Chapter 1 and 2. However, before comparing the various labour practices used in each country we need a broader idea of the structure of the banking sector and contemporary concerns within it. This chapter sets out to present such a picture: it compares the composition of the banking sector in the two countries. It examines the impact of deregulation and automation on the branch networks and clearing centres, and on employment practices in general. By outlining the stimulus for growth and the pressures for change, we can identify areas where the banks want to restructure their operations and, possibly, introduce flexible working practices.

In France much of the retail banking system was nationalized by De Gaulle after the second world war, and the banks were severely restricted in the services they could offer[2] (Burgard 1988; AFB 1986; Green 1986). Since the late 1960s these restrictions have progressively been lifted. In 1986 the Chirac government privatized the Société Générale, and some other smaller banks (Fabra 1985); the re-election of the right has led to further discussions of future privatisation including the Crédit Lyonnais. The banks in France have traditionally been used as an instrument in government financial policy to provide a source of cheap funds to industry, although since 1983 there has been less pressure on the banks to do so (Marsh 1985; Lewis 1987; Shreeve & Alexander 1991; de Quillacq 1987). The close link between the banks and government can be seen in the appointment of senior managers of the nationalized banks who are often political appointments. Despite state ownership there is intense competition between these rival groups. The prospects of future privatisation is likely to exacerbate this.

The main banks in France are the Société Générale, the Crédit Lyonnais, and the Banque Nationale de Paris (BNP), which all belong to the employers federation, l'Association Française des Banques (AFB). There is also the Crédit Agricole, a co-operative bank and one of the largest in France. The Crédit Agricole was originally set up to provide cheap credit to the agricultural community, and it operates under regulations distinct from those of the AFB. The Banques Populaires were also established for similar reasons for the urban artisans. Although the Crédit Agricole benefits from offering preferential credit, like other mutualist banks, the state is active in their lending policy, and the government can nominate members for the national Management Board (caisse).[3] The 1984 Banking Act in France set up regulatory bodies to separate "prudential control" of the banks from the apparatus of state ownership (Economist Publications 1989:6). This system of regulation also sought to bring the savings banks, co-operative and mutual banks under the same regulatory umbrella as the commercial banks. Green argues that,

> Despite this (state) control, the activities of the cooperative and mutual agencies have altered to such an extent that it is increasingly difficult to sustain the distinction between

them and the commercial banks. (1986:90).

As the mutual and cooperative banks have expanded their services they have become the major source of competition to the main commercial banks like the Société Générale, the Crédit Lyonnais, the Banque Nationale De Paris (BNP), and the Crédit Industriel et Commercial (CIC).

In Britain, by contrast, the fierce historical independence of the City of London together with a liberal political culture have acted as obstacles to state control and governmental direction of financial capital (Zysman 1983). The retail banking sector in Britain has been dominated since the 1970s by the 'Big Four': Barclays, NatWest, Lloyds and Midland, although deregulation has widened the number of players contesting for business. Until quite recently one could distinguish between the Clearing Banks, which dealt with transferral of funds, and the Building Societies which financed house purchases. However, deregulation has now blurred these boundaries. The same degree of market segmentation between consumer credit and housing finance does not exist in France, and there are a wider range of institutions active in the field of retail banking (Frazer and Vittas 1984: 158-60).

The differences between the institutions operating in the retail banking system are attributable to the historical development of the banking system, government intervention and the process of industrialisation in each country (Zysman 1983; Cox 1986; Green 1986; Hu 1975). Table 3.1 presents the number of companies in each type of establishment, the number of branches and the percentage of the market they controlled in 1987.

In Britain the market is dominated by the authorised commercial banks. In France the market is divided between the commercial banks and their main rivals the co-operative banks and the savings banks. Until quite recently the British system was concentrated in the hands of a few of the major clearers. In France there have been a significantly larger number of players since 1945. For example in 1983 in Britain, there were 13 Clearing banks, which controlled 52% of the accounts market; in France during the same period there were 406 companies defined as commercial banks, controlling 40.8% of the market (Banque des Règlements Internationaux et La Banque de France 1986). However since the 1987 Banking Act a larger number of institutions in Britain can now offer banking services.

Table 3.1
Structure of the financial sector in Britain & France

Type of Establishment	No. of Institutions	No. of branches	% of the Market accounts	value
BRITAIN 1987				
Authorised Banks	567	14,994	54.0	45.4
Building Societies	137	6,967	34.0	53.6
Post Office (NSB)	1	21,211	12.0	1.0
FRANCE 1987				
Commercial Banks	377	9,939	22.1	36.0
Cooperative Banks	190	11,175	33.0	30.7
Savings Bank	364	4,378	26.2	18.3
Post Office	1	17,089	18.7	15.0

(Source: Banque des Règlements Internationaux et La Banque de France (1989) Table A.2 page 302 & 344, B.1 page 303 & 345.)

1.2 Regionalised versus centralised clearing

The clearing system refers to the administrative support used to treat the paperwork generated by customer credit and debit transferals. Banking in Britain tends to be divided into three regionally distinct markets which correspond to Northern Ireland, Scotland, Wales and England. In France whilst the main banks have head quarters in Paris, there are a significant number of regional banks. This organisation is more decentralised than in Britain; Child (1988) notes that the British system, in comparison to other European countries, is exceptionally unitary. In Britain the clearing system has been controlled and dominated by the London clearing banks, except for minor systems used in Scotland and Northern Ireland. The British clearing system is centred around London. It was set up in 1770 and was formed into a private company in 1895 as the "Banker's Clearing House Ltd." This body was controlled by the six members of the "Committee of London Clearing Banks" who operated as a cartel. This arrangement recently broke up in 1987 over a dispute concerning the national salary levels of bank employees (Gapper 1987).[4]

The French system tends to be more decentralised than in

Britain. A number of factors account for this. Firstly, many of the banks are organised on a regional basis. Secondly, the administrative organisation of processing is encouraged to operate at a departmental level.[5] This is because of legislation which established that the exchange of cheques was to take place at a local clearing house, not as in the centralised British system (Lasfargues 1980). In France exchange can take place on a bi-lateral or multi-lateral basis, in private or official "chambres", directly or through an intermediate representative. Since 1984 the government have attempted to reduce the number of bilateral exchanges encouraging banks to go through the official channels. Originally the sorting machines reading the electronic codes on the cheques were operated from specialised centres. However together with,

> technological evolution and a modification to the rules governing cheque treatment they have on the whole been decentralised to the level of departmental clearing centres. (La Banque des Reglements Internationaux 1986:202).

The Bank of France decreed that clearing should be decentralised because 95% of all cheques were drawn on and paid into accounts within the same department. Since 1980 there have been 104 'principal' "chambres de compensation" (clearing houses) corresponding approximately to the administrative departments. Cheques can be presented at the clearing centres situated near the bank where the cheque has been drawn (Lasfargues 1980).

In France the cheque clearing institutions include the Paris based Bankers Clearing Office, the provincial clearing offices run by the Bank of France, the "Club of Nine"/Scenario Trois in which the major banks exchange cheques payable both locally and in the provinces at Paris, and finally the automated clearing centres operated by the Banque de France in Paris, Lyon, Strasbourg, Rennes, Nantes, and since 1983 in Lille, Marseille and Bordeaux. This system is far more decentralised and diverse than that found in Britain where most cheques have to pass through London.

Overall, in Britain the retail banking sector has been dominated by a small number of major clearing banks, whose organisation has been centralised through London. In France, a significantly larger number of commercial banks have been operating in the retail banking sector, where regional organisation has been a more common characteristic.

2. The retail market

2.1 Market expansion

Banks have moved away from catering for an elite, to offering their services to a mass market. Rising standards of living in most of Western Europe have stimulated these changes (Fraser & Vittas 1984). The increasing trend for employees to hold bank accounts was popularised by the move to pay wages on a monthly, as opposed to a weekly basis. In France "mensualisation", the monthly payment of wages encouraged manual workers to open a bank account.[6] A similar situation occurred in Britain with the abolition of the Truck laws which removed the right to demand payment in cash, so cheques or credit transfer became legal tender. The growth of a mass market in retail banking corresponded to the decline in the use of cash. For example the number of employees paid in cash has fallen from 75% of all employees in 1969 to 44% in 1981. The growth in banking services was effectively managed by the increased automation, which made the transferral of credit cheaper and more popular than direct cash payments (Rajan 1984:62).

The increase in account holders pressed the banks to open more branches. In the mid sixties the Debré reforms in France lifted the post-war segregation of savings banks, deposit banks and commercial banks which encouraged universal banking and the expansion of commercial bank networks. Nationwide banks doubled their network, whilst smaller regional banks, in some cases, nearly trebled the number of branches (Frazer and Vittas 1984:158). British banks also expanded their branch networks in the same period. However this growth was constrained, in both countries, by the economic crisis of the 1970s and has subsequently led to re-evaluation and restructuring in the 1980s.

Whilst the trend towards account holding has been increasing there has been a considerable difference in the degree of market penetration between the two countries, although the gap is gradually closing. In France the chequing account market is practically saturated. In 1981 over 90% of adults had a chequing account compared with 60% in Britain. The banks in Britain were comparatively sheltered from the brunt of competition during the early 1980s because the lower density of personal bank accounts left them with room for market expansion (Frazer and Vittas 1984). However, as market penetration has increased this advantage has been gradually whittled away: by 1989 the number of people with a bank account in Britain had risen to approximately 80% (Bailey 1990). In France recent figures show that 99.3% of all adults have a bank or savings account, and 95% a chequing account (Graham 1988).

2.2 Increased competition and product diversification

Retail banking has lacked the glamour of other realms of the banking world and has been seen largely as a processing operation.

> Retail banking was for many years a bit of a back water in the financial services industry - routine and rather unenterprising. There wasn't much competition between the major banks, and not much from outside, either. (Blanden & Laurie 1989).

The consumer credit market has become more attractive for the banks in both countries, because of the decline in traditional sources of revenue earned in the corporate sector.

> The corporate sector, their main focus during the long years of credit controls, has become increasingly difficult to milk, under the influence of increased competition and the process of securitisation. (Graham 1988).

Deregulation of the securities market removed the barriers which had given the banks a monopoly on raising company credit.[7] Corporations have had direct access to the money markets, or, have acted as lenders between themselves thereby squeezing out the bank as intermediary (Lewis 1987:45). The declining profits to be made on corporate lending encouraged the banks to look elsewhere for new markets. The personal sector was attractive because of the degree of stability in revenue transfers. Whilst corporate accounts have larger amounts of money coming into them, they also tend to have a high degree of cash flow leaving the account. Banks can minimise their risks by spreading them over a wider range of small borrowers rather than concentrating them in a few large companies; a logic which is especially relevant in a period of economic recession and bankruptcy (Blanden & Laurie 1989:171; Lascelles 1989).

However, the banks were not the only ones to notice this untapped source of profit in the personal sector. In Britain, domestic competition has increased especially since retail banking services were opened up to the building societies by the Banking Act in February 1987. Competition has also come from retailers, in both countries, offering charge cards (Barchard 1988). Also, in France the co-operative banks, like the Crédit Agricole, have been moving from their traditional agricultural based clients into metropolitan markets (de Quillacq 1987; Gueslin 1988).

The main clearing banks have found themselves burdened with processing cheques and maintaining branches. According to a report by Shearson Lehman (The Banker, Feb 1991:10) French banks have particularly high operating costs in the areas of cheque clearance. The benefits of deposit holdings have been going to the savings banks and co-operative banks in France, and in Britain the Building Societies have been the main beneficiaries (La Banque des Reglements Internationaux 1989:302; Lewis 1987). Between 1963 and 1983, the four main banks in Britain held approximately 35% of all personal savings.[8] The building societies have seen their deposits rise rapidly from 22% share of the market in 1963, to nearly 50% in 1983 (La Banque des Reglements Internationaux 1985:281).

> For longer than bankers can remember price competition in most European countries was constrained by official regulation or voluntary agreement. So competitive efforts tended to focus on increasing branches and services. With competition intensifying, the chief need now is to cut costs and either prune over-extended branch networks or get more value out of them by adding insurance or other products to the services provided. (The Banker, Top 1,000, July 1990:77)

The banks have been looking to offer services in new areas.

To increase profits and retain customers the banks have sought to extend their services beyond simple money transmission. They now offer advice on management of estates and private trusts, life assurance, brokering, factoring, leasing and other advisory services. Cross selling is becoming a high priority strategy together with an emphasis on the quality of personal service (Lewis 1987). A more pro-active policy of cross-selling is evident from the recent use of telemarketing. Frazer and Vittas suggest that,

> ancillary services will go from being an additional revenue-earning activity to being eventually the entire raison d'etre of the branches(Frazer & Vittas 1984:xiv)

This will make a significant change to the face of retail banking (Reed 1988).

2.3 Mergers, economic instability and deregulation

As the banking sector has grown there has been a trend towards concentration, as larger banks have bought up smaller regional banks and merged their operations. In 1963 there were 11 clearing banks in England and Wales, by 1985 there were only 9. Although the late 1960s were characterised as a period of "mergermania" when the number of major clearers was reduced, in the last 20 years there has been an increase in a number of smaller banks in Britain. (Wright & Valentine 1988:39; Savage 1989).

A similar trend has also developed in France although under the auspices of state control. One of the repercussions of the 1966-7 reforms[9] led to a greater concentration of banks and the disappearance of small local banks (AFB 1986:4). Despite mergers, competition increased. This was encouraged by government economic policy and a boom in consumer spending. With the advent of the Socialist government further nationalisation of deposit holdings of over one milliard francs took place in 1982 (Fabra 1985). However, in 1986-7, with the election of right, the Société Générale, Paribas and Suez banks were privatised. The re-election of the right has led to discussions of further privatisation. The development of the Single European Market is likely to encourage further mergers to protect the sector from foreign competition. Mergers have already taken place between the banks and insurance companies, often under the heavy guidance of the state in France. The cost of and investment required by electronic processing is really only affordable by the big banks, and as a result will further encourage such mergers.

One impact of the close relationship between government

and the banks in France has been to produce low capital/assets ratios for French banks (Table 3.2). If we compare this measure of financial stability with the British case we see that banks in the UK have tended to be in a stronger financial position. However, this data needs to be understood in the context of French industrial organisation. The close relationship between the banks and government has meant not only that the government relies on bank funds, but that it also steps in to support banks, like the Crédit Lyonnais, when they are in difficulties. When the Crédit Lyonnais showed a loss of FF6.9billion ($1.2 billion) in 1993, the conservative government was willing to provide FF4.9 billion new capital (Economist 26/3/94:98).[10] Therefore, capital/assets ratios only tell part of the story, about the economic vulnerability of the banks in each country. Profitability portrays a different picture.

In Britain Rajan (1984) argues that, despite continuous growth, the banking sector has increasingly experienced periods of instability and fluctuation:

> ..the last decade witnessed some fairly sharp changes in banking activity in two distinct periods: 1971-74, which saw an upsurge in international banking and the introduction of Competition and Credit Control; and 1975-77, when there was relative slackness because the "Corset" was biting severely on banks' eligible liabilities in the aftermath of a series of sterling crises. (Rajan 1984, 60)

Banks in Britain make their profits roughly equally between chequing accounts and savings accounts, and they are more sensitive to changes in the interest rate than in France (Frazer and Vittas 1984:171). The growth of financial services during the late 1980s in Britain was fuelled by the consumer boom and increased profitability in personal lending. The Chief Economic Adviser to Lloyds Bank stated that in Britain 'Home ownership and the City have been two poles of banking growth.' (Johnson 1988). However, profit rates in Britain have been subject to greater fluctuations than in France. Although profit levels are lower in France they have also been more stable than in the UK (Table 3.3). The recent decline of profits in Britain has been one of the causes for the banks attempts to cut back on labour costs. These differences indicate that market pressures to develop labour flexibility in each country have come from different sources. This in turn affects the way the think about the type of labour flexibility they need to develop.

Table 3.2
A comparison of the capital/assets ratio of leading banks
in France and Britain

BRITAIN		FRANCE	
NatWest	5.23	Crédit Agricole	4.88
Barclays	5.23	BNP	2.67
Midland	4.36	Crédit Lyonnais	2.67
Lloyds	3.81	Société Générale	3.36

(Source: The Banker 1990, The World's Top 1,000 Banks.)

Table 3.3
Pre-tax profits 1986-91 for banks in Britain and France
(in $m)

	1986	1987	1988	1989	1990	1991
BRITAIN						
Barclays	1,319	634	2,517	1,111	1,465	997
NatWest	1,491	1,318	2,546	649	972	251
Midland	640	-945	1,254	989	21	67
Lloyds	1,032	-464	1,723	-1,148	1,139	1,291
FRANCE						
Crédit Agricole	529	852	852	1,266	1,381	1,599
BNP	772	852	876	918	603	862
Crédit Lyonnais	629	918	811	940	1,513	1,048
Société Générale	624	701	863	1,013	720	1,086
CIC Group	266	224	255	387	387	306

(Source: The Banker 1987-1992, July)

Overall, we can see that market competition and product

diversification have increased, and that the banks have been increasingly vulnerable to greater profit instability.

3. Automation and the clearing system

New technology has made a profound mark on the face of retail banking, and it has been suggested that without it current levels of activity could not have been dealt with, without entailing massive recruitment (Cooke 1986). The banking sector has been one of the major industries to invest in micro electronic technology (Ressources Informatiques No.5 Sept 1989:59; Sarrazin 1987), although it is difficult to get precise figures on levels of investment by individual banks. The French have been particularly successful in harnessing high technology to serve the personal sector (The Banker Jan 1991).

Automation, in both countries, has gone through three phases. Initially mainframe computers were introduced for administrative processing at the central headquarters. Automation was then extended to the branch networks with the use of Automated Telling Machines (ATMs) and cashier terminals. More recently the development of homebanking and Electronic Funds Transfer Point of Sales (EFTPOS) has encouraged banking outside of the traditional branch structure (Rajan 1984; de la Mothe 1985).

3.1 First Phase: Mainframe computerised accounts

Mainframe computers in both countries were introduced at the centralised processing centres in the 1960s. In 1968 the Bankers Automated Clearing System (BACS) was introduced into General Clearing in Britain which centralised the processing of accounts, and took work away from the branches. In Britain clearing is divided between "Town Clearing" for amounts over £100,000 [11] transferred within the Central London area, and "General Clearing" for the rest of the country. Since 1984 the Clearing House Automated Payment Service (CHAPS), a form of electronic transfer of funds, has been used for Town Clearing.

In France the clearing system can be distinguished between traditional and automated methods. In 1985 the traditional system accounted for 81% of the total number of transactions, and 94% of the total value. The new automated system at that time only accounted for 19% of the number of transactions and

6% of the total value (La Banque des Reglements Internationaux 1985:300). Table 3.4 compares the development of different payment systems in each country since 1978.

Table 3.4
The relative importance of cashless payment instruments

Instrument	Percentage of total transactions		
	1978	1983	1987
BRITAIN			
Cheques	74	63	57.0
Credit Cards	4	8	11.5
Paper-based credit transfers	9	12	9.0
Paperless credit transfer	8	11	13.5
Direct Debit	4	6	9.0
Interbank transfers	>1	>1	>1.0
FRANCE			
Cheques	86	82.5	65.4
Credit Cards	>1	2.1	na
Paper-based credit transfers	3	1.5	1.9
Paperless credit transfers	4	7.6	15.4
Direct debits	6	6.2	9.4
Interbank transfers	>1	0.1	na
Debit card at EFTPOS	na	na	7.9

(Source: La Banque des Règlements Internationaux - La Banque de France (1986) and (1989) "Systèmes de Paiement dans Onze Pays Developpes".)

Automated transferrals are developing gradually. Although cheques represent well over 50% of all transactions in each country, slightly more in France than in Britain, their use has been slowly declining. During the 1970s, in France cheque payment increased enormously, and more recently the French banks have been trying to encourage customers to use plastic cards. In 1981 there were 18,850 credit cards in Britain compared with 5,500 in France (Fraser & Vittas 1984:167 and 259). In Britain credit card use is more extensive but these transfers also involve considerable paper work.

3.2 Phase Two: Automatic tellers and cashier terminals

During the 1970s automation developed primarily in the back office. The use of ATMs was directed at providing cash dispensing services outside the branches and at irregular hours (Rajan 1984). Their use was only slightly higher in Britain than in France: at the end of 1987 there were 12,500 cash dispensers and ATMs in the UK, compared to 11,500 in France (Banque de Reglements Internationaux et La Banque de France 1989:304 & 346). The Chairman of Barclays Bank estimated that ATMs would halve the number of cashiers required. The Banking, Insurance and Finance Union (BIFU) in Britain was more pessimistic: '*It has been estimated that one ATM avoids the need for between 0.7 and 2 cashiers. At the end of 1984 6,470 were in use.* (BIFU 1985:6). Some banks in Britain have decided to use ATMs at the quick service counters, this is because of perceived customer hostility to them, and because the banks want to maintain a personal service and develop cross-selling. Cashiers are increasingly encouraged to draw clients attention to the other services the bank offers, for example, credit cards, insurance, or small loans; stand alone ATMs are also used for this purpose of cross-selling by advertising loans and insurance products.

One noticeable difference between the application of new technology in the two countries is the use of computer terminals by cashiers. It is common in France, in most of the major banks, for cashiers to have direct access to an on-line terminal, through which they can interrogate a customers' account to credit, debit or give instant information on their balance. They can also check to see what loans the client already has before granting a loan. In Britain on-line terminals are more popular in smaller building societies and were not in operation in the larger bank at the time this study was being conducted, although some banks have been introducing these selectively and their use is likely to increase; the implications of this are discussed in Chapter 4.

3.3 Phase Three: Banking without branches

As automated payments, in the form of direct debit, standing orders, or "Lettre de Change Releve" (LCR) and the "Titre Universal de Paiement" (TUP), become more popular this reduces the need for banking to be tied to the branch network structure.

3.3.1 Homebanking marks an important move away from direct face-to-face customer contact in the branches, and as it becomes more popular this will have serious repercussions on employment in the banks. Homebanking involves being able to access the main bank computer to obtain balances, transfer funds and pay bills from home; some companies also accept foreign currency and cheque book requests. In response to the establishment of Firstdirect, a bank without any branches (Barchard 1990), all the other main banks started to offer some form of account interrogation by phone.

French homebanking is conducted through the services provided by Minitel. Since 1987 bank cashiers have been able to deal directly, over the counter, with customer requests to buy and sell shares through brokers on the stock market using Minitel for quotations and electronic mail. The obstacles to this type of banking being adopted on a more extensive basis are the existence of branch networks, public indifference and possible security problems. The conservative habits of clients are hard for the banks to change. Rough estimates expected that it would take between 10-20 years for customers to break their banking habits (Vaughan 1990), however, customers have been surprisingly receptive to these technology developments.

3.3.2 Electronic Funds Transfer at Point of Sale is the second major development encouraging a move away from branch banking (de la Mothe 1985). This is the electronic equivalent of using cash or cheques. BIFU claims that,

> The major Banks are pursuing a joint scheme to cover the entire country. If this goes to schedule there will be 18,000 terminals in shops handling 130 million transactions by 1990, rising to 100,000 terminals and 750 million by 1995 or one eighth of estimated transactions. (BIFU 1985)

Child (1988) sees this as the greatest threat to low grade clerical jobs. However, such a scheme requires massive capital investment and a collaborative standardisation between banks and retailers. EFTPOS is also being experimented with in France where there is a preference for an off-line system (Frazer and Vittas 1984). This means it is cheaper to install and run, and allows the customer the same benefit of a two day float before payment, as with a chequing account. However they are also more difficult to integrate with the homebanking on-line system and it makes it difficult to control fraud of unauthorised cheque usage. The development of a "memory" card, or "smart" card, is seen as a means of linking on and off-line systems.

Technology solutions have been accepted in relation to the institutional structure of the banking system in each country. In Britain BACS was developed to meet the needs of the centralised cheque clearing system. In France, where the system is more decentralised, automation has been located at regional clearing houses, after government intervention in 1980 to regulate the exchange of cheques. Cashier computer terminals have been more popular in France than in Britain. This is partly because the branches in France are smaller and because the French banks have been developing a policy of service integration; in Britain the branches are larger and service policy has been more segmented. Technological developments have not created uniform solutions for the banks in either country, instead technology has been grafted on to existing practices and organisational constraints. Austrin (1991) argues that the banks have been able to "mix and match" a range of technology options related to their policy on service provision. As automation becomes increasingly decentralised, how will this affect the type of flexibility employers want? And, how will it affect staff numbers, and the qualifications expected of bank employees?

4. Restructuring the branches

The possibilities created by new technology together with increased competition have pushed the banks to reconsider the provision of branch services. During the late 1960s and early 1970s there was a massive expansion of branches. Today technological developments are allowing the banks to rationalise and restructure branch networks. In Britain and France branches tend to be organised on the basis of a central branch and its' satellites. These are run by local managers who have some autonomy, depending on the status of the branch. These branches are managed by a regional office who in turn reports to central office. This highly centralised structure conceals the diversity of units within the bank. For example at the Midland the Conventional Branch offers a wide range of services, the Service Branch caters mainly for individuals and small businesses, and the Automated Branch is designed specifically for the personal sector. Extensive use is made of self-service electronic machines and these branches are often found on University/Polytechnic campuses or in large shopping centres or train stations. This model has largely been adopted by the other banks in Britain.

New technology has facilitated this restructuring of the branch networks in at least two ways. Accounts can be opened at a small local branch and run from the regional central office so that smaller branches can be opened at less cost. Secondly, ATMs reduce the number of staff needed to run a branch. In France a similar pattern is taking shape which is a product of new technology and market segmentation. New technology allows banks to operate smaller agencies and to separate their corporate and personal customers. Table 3.5 gives an indication of the relative size of branch staffing in the two countries.

Table 3.5
A comparison of the number of employees to branches in 1987

	No. permanent /non-permanent branches	Employees	Employees to branches
Of the top ten French banking groups	26,307	352,576	13.4
Of the top six British banking groups	16,705	398,071	23.8

(Source: CNC in JP Moussy (1989))

In France there tends to be more branches with fewer staff employed in them, compared to Britain. The average number of staff at a branch in France was 13.4 compared to 23.8 in Britain. This lower figure for France may be a reflection of the attempt to reduce the number of "back office" administrative jobs done in the banks.

In Britain, Barclays set up 300 business centres for corporate clients, offering specialised services which were formerly only available through the branches; the branches now specialise in the personal sector (Barchard 1988). In both countries the banks have been rationalising their branch structure. In Britain this has been developed along the lines of service segmentation between and within the branches, whereas in France the banks have been trying to integrate the services provided by their branch staff. This reorganisation has been directed to meet local business needs.

4.1 Opening hours

Opening hours has been a key issue in restructuring the branches. The banks want to be able to open according to local needs. In France flexibility in opening hours is facilitated by the different types of branch. According to Burgard (1988) the types of "guichets", defined as "les points de vente bancaires", are as follows. "Les guichets permanents": these are open on all working days and offer a full range of services although their size can vary considerably. The terms 'agence' and 'succursale' are used arbitrarily between different companies. They are collected together under a "group d'agences" placed under the same management. "Les guichets non-permanents": these are only open either during the week on market day, or in the busy season. They are often found in fixed buildings or even on "camion-bancaire", bank lorries. "Les guichets spécialisés": these only offer specific services like a bureau de change in train stations and at airports. Or, they are open for a specific clientele, for example, the "guichet d'entreprise" is only open to employees of the specified company. "Les guichets automatiques" are either found in the bank "in situ" or off site. They can be either staffed with personnel who advise on their use or else they are completely automated.

The opening hours in the two countries tend to differ. French banks are open throughout the day and closed at lunch time whereas in Britain it has been traditional for banks to shut at 3.30pm although this has been changing and many are now open until 5pm, as well as opening on Saturdays too (Bernoux et al. 1990). Banks are responsive to their local markets; in some areas, they remain open over lunch whereas in others they are shut. Extended opening hours have been introduced to offer advisory and selling services, and the use of new technology in the form of ATMs facilitates cashier services at irregular hours.

Branches are being significantly re-organised to offer a diversified range of services with extended opening hours. Where employers are seeking to improve the skills of their staff it is possible they are looking for functional flexibility. Where branches are being kept open for longer it is possible that the banks are looking to use numerical flexibility; these issues are examined more closely in subsequent chapters.

5. Employment and recruitment

The old days of paternalistic, cradle-to-the-grave employment are not quite dead but they are on the way out as banks become more market driven. (The Banker Jan 1991)

5.1 From employment growth to redundancies and restructuring

During the 1970s the expansion of branches and bank work led to a massive recruitment of essentially low grade administrative staff. *"We employed anyone so long as they could stand up"* (Personnel Manager, Britain 1989). One noticeable difference between the two countries is related to the higher levels of female employment in financial services in Britain compared to France. During the 1980s the financial sector experienced a period of continuous growth in employment. (Table 3.6).

Table 3.6
Male and female employment in the banking and finance sector in Britain and France 1979-1987
(in thousands)

	BRITAIN		FRANCE	
	Men	Women	Men	Women
1979	194.0	246.8	211.1	205.6
1980	197.9	263.3	213.8	207.8
1981	201.5	273.1	215.8	208.9
1982	206.3	268.5	218.2	211.0
1983	213.9	272.5	222.3	217.0
1984	221.5	285.1	223.6	220.2
1985	231.0	286.4	223.5	220.5
1986	237.5	292.5	228.9	226.8
1987	247.5	301.7	229.9	228.2

(Source: Eurostat, Employment and Unemployment 1989, Table III/4, NACE class 81)

However, the banks are increasingly concerned with reducing personnel. This concern started earlier in France than in Britain. In France, the Nora-Minc report in 1978 warnings of over-staffing sent a shock wave through the industry. This report predicted a 30% reduction of personnel by 1988. However falls in employment levels have not been so severe, even though there have been cases of redundancies in France, for example at the Crédit du Nord. According to Bertrand & Noyelle (1988), the market for banking in France is saturated and constrained by increased competition - its' production exceeds the capacity to consume; there has been an increase in the costs of raw materials (decline in non-remunerable deposits); there is insufficient investment and thousands of low qualified employees; banks have faced a reduction in structural profitability and are exposed to increasing risks. Until quite recently this concern had been more pressing in France than in Britain.

Even though there has been greater pressure to reduce staff numbers in France in the 1980s, this experience has not affected all the banks in the same way (Table 3.7). These figures highlight the differences in employment within the sector. The popular banks have suffered the most. The larger AFB Banks and the Crédit Agricole have been reducing their numbers whilst the Crédit Mutuel and the Caisses d'épargne have been protected from this trend.

Table 3.7
A comparison of the percentage change in employment in the retail banking institutions in France from 1979 to 1986

	1979	1983	1984	1985	1986
AFB Banks*	0.49	1.04	0.50	0.40	-0.29
Crédit Agricole	1.84	2.55	1.70	-0.20	-0.76
Banques Populaires	0.96	2.11	1.40	1.0	-1.79
Crédit Mutuel	8.30	5.95	6.60	4.10	3.37
Caisses d'épargne	8.27	9.53	4.20	3.10	2.50
TOTAL	1.41	2.10	1.27	0.70	-0.11

(* Banks attached to the Association Française de Banque i.e. they are universal banks. Source: Rapport 1987 du Comité des Etablissements de Crédit, AFB.)

Job security has become a growing issue in the banks in Britain. In 1990 Barclays reduced their staff by 1,500 and envisaged loosing between 13,050 to 17,400 *"over the next few years"* (Financial Times 26/2/91). Lloyds cut their staff by 2,000 in 1990 and Midland reduced theirs by 1,000, and planned to loose a further 1,400 in 1991. NatWest with a total staff of 80,000 announced, in 1989, a seven year programme to loose 15,000 jobs (Willcock 1991; Bennett 1991). Most banks have preferred to reduce personnel through "natural wastage" or voluntary packages. Predicted job losses at Barclays are expected to amount to 9,000 by 1995; Lloyds expect to reduce personnel by 3,000 by 1996, and NatWest intend to cut their personnel by 4,000 by 1994 (BIFU Research 10th February 1993).

Table 3.8
Confirmed redundancies in the UK insurance, banking and finance sector

1988	1,151
1989	2,109
1990	4,112
1991	11,690

(Source: BIFU Research Department 28th September 1992.)

The possibility of market growth had in the past protected employment in this sector. Pressures to cut back, especially on labour costs, have come about as the result of the recession, the collapse of the property market, the increase of bad debts at home and abroad (Parker-Jervis 1991, Brierley 1991). The areas most threatened by these announcements are in low grade administrative jobs. In Britain the unions have tried to encourage a policy of allowing staff numbers to fall through "natural wastage", although compulsory redundancies have been made at NatWest. In both countries where branches or departments are being closed down the unions have tried to negotiate redeployment and retraining, with limited success.

5.2 Changing staff skills

The banks are increasingly emphasising pro-active selling. Barsoux and Lawrence (1990a:119) argue that management in the British banks has moved away from the "traditional 'bankly' virtues of restraint, literate orderliness, and judgement". The emphasis is now on managers *'grasping nettles'*, taking initiatives and pursuing business opportunities: *"You're running a business, not minding a branch"* (Bank managers cited in Barsoux and Lawrence 1990a:120).

In France the increased pressure for staff to be more commercially orientated has pushed up the qualifications the banks require of their staff. Bank employees in France tend to be more highly qualified than those in Britain. For example, in 1975, 14% of bank employees in France had completed their full-time education up until the age of 22-3 years. By 1995 it was predicted that there would be 31% of all bank employees in this category (Moussy 1988). In Britain only 1-3% of bank staff had a university degree, 8-15% had A-levels and 15-20% had 0-levels. This difference was not only due to the French education system producing more people with higher qualifications than is the case in Britain. The French banks also actively recruited higher qualified, commercially orientated staff who they considered would be more adaptable to future change, compared to the low grade clerical workers they used to recruit.

In Britain the banks continued to focus most of their recruitment on young school leavers at 17+. Although there have been moves to introduce tiered entry in the British banks, post A-level entrance accounts for a minority of total annual recruitment, and women with few qualifications are predominantly employed in the lower grades (Crompton 1989:148-9). This pattern has been perpetuated in the banks in Britain because of the reaction to demographic trends which encouraged the British banks to offer women low grade part-time work. In Britain, at the end of the 1980s, employers were particularly concerned by the predicted 25% fall in the number of school leavers entering the labour market (Manpower Policy and Practice 1987; Parsons 1990). This was not a major concern to French employers. First, because it was expected that the decline in school leavers would only amount to 10% fall; and secondly, the impact of this trend was delayed for the French banks because they tended to recruit older, more qualified people than their British counterparts.

Employment issues in the banks have become of central significance as the impact of increased competition, falling profits, product diversification and technological change which have forced the banks to reconsider the way they provide financial services. The instability and change which has crept into the once cosy and stable environment of retail banking makes this sector a particularly apposite arena in which to examine the issues raised by the debates on labour flexibility.

6. Conclusions

This chapter has outlined the growth, structure and change which has occurred in the retail banking system in Britain and France. This has enabled us to identify where the banks in both countries have experienced similar pressures to re-evaluate and restructure the services they provide. Traditionally the banking sector was typified by a stable business environment, where the banks were rigid, hierarchical organisations. Today this environment is subject to greater competition, product diversification, falling and unstable profits. Technological innovation has allowed the banks to offer new services, and reduce the cost of labour intensive administrative work.

Nevertheless, there are important differences in the organisation of retail banking which suggest that the banks in each country are likely to adopt different labour strategies. The French system is more decentralised than in Britain, and has been subject to state control which has left them relatively undercapitalised, although profitability has on the whole been more stable. In France, where there are a larger number of financial institutions, the market for personal accounts is completely saturated. In Britain, where until quite recently the major banks operated as a cartel, the effects of competition have been curtailed because the limited degree of market penetration has left the banks room to compete for new clients. However, more recently they have been subject to increasing fluctuations in their profitability. Technological change has been grafted on to the existing organisational structure, and the banks have been able to "mix and match" technology solutions in relation to their service policy and recruitment practices.

Given these changes in what ways have the banks sought to achieve labour flexibility? Have changing product market demands encouraged the banks to introduce functional or task flexibility? Or, have they sought to deploy a strategy of numerical flexibility to meet the unpredictable fluctuations, extend opening hours and restructure their organisations? To what extent are jobs previously considered to be in the core sector of the labour market now threatened? These are central questions this book seeks to address. We start first with a discussion of functional flexibility in Chapter 4.

Notes

1. Taken from the title of "The white-blouse revolution: Female office workers since 1870" Gregory Anderson (1988), Manchester University Press.

2. Sharp distinctions were made between the services offered by different financial institutions in France so as to avoid the circumstances which led to the economic crisis of the 1930s.

3. Although the structure of the bank is decentralised and run on an independent regional basis the national caisse can provide financial support for local caisse by issuing bonds in its own name (Green 1986:89)

4. NatWest wanted to offer higher salaries to attract staff in a tight labour market, which the other banks opposed. NatWest unilaterally raised their salaries and this effectively made the Committee of London Clearing Banks redundant. Some of the implications of this are discussed in Chapter 9 of this book.

5. A department is the administrative unit used for the purposes of local government administration. There are 22 regions in France, 96 departments (divided into 320 arrondissement and 3530 cantons), and 36,034 communes. The departments date back to 1789 (Wright 1983:257).

6. This was reinforced by a pre-war law stating that employers had to pay any salary over 2500 francs a month by postal, bank or credit transfer to a postal or bank chequing account. It is possible to opt out of the system and have twice monthly payments (Frazer and Vittas 1984: 160-1).

7. Companies can negotiate credit stocks into transferable credit (paper drafts or securities) which has the same value as money. In this way a borrowing establishment can ease its problems of cash flow without liquidating its assets, at the same time avoiding bank charges.

8. This figure remained largely unchanged except for a fall in 1977 to 32%.

9. These reforms removed many of the restriction imposed by De Gaulle between merchant banks, credit banks and deposit banks. A money market was established, and more freedom was given to the banks to open branches.

10. A "bad bank" will be set up to allow the Crédit Lyonnais to off-load its bad loans, and the government will guarantee any losses on these loans for five years.

11. Before 1989 this was 10,000 pounds sterling. Raising the threshold reduced the amount of work in Town Clearing.

4 Functional flexibility

1. Introduction

The issue of task or functional flexibility has been of major interest in debates concerned with restructuring skills and training. Research on labour flexibility has debated whether or not technological change has led to de-skilling, in the way suggested by Braverman (1974). Researchers who argue that employers are increasingly concerned with the development of functional flexibility have associated this strategy with a general up-skilling of employees (Atkinson and Meager 1986). Critics, however, argued that this concept disguises the reality of restructuring and the practice of work intensification (Pollert 1987, 1991; MacInnes 1987). Gallie (1991) has examined the debate on changing skill levels at an aggregate level. He suggests that in Britain, during the 1980s, there has been a polarisation of skill. Further, an extensive literature, based on comparative research, argues that there are significant differences in the industrial organisation of different West European countries (Gallie 1978, 1983; Lane 1989; Maurice, Sellier and Silvestre 1982; Gregory 1989). Given these cross-national differences, has the "search for flexibility" been experienced in a similar way in different countries?

The aim of this chapter is to examine these debates and the concept of functional flexibility empirically. This is done with reference to in-depth case-study research conducted in the retail banking sector in Britain and France. This research looks specifically at where bank employees in each country have increased their task variety, and how this is related to training and skill. The central argument developed in this chapter states that a clearer distinction should be made in the concept of functional flexibility. This should distinguish between an increase in training and an upgrading of skills, in contrast to ad hoc practices used to meet shortages and intensify work. Second, this chapter introduces the empirical evidence used to support the argument that employers' use of labour flexibility needs to be understood within a societal context.

2. The concept of functional flexibility

Employers' motivations to look for labour flexibility have been attributed to a number of sources (Atkinson & Meager 1986; Boyer 1986; Piore & Sabel 1985; Berger & Piore 1980; Doeringer & Piore 1971). According to these theories, product market volatility has increased, and competitive marketing strategies in saturated markets have re-shaped consumer demands. Restructuring and decentralising operations have been motivated by a desire to control costs, regain control of the shopfloor and undermine union strength. Increased economic uncertainty has undermined the former stable trading environment, coupled with government inadequacies in managing the economy, inflation and recurrent periods of recession. Technological change has led to a displacement of staff, a blurring of skill boundaries, and generated the need for highly specialised personnel. It is in this turbulent atmosphere that discussions on the development of functional flexibility have been formulated.

The concept of functional flexibility, in its widest sense, refers to employees performing more than one function or task, or being able to do jobs other than the one they do regularly.[1] This is a new strategy, it has been claimed, because the extension of skills cuts across traditional job boundaries and skill demarcations (Piore and Sabel 1984; Atkinson & Meager 1986; Child 1985). Functional flexibility can exist at several levels. Horizontal job enlargement aims to broaden the number of tasks performed by employees at an equivalent skill level: a sideways expansion of a job, by the addition of a few extra tasks, can create a multi-skilled "craftsman" (sic.) (Atkinson & Meager 1986). Functional flexibility is also defined as vertical job enlargement. This involves either increasing the skill and competence of a worker (upward enlargement), or it can involve a skilled worker taking on semi-skilled operative functions (downward enlargement). Here is where the controversy in the debates on functional flexibility lie. Is functional flexibility only about an expansion of high and low grade tasks performed by employees in a given job? Or, should the claims that employers are developing functional flexibility be more closely tied to the conscious intention to increase training and skill? The problem in these debates has been that the two developments have been classified under the same conceptual category.

Developing functional flexibility is a strategy closely associated with core sector or permanent employment because employers seek to maximise on their investment in training (Rosenberg 1989: 393).

> Functional flexibility is achieved in the core, supported by appropriate incentives and rewards, possibly including enhanced employment security. In theory this is possible because the peripheral groups soak up numerical fluctuations in demand. (Atkinson & Meager 1986:5)

In some senses this is a continuation of the idea of internal labour markets developed in early dual and segmented labour market theories (Doeringer & Piore 1971; Berger & Piore 1980; Wilkinson 1981; Edwards 1979; Gordon et al. 1982). These theories postulated that large companies, in a privileged market position, provided training to obtain the skilled staff they required, in order to operate the advanced technology they used. The secondary labour market, in contrast, was relatively unskilled because companies operating in this sector were more labour intensive, with a lower investment in high technology. The flexible firm model transfers these labour market characteristics to within firm strategies.

Duration and location also affect the distinctiveness of these definitions. The span of time over which staff are expected to be functionally flexible can vary significantly: employees can be required to perform a wide range of tasks continuously, or only when required, or even on a short-term basis, all of which could be defined as being functionally flexible. Location, as well as skill performance, could also be included in the definition. For example, bank staff being moved between branches, or nurses working on different wards, or different shifts, could be a use of functionally flexibility (Atkinson & Meager 1986: 42-3). According to Atkinson and Meager (1986) functional flexibility does not, however, include permanent redeployment from one job to another, unless that worker is expected to do the former job "as required". Where technological change eliminates jobs, and the automated process is performed by another employee, this does not qualify as functional flexibility (Atkinson & Meager 1986: 43).

2.1 Problems with the concept of functional flexibility

Despite the enormous popularity of the literature on flexibility in commercial and academic circles, there are several conceptual problems with the concept of functional flexibility. Firstly, MacInnes (1987) points out that this concept is particularly difficult to measure, although Atkinson and Meager (1986: 39) are aware of this. Equating functional flexibility with core employment can also be problematic because of the difficulties in defining core employment: is it job security, training or promotion opportunities, and how are these linked to the development of functional flexibility? Who belongs to the core, and how do we identify them? Pollert (1987) argues that it is misleading to equate permanent employees with those in the primary sector, and cites examples of low grade, low paid public sector workers whose jobs are permanent. If the real difference between core and secondary sector employees is to do with their levels of job security, recent redundancies in the banks, calls into question the development of functional flexibility amongst core workers in the banking sector (BIFU 1993; Financial Times 11/1/94). Will employers expect the remaining staff to work harder to make up for the reduction in staff, or, are the banks training their staff to take on a wider range of skilled tasks?

Secondly, we are faced with the claim that functional flexibility represents a new strategy on the part of employers. As with much of the recent Human Resource Management literature there is an intense debate as to whether or not recent developments mark a paradigm shift in organisational strategy and practices (Blyton and Turnbull 1992; Storey 1991; Legge 1988). The concept of strategy, as discussed in chapter 2, is also problematic when applied to empirical research. Unfortunately the term flexibility has been used so diversely that it is difficult to identify where it is new. On the one hand Atkinson and Meager (1986: 38) say that the "*reorganisation of the way in which jobs and people are deployed is a continuous process*" and to this extent "*such a requirement is nothing new*". Whilst, on the other hand, they say that the development of functional flexibility is "*about real changes which in some cases mark major breaks with past practice and convention"* (Atkinson & Meager 1986: 68). Their claims that this represents a new strategy are ambiguous. Pollert (1989 & 1991) argues that change has to be seen in terms of a continuum rather than a radical break. Functional flexibility, she claims, is little more than a revamped version of the rationalisation programmes at the end of the 1970s. These involved using new technology and changing working practices to increase productivity. She argues that there is little evidence of companies developing core-periphery strategies in the way outlined by the flexible firm. MacInnes and Hunter (1991) also find little evidence to support the flexible firm model. They argue that personnel strategies are a subsidiary to business and financial strategies which may have unintended consequences on the organisation of work. Child (1985) points out the importance of distinguishing between senior managers, who devise strategies without a necessarily detailed knowledge of the production process, and the influence of middle managers who implement such strategies. The emphasis on strategy poses significant conceptual problems and the claim to be "new" is also ambiguous.

Thirdly, the concept of functional flexibility has been developed from studies based on the manufacturing sector. This raises questions concerning its appropriateness when applied to service sector work. Can jobs in the service sector and banks, in particular, be compared with car assembly workers? Child and Loveridge (1990) are critical of the arbitrary extension of global theories based on the manufacturing sector being extended to the area of service work. They argue that the service sector is distinctive from manufacturing,

> If the service product expected by the consumer includes an element of personal service, such as providing advice on alternative retailing purchases, then labour is not simply a cost-creating factor of production but is also intrinsic to the value of the product. (Child and Loveridge 1990:10)

This is relevant to the banks when we compare the practices in the branches, where staff are in direct face to face client contact. In contrast the administrative processing centres bear a closer resemblance to factory operations. This highlights the diversity of employment situations in the service sector. Gallie and White (1991) point out, that generalisations about this sector often assume a unrealistic degree of homogeneity.

Fourthly, a further problem in conducting comparative research relates to the use of concepts generated from single country research (Child and Loveridge 1990). Maurice et al. (1982) have shown how the organisation of work varies between countries. In their study of Germany and France they point to variations in hierarchical relationships at work, and the differences in qualifications between similar workers in the two countries. If there has been a change in managerial strategy, how do we measure this? Also, how do we make meaningful the disparity in the educational and training systems, the nationally specific occupational structure and the varied grading schemes between companies?

The research presented here tries to overcome some of these obstacles. It sought to focus on the location of specific tasks in retail banking, and identify which type of staff performed these tasks. In this way we can examine which tasks are separated into different jobs, or if they are accumulated under the one job title (see also Prais and Wagner 1983; Steedman and Hawkins 1993). This approach is particularly useful when the grading structures vary and the structural organisation of the sector is also different (Bernoux et al. 1990; Burgard 1988; Frazer & Vittas 1982). In this way we can examine whether task expansion has been accompanied by training to create a 'multiskilled craftsman' (sic.), or if it is purely a form of work intensification.

3. Functional flexibility in the past?

A retrospective view on employment practices in banking can allow us to assess how "new" a strategy functional flexibility really is. In the post-war period three central characteristics stand out: increased bureaucratisation, feminisation and automation. Each is considered in turn.

3.1 Bureaucratisation

The traditional image of bank employment began to change with the advent of mass recruitment, automation and rationalisation.

When the mechanization and rationalization of office work has proceeded to the extent that relatively large groups of semi-skilled employees are concentrated together, separated from managerial and supervisory staffs, performing continuous, routinised and disciplined work, often rewarded in accordance with physical output, with little chance of promotion - then clerical work becomes, in the terms of social and physical environment, extremely like that of the factory operative. (Lockwood 1989:92)

Personal discretion was gradually replaced by administrative rules and procedures (Edwards 1979). Bureaucratisation required a system of formal qualifications for employment and promotion. This replaced the system of paternalistic nepotism and personal contacts which had previously existed. Even so, Lockwood (1989) points out that the persistence of small work units, even within large organisations, served to perpetuate a work relationship characteristic of some of the older features of paternalism.

In highly bureaucratised systems, personal relations and the culture of paternalism were replaced with a formal rule-governed hierarchy, and a stricter division of labour and task fragmentation. In smaller work units, where relations were more personal, the use of functional flexibility has been more common. This is because job demarcation and the division of labour is less extensive. Therefore the size of an organisation is significant for the type of relations developed at work: in smaller work units functional flexibility is more likely to be developed, and, in larger bureaucratised organisations we could expect to find a more extensive division of labour and task fragmentation.

3.2 Feminisation

The feminisation of bank work came about at approximately the same time as the social status of the industry deteriorated. Strober and Arnold (1987) show how the status of bank tellers in America moved from being a very specialised job to one of lower status with less training, and how this was related to occupational segregation. They cite evidence from 1948 where bank tellers in the US were held to be, *"men of the highest type, whose personality is well adapted to meeting the public, and have proved their efficiency in other parts of the bank."*[2] Bank clerks were traditionally skilled in various areas of bank work and their personal qualities were also an important part of the "skills" required for the job. By the early seventies the job was described as tedious by the "Occupational Outlook Handbook": *Although tellers work independently, their record keeping is closely supervised. They work with detail and are confined to a small work area.* (Strober and Arnold 1987:129). In a period of twenty years the perceived status of the job declined considerably,[3] with the implication that it has become more specialised and controlled.

As bank employment became less attractive to men, because of the relatively low pay and status, it was easy for the banks to employ women. Extensive bureaucratisation and the division of labour led to tasks becoming more specialised and of lower status. In Britain, according to the evidence presented by Lockwood (1989), Crompton (1989) and Savage (1989), a similar trend was taking place. In France, wages and the deterioration of occupational status were the main issues of conflict after the war.[4] Bank employees demanded a "revalorisation" of their profession.

3.3 Automation

Automation had a limited impact on cashiers' jobs, even with the introduction of adding machines in the 1940s. These machines made the cashier's job faster and more accurate, although it did not reduce the number of tasks they performed. This also applies, for example, to administrative jobs like those of the balance clerks in France, who kept up-to-date records on clients' accounts (Appert 1977). The work of these female balance clerks integrated the tasks of manual sorting, adjustment of hand written records and surveillance of customers' balances. This changed with the introduction of perforated paper adding machines used in conjunction with centralised computers. Initially, the low grade work of data entry on perforated ribbon, was performed by a variety of branch staff in rotation ("à tour de rôle"), in the French banks. The French balance clerks were then given other low grade administrative work to perform. This shows how a strict task demarcation never really existed in the banks as it had done in manufacturing; traditionally bank staff have been expected to be adaptable. At the same time there was evidence to show how tasks were re-allocated along gendered divisions. For example, the analysis of balances on customers' accounts became the responsibility of a more senior member of staff, usually a man, and the low grade data entry work was done by women (Appert 1977: 50).

In both countries during the 1960s magnetic tape was

attached to cheques which allowed them to be read and recorded by automatic sorting machine. The laborious manual work of sorting and recording cheques was removed from the branches, and pools of data entry operators, usually women, were employed at a central location to encode the cheques.[5] Automation primarily affected administrative jobs and it was not until the 1980s that information technology began to have a radical impact on cashiers' jobs. This took two forms: computer terminals and Automated Teller Machines (ATMs), which are examined in more detail later.

Thus, we can identify two trends pulling in different directions. On one hand, the work of bank clerks has traditionally incorporated a variety of tasks performed by the same employee. When work procedures were standardised or automated, this did not always lead to task separation. The case of the balance clerks in France shows how other low grade tasks could be integrated into their jobs. However, where automation led to the displacement of jobs from the branches to large administrative centres, there was evidence of task fragmentation. For example, the pool of women data entry clerks at the clearing centres had more in common with a factory than a branch. The size of operations has an important effect in the development of specialisation or functional flexibility, as pointed out by Lockwood (1989). The persistence of small work units, like branch banks, resisted the ultimate development of bureaucratisation and an extensive division of labour, although cleavages in job allocation were heavily influenced by gender. The relative smallness of the branches as work units maintained a tradition of paternalism and sought to encourage staff to be adaptable.

4. Functional flexibility in the branches

As increased competition has forced the banks to diversify the services they offer in the branches in both countries, this emerged as an apposite site for studying the development of functional flexibility. Essentially the job of a cashier is to serve the public, pay out and receive money. It is administrative and routine, in the case of filling out forms, but it is becoming increasingly commercial with the emphasis on "selling" a wider range of financial services.

We are thinking of trying to make the cashiers more aware of the other commercial services we offer, so as to draw clients' attention to credit card facilities etc... but this hasn't yet been put into practice (Assistant branch manager, Britain).

The most recent stage of technological development, with the use of ATMs and cashier terminals, has given the banks considerable scope to "mix and match" these systems in the way they offer their services (Austrin 1991: 204). However, this research suggests that French banks have chosen the route of offering an integrated cashier service in their branches, whereas service delivery in Britain has been more segmented.

4.1 Service integration in France and segmentation in Britain

In France cashiers were expected to offer a more integrated service. For example, they could buy and sell shares for clients over the counter using the Minitel system. They could provide clients with balances on their accounts by using their computer terminals. They could arrange appointments with customers who wanted to take out a small loan and they could check their credit record, again through their computer terminals. They could buy or sell foreign exchange directly over the counter as well as accepting ordinary credit and debit payments. (This observational evidence is supported by the CNC report 1989: 69; Bernoux et al. 1990: 28; Cosslater 1990; Moussy 1989). French cashiers, in the banks studied, were also expected to do low grade administrative work like encoding cheques. In Britain this work was done at the clearing centres by shifts of morning part-timers; more recently, however, the bank studied in Britain had started to decentralise some of these tasks to the branches. In France this work used to be done by large pools of data entry staff, but now it was either completed in the branches, or it was subcontracted (this case study evidence is supported in the research of Brunhes 1989). Access to computer terminals also allowed cashiers to input and access data directly from the main computer files[6] (see also the evidence of Bernoux et al. 1991: 23). Overall French cashiers were expected to be more functionally flexible than cashiers in Britain.

In Britain a typical branch would have "personal bankers" at the front of the banking hall, seated behind ordinary desks, wearing a distinctive uniform. These staff provided general information and enquires services, and directed clients to the specialist range of bank services. In the middle of the branch it was common to find "Quick Service Tills" for transactions under £300. These cashiers had access to an ATM locked till. Finally, at the back of the branch traditional cashiers, seated behind glass security screens, handled higher value transactions. This was the central model around which the banks in Britain have been developing their staffing policy. This model varies depending on the size and status of the branch. In some smaller branches there are no "Quick Service Tills", and in very small branches there may be no "Personal Banker". Cashiers in smaller branches are expected to perform a wider range of tasks because there are fewer staff, so, for example, they refer customers to specialist services in other parts of the bank or at other larger branches. However, the overall emphasis in Britain is towards service segmentation.

4.2 A common practice: locational functional flexibility

Despite identifible differences, common practices could also be seen, for example in the use of locational flexibility. This refers to the banks' use of special relief teams of full-time permanent staff who are used to meet short-term staff shortages in the branches, usually for illness, holidays or absence. These employees could be asked to work for a day, or longer, in different branches within a region. Their company specific experience guaranteed a better quality service, compared to using expensive agency temps.

> There is approximately one relief staff for every two branches, that's a 'natural' balance. Branches with very few staff get priority in the allocation of relief staff. A large branch won't get relief staff, they are expected to cover themselves with their existing staff. Relief staff are usually in the lower grades, but have worked for the bank for some time. (Manager for the relief team, France).

In one of the French banks studied, these relief teams were still in operation, although this was not the case for all the banks in France. The bank wanted to use this system to provide training as well as covering for staff shortages.

> Joining one of these teams is a good way to get promotion,

because staff can widen their experience. But unfortunately there are some staff who once on the team are reluctant to go back to work in one branch because of the extra bonuses they get. (Manager of relief teams, France)

Travel and food bonuses had been offered to attract staff to work on these teams. As a result certain employees preferred to work on a team, rather than be based at one branch on a lower salary. The French manager of this service perceived this as an obstacle because it prevented other people getting on the teams and getting experience. However, in both countries, most banks appear to have disbanded these teams because of the high costs involved.

We used to have relief teams, but we decided to disband them when we re-organised the branch networks because they are a very expensive auxiliary workforce. (Senior Personnel Manager, Britain)
No, we no longer have any relief teams, they were very expensive. (Senior Personnel Manager, France)

These teams were a relatively expensive auxiliary work force who benefited from the advantages of permanent employment status. In smaller banks in France greater recourse is made to temporary agencies because they do not have the same reserve of labour to draw upon.
In Britain, where the teams had been disbanded, the re-organisation of the branch network into a satellite system has been one way of catering for the service these teams provided. The senior manager at the "parent" branch was responsible for meeting staffing needs in the smaller branches. Often staff were "lent out" between branches for a few hours, a day, a week, or longer depending on the case.

We'd be more likely to send a full-timer to another branch rather than a part-timer. The full-timers don't like being moved about though, they have a misconceived idea that they're been pushed around. But for them it's better for their career if they get a wider experience. (Branch Manager, Britain).

The system used in Britain was less expensive than using a relief team. Staff were not paid extra benefits for the inconvenience of travelling; they were persuaded to co-operate on the basis that it would broaden their training and experience. Nevertheless, many staff were often reluctant to move between branches. In Britain full-time staff were lent between branches; in France relief teams were employed to meet these temporary needs.

Borrowing staff between branches constrained the demands for extra staff, as sub-managers were made aware of the pressure they were placing on the senior manager and his central branch. During field work, one sub-manager, who phoned the central branch to request an extra member of staff to cover for sickness, was reminded, by the central office manager, that his previous request had not been justified, according to the comments made by the cashier sent out.

> Young Brian told me he was twiddling his thumbs last Friday and that you ended up giving him a training manual to read, to give him something to do! I'm not sure I can spare one of my staff, if that's what they're going to be doing. (Overheard telephone conversation between central office manager on the phone to sub-manager, Britain).

This type of system puts much greater pressure on the personal relations built up between management staff in different branches. It makes junior sub-managers reluctant to ask for extra staff if they think that they will encounter a certain degree of hostility to their request, and in order to get a good reference and future promotion they want to be seen as being able to cope, even under difficult circumstances. In such cases they are more likely to make their existing staff work harder, when they have staff shortages.

In sum, French cashiers were expected to perform a wider range of tasks than British cashiers. The banks expected full-time permanent staff to be locationally and functionally flexible on the basis that wider experience was a means to promotion. However, this did not entail a formal enhancement of skills or training. This system allowed the banks to meet temporary requirements using qualified and reliable staff. The use of this policy has significant implications for the flexibility debates. The sharp distinction between the rationale to use numerical or functional flexibility is more blurred than dichotomised flexibility models suggest.

5. Functional flexibility in the clearing centres

The cheque clearing centres provided the administrative back-up for the work generated in the branches. In Britain thousands of employees poured in daily to the "clerical factories" located in central London. Row upon row of clerical staff, usually women, encoded cheques, entered data into VDUs, checked figures, sorted mail, or operated the sorting machines in the daily process of clearing cheques. In France the system of cheque clearing is more decentralised than it is in Britain: cheques are presented at regional clearing houses, whereas in Britain they all have to pass through the central clearing house in London (see chapter 3). As a result French banks have smaller clearing departments compared with the British banks. In France diverse forms of cheque exchange developed after the rapid expansion of banking activities in the 1970s. Government and interbank agreements sought to regulate and unify these clearing houses ("chambres"); the present system is organised around the administrative "départements" and regions[7] (Lasfargues 1980).

The bank's clearing centre in Britain usually handled in the region of 3,500,000 cheques on a busy day like Tuesdays[8]; by Friday this usually fell to 2,000,000 cheques passing through the building. The smaller clearing departments in France treated fewer cheques and had less extreme fluctuations. For example, in one of the clearing departments in the Ile de France region, on a busy day like a Tuesday it was normal for them to treat 270,000 cheques, this fell to 200,000 on a Friday. The British clearing house had to manage daily variations of as much as 1,500,000 cheques, while the daily work load at the French centre varied by 70,000 cheques a day. These volumes posed different problems for management in terms of labour requirements in the clearing centres. Also, the work load in France was more staggered. For example, the exchange of cheques at the Clearing House in Paris took place at various intervals during the day: 9.15am, 12.15pm and 3.15pm; 12.15pm was the most important. In Britain there was one major exchange at 11am; on Tuesdays this was at 11.30am. These differences affected the type of flexibility employers needed: British employers were under more pressure to meet one deadline, whereas the French could prepare the work to be sent in batches at different intervals.

5.1 Task integration in France and segmentation in Britain

In France where operations were considerably smaller than in Britain, staff were expected to perform a wide range of tasks within the one job. For example, before a cheque can be exchanged it needs to be encoded, sorted, the data entered onto the computer, and prepared with other cheques being sent to the same bank. In Britain it was common practice for all these tasks to be performed by different employees. In France it was more common for them to be integrated and performed by the same employees. For example, the staff who opened and prepared the cheques for sorting in the morning, would spend the afternoon entering rejected cheques[9] manually into the VDU system. On quiet days these staff would help with the research jobs which involved looking up old records of cheques which had been queried because they had bounced or because of an accounting error. As a result, a copy of the original cheque was required. In this way staff in France were expected to perform a wider variety of tasks compared to the staff employed in Britain.

In Britain, partly because the clearing department was so much larger than in France, there was a more extensive division of labour. There were distinct teams of part-timers employed to do encoding work only. In France this work was either performed by cashiers in the branches, or was subcontracted. In the central London offices an entire floor was given over to the work of tray agreers and VDU operators. On another floor the large sorting machines were operated by shifts of full and part-time staff. In a separate room in the basement mail going to and from the branches was sorted by shifts of part-timers in the afternoons and full-timers at night; during the day full-time male messengers did manual moving work.

The nature of the operations in each country was quite distinctive. The way jobs were organised meant that the staff in the smaller operations in France were expected to perform a wider range of tasks compared with those in Britain. This observational and management interview data was supported by the experience of employees. Interview data was collected from 126 full- and part-time women employees from both countries, working in similar jobs. This indicated that French employees were more likely to describe themselves as performing a wide variety of tasks, compared with the British women. These employees were asked how repetitive or varied their work was, as a measure of existing functional flexibility. The responses are presented in Table 4.1.

These results reinforce the differences identified between the two countries. Three-quarters of the British respondents, compared to only a fifth of French employees, described their job as either very routine and repetitive, or enabling them to occasionally do new things. Approximately 80% of the French employees, compared with only a fifth of the British respondents, said they did new things quite often, or that their job was very varied. Together this quantitative and earlier qualitative data suggest distinct patterns in each country: in France there was more task integration than in Britain where tasks were more segmented.

Table 4.1
Perceptions of task variety

	British Clearing %	British Branch %	French Clearing %	French Branch %
very routine & repetitive	36	36	3	3
routine, occasionally do new things	39	39	19	15
routine, quite often do new things	13	6	52	55
different every day often do new things	9	6	23	27
don't know	3	13	3	0
Total (%)	100	100	100	100
total responses (n)	31	31	31	33

(Source: Employee questionnaire)

5.2 Common practices: borrowing staff

Employers, in both countries, have been expecting staff to perform a wider range of tasks, although it is debatable whether we could call this functional flexibility. If we take a broad definition, to include the performance of different tasks in different locations "as and when required", these developments in banking can be classified as functional flexibility. But if we were to adopt a tighter definition, which specified the need to include an element of training and upgrading of status together with evidence of a direct managerial strategy as implied in the literature, then recent developments in clearing would fall far short of this meaning. Our categorisation of functional flexibility inevitably affects the conclusions we draw. Here we will use the broader definition as a way of allowing for the possibility of any development towards the use of functional flexibility. However, a tighter distinction in relation to the provision of training needs to be integrated more fully into this concept.

From managerial interviews and observational material from both countries it became clear that, as in the branches, it was common practice to borrow staff between different services within the clearing department. This usually happened when there was a build up of urgent work. In France this had developed as a result of staff shortages created by the bank's policy to restructure and subcontract certain services. Staff were "borrowed" for as little as an hour or as much as a week or more, depending on the mutual co-operation of section supervisors. For example, in France if the section finalising the cheques to be exchanged at the clearing house was short of staff, they could borrow tray agreers to help them meet the deadline. Tray agreers normally performed low level accounts work, checking the total produced by the sorting machines against the totals sent in from the branches, and those exchanged at the clearing houses. They used the same skills of accurate accountancy when lent to other sections. The service which finalised the preparation of the cheques for clearing was short of staff because the bank planned to subcontract some of this work in the next few years. As a result, no new staff were being employed in these sections in France, and staff who were re-deployed or who left, were not being replaced.

In Britain staff were also borrowed between sections in the clearing department. This was facilitated by the use of a work flow-staff measurement table which had been devised for the clearing department by an external management consultancy. This measure indicated the number of staff needed in each set of operations at specific times of the day. For example, VDU staff could be sent down to help out the encoders if they were short-staffed and it looked as if they would not be able to "meet the house".[10] It was a consultancy measure, rather than an strategy developed by the bank's own managers, which led to the use of staff in this way.

Decentralisation of encoding work in Britain also led to the tasks of the encoders being expanded. It used to be the case that the women encoders only encoded cheques. More recently, after they had finished the encoding work, they had to enter the data of rejected cheques into the computer. This required skills of accuracy and speed, similar to those of encoding. On busy days the women were fully occupied with encoding, and on quieter days their contractual hours were filled by doing less urgent data inputting. The decision to diversify the tasks of these encoders in Britain came about in an ad-hoc way as a result of a senior management decision to introduce encoding machines into certain branches. One of the unforeseen repercussions of this decision was that the work load of the encoding staff had decreased significantly and the managers of the centre had to find new ways to redeploy their staff. One manager made an aside remark about this decision taken at senior level: *"They didn't bother letting us know about it!"*, and was obviously quite angry that they had not been sufficiently warned of the decision and the likely repercussions this would have on the work for which they were responsible. The encoders, although part-time, were on permanent contracts and the banks were reluctant to make redundancies, preferring "natural wastage" or voluntary packages. These practices have not involved an increase in skill and although they could be described as a horizontal extension of tasks, they have not involved up-skilling and come nowhere near the image of the "multi-skilled craftsman" (sic.) which is central to the idea of functional flexibility.

Evidence of a more general move to task expansion in both countries was supported by the questionnaire responses. Employees were asked if the variety of tasks they performed had increased, decreased or stayed the same. An increase could loosely be taken for a move to increase functional flexibility.

The results presented in Table 4.2 show that a majority of respondents thought the variety of tasks they performed had increased, and this was marginally higher in France than in Britain. More staff in the clearing department reported an increase in task variety compared to the staff in the branches. This suggests that there has been a general trend towards increasing the task variety of staff in both countries, although the French appear to be at a more advanced stage than the British (see also Table 4.1).

Table 4.2
Change in the variety of tasks performed

	British Clearing	British Branch	French Clearing	French Branch
	%	%	%	%
increased	68	55	81	58
stayed the same	19	26	16	30
decreased	7	6	0	9
don't know	6	13	3	3
total (%)	100	100	100	100
total responses (n)	31	31	31	33

(Source: Employee questionnaire)

From the evidence presented so far we have seen a more extensive use of functional flexibility in France. At the same time there have been moves towards an expansion of employee tasks in both countries. But how should we interpret this type of functional flexibility? What kind of training and skills have been developed? And has this development been used strategically by employers?

6. Explanations for the differences and similarities in the use of functional flexibility

If we look first at the explanations for the differences between the two countries, we can identify a variety of factors. These include the level of qualifications of the available labour force, recruitment practices, the training systems employed, the use of cashier computer terminals, the size of branches and work units, and finally the differences in the way security issues are treated. Each of these will be examined together with the explanations for similarities, to show how independently and accumulatively they have affected the context within which employers have developed functional flexibility in each country.

6.1 Qualifications

The qualifications and skills of the available labour affect the type of flexibility developed by employers: where the work force are more highly qualified it is easier to introduce functional flexibility. There is a significant difference in the qualifications and educational level of the staff employed in the banks in Britain and France. In general, French women are better qualified than women in Britain (Barrère-Maurisson et al. 1989; Benoit-Guilbot 1987) and this was confirmed in the sample of women interviewed for this survey as can be seen in Table 4.3.

Table 4.3
Exams obtained at school

(column %)	British Clearing %	British Branch %	French Clearing %	French Branch %
none	36	7	10	0
GCSE/Brevet	58	87	61	30
A Levels/Bac	3	3	26	67
not answered	3	3	3	3
Total (%)	100	100	100	100
Total (n)	31	31	31	33

(Source:Employee questionnaire)

The French women interviewed were more likely to have a baccalauréat, the equivalent of A-levels, whereas most of the British women had GCSE equivalents. The most highly qualified women were employed in the French branches and the least qualified in the clearing department in Britain.

The difference in educational qualifications are a reflection of the fact that British women are more likely to leave school at an earlier stage than French women (Sullerot 1973). Of the British women interviewed in this research, 100% of those employed in clearing and 97% of the cashiers had finished their full-time education by the age of 17. In France 39% of those working in clearing had stayed on until they were 18, and 19% had stayed on until they were 19 or 20. The cashiers in France had a much higher level of education with 52% having left full-time education between the ages of 19 and 22.

Educational levels affect career expectations: where employees have higher qualifications they are more likely to have higher career expectations (Lane 1991). This was borne out in the attitudes of the respondents in this sample. In Britain only 55% of cashiers said they wanted promotion compared to 76% of the cashiers interviewed in France. More highly qualified staff generally expect greater job diversity than those with less qualifications. The fact that French employees perform a wider range of tasks could be a product of employers adapting jobs to meet these demands. This flexibility on the part of French employers to adapt jobs to employees' needs is also supported in the work of Gregory (1987, 1989 & 1991).

6.2 Recruitment

For a long time in France the banks, like the banks in Britain, recruited thousands of people with few if any educational qualifications. *"In the '70s we would employ anyone, so long as they could stand up."* (Personnel Manager, Britain). The traditional single port of entry into the bank led male junior clerks to aspire for the ultimate promotion to the post of branch manager (Savage 1989). As the organisation of banking services has changed, this system has gradually been replaced, in both countries, by multi-tiered entry, related to educational or professional qualifications (Quack et al. 1993). The re-organisation of branch networks and business units, especially in the UK, has resulted in the declining status of branch managers within the banks.

Nevertheless, there are significant differences in current recruitment practices in Britain and France. The banks in France have made a deliberate strategy to raise the standard of entry requirements in their attempts to find staff who will be more adaptable to future change (CNC 1989: 63). The banks in Britain have put more emphasis in recruiting part-timers (Rajan 1984) and young school leavers. Before the 1990s recession the banks in Britain focused their recruitment on 17 years plus school leavers, whereas in France new recruits are expected to have two years' post baccalauréat higher education, with preference being given to those doing commercial studies (Moussy 1989; CNC 1989; Cossalter 1990; Betrand & Noyelle 1988; Brunhes 1989; Quack et al. 1993).

We have too many staff with low qualifications, we need to recruit people with higher qualifications because they will be more adaptable to the changes which are taking place in the bank. (Personnel manager, France)

According to the banks in France, staff with higher qualifications and with greater commercial awareness will be better able to provide advice to customers on the varied range of ancillary services the banks are increasingly selling in their branches. The widespread nature of this trend was supported by a survey conducted in 1987 (CNC 1989: 64). This showed that the number of staff recruited to French banks with two or more years' post-Baccualauréat studies had increased by 10%, whilst the number of staff without qualifications decreased by a similar amount. The report by the National Credit Council (CNC 1989) concludes that the French banks have, in general, made a significant change in their recruitment policy in favour of higher qualifications.

6.3 Training

Training systems also affected the way employers developed different forms of flexibility. Lane (1987) has shown how in Germany a broad based pre-entry system of certified qualifications has provided the basis for German banks to develop a policy of functional flexibility amongst its clerical personnel. In Britain there is less encouragement to develop these broad commercial skills. It is more difficult to transfer post-entry training between different companies and sectors. Although NVQs may reduce these barriers, the banks have been slow to develop recognition beyond level 3 (Quack et al. 1993). The skills provided in Britain are considerably narrower than those available in the German system. This leads Lane (1987:67) to argue that whilst in Germany there is evidence of task integration amongst clerical workers, in Britain there has been a polarisation between career and non-career staff, with the work of the latter becoming increasingly fragmented.

In Britain a typical school leaver entering a branch bank would expect to start work in the back office/machine room. Training is given on-the-job and staff are sent to other branches.[11] After approximately two years they could be moved to the post of cashier. At this level the main emphasis is on company-specific on-the-job training. Women were more likely to stay on these tills whilst the men would go on to the foreign till or securities. Many of the women interviewed in Britain, especially the younger ones, complained of sexual discrimination in training and promotion.

It's always the boys who get pushed on. They end up doing securities and stuff like that, whilst we get left here on the tills. (Full-time cashier, Britain)

The boys never seem to spend long in the machine room, they think it isn't really men's work. I think they get pushed through quicker because they're expected to have a career. (Supervisor of the machine room in a branch, Britain)

Despite attempts by the bank in Britain to improve its record on equal opportunities, in practice there was a clear sense of discrimination amongst the cashiers at the branch level. Men had careers and women did a job. This expectation was reinforced by the use of part-time work in Britain. In contrast French women had a longer and more continuous pattern of work. As a result slightly more women in France were in higher managerial grades (Moussy 1989; Bernoux et al. 1990; Springer 1991).

In France branch staff, who were increasingly being recruited with BAC+II or even BAC+IV,[12] would start as a cashier ("guichetier") expecting to become a commercial agent[13] within a few years. The "back office" jobs that provided a training ground for new recruits in the British bank did not exist in a comparable way in the French branches. In 1986 the Centre de Formation de la Profession Bancaire (CFPB) set up pre-entry schools for potential candidates of the level BAC+I or higher. These involved four months of study supplemented by a practical training cycle at different posts inside a bank. This was a move to develop a training system comparable with the German one. However, in Germany certification allowed employees to transfer their qualifications between companies and sectors, whereas in France this training did not receive any qualifications or certification (CNC 1989:75; Lane 1987). The French have made limited developments to improve their provision of training along German lines.

As the qualifications demanded by the banks increase, the numbers enrolled for basic level qualifications, like the Certificat d'Aptitude Professionel (CAP) and the Brevet Professionel (BP), have fallen.[14] On average only 0.8% of all the employees in the banks in France qualify each year for a CAP or BP. This is less than in Germany where between 3-3.5% pass an equivalent exam (CNC 1989:75). The difference between France and the UK is highlighted by Bernoux et al. (1990: 20-21). They show in their case-study research, that a regional French bank spent the equivalent of 7.9% of the total salary bill on training, while a comparable regional bank in the UK spent only 2.5%. Training in France has been seen as a means to re-shape the profile of their personnel. In Britain this concern has not yet developed the same momentum.

6.4 Security, service policy and technology

In the branches in Britain the banks were developing a segmented service delivery policy, compared with France where functional flexibility was more widespread. This was partly related to the way security arrangements were dealt with. In France, as a result of a series of armed robberies in the 1970s, the banks installed locked double doors which can only be opened by the cashier inside the branch, making it more difficult to enter a branch. In Britain it is much easier to walk in and out of the main lobby. In France, the higher level of security controlling entry into the branch means that there is no need to segregate services in the same way, as all staff are relatively secure. This has encouraged the banks to maximise on the services each cashier offers.

Technology, in the shape of computer terminals for cashiers, has also facilitated an integrated service policy in French branches. Comparable terminals were not widely used in the British bank although they have been introduced into some of the smaller banks and building societies in Britain. There was less pressure to use computers for competitive advantage in Britain during the 1980s because the levels of competition have been less intense than in the saturated market in France. In larger branches there is a higher degree of task separation than in smaller ones where staff are expected to be more flexible; the selective development of cashier terminals could also be related to the fact that branches in Britain are generally larger than those in France (Moussy 1989; Bernoux et al. 1990).

6.5 Explanations for common practices

Despite significant differences observable in the two countries, it would overstate the case if we failed to recognise the factors pushing the banks to adopt similar practices. The general move towards an extension of employees' tasks was noticeable in each country, especially in clearing (see Table 4.2). In both countries competitive pressure and technological developments have forced the banks to reconsider how they operate their services. Restructuring has led to a displacement of work and an attempt to reduce staff numbers. As a result staff are expected to be more flexible in order to "fill in the gaps". Plans to subcontract services had curtailed recruitment in the clearing department in France. As a result tray agreers were used to help meet deadlines for the exchange of cheques. In Britain encoders were expected to do VDU work, when part of their encoding work was decentralised to the branches. These developments did not entail a significant level of training and came closer to a horizontal enlargement of tasks. Pollert (1991:12) talks of an 'endangered core' who are threatened with being expelled from core status, and this appears to be a more accurate description of the experience of these women in the clearing department in both countries. New technology and competitive pressure to reduce administrative costs have pushed the banks to find solutions to reduce this area of work; one of the repercussions has been to increase the tasks staff are expected to perform as work loads and staff numbers fluctuate.

With regard to the branches, locational functional flexibility was a common practice in both countries. Staff were expected to move between different posts as a way of broadening their experience and gaining co-operation. At the same time the banks benefited from this by being able to re-locate their staff to meet unpredictable flows of work in a way which calls into question the distinction between functional flexibility for core employees and numerical flexibility for those in the secondary sector.

7. Re-evaluating the concept of functional flexibility

Throughout this chapter it has been argued that functional flexibility refers to a diverse set of developments. Tight or broad definitions of the concept can be operationalised with different implications for the conclusions we draw. If we decide to use a broad definition as a means to detect change in the organisation of work, we cannot assume that this means a general up-skilling of workers. Just because workers say they are performing more tasks than before may not mean that this has been supported by further training or skill enhancement.

To examine the relationship between the strategy of functional flexibility, up-skilling and work intensification, the concept of functional flexibility was operationalised to analyse the quantitative data collected in the employee questionnaires. This took a measure of existing functional flexibility and a measure of change by combining the variable describing job variety (Table 4.1) with the variable asking about increase in task variety (Table 4.2). Respondents who said they either had a varied job or that their task variety had increased, were taken as having a positive degree of functional flexibility in the widest sense. Respondents who scored negatively on both of these two measures, i.e. they had routine jobs and had no increase in task variety were defined as not being functionally flexible.

In France 83% of the interviewees were included in the functional flexibility category compared with only 63% in Britain. This supports the observational and interview data presented earlier, which showed how the functional flexibility was more developed in France than in Britain. In Britain 26% of the sample were categorised as not functionally flexible, i.e. they were in repetitive jobs and had not experienced any increase in task variety, compared with only 12% in France. Eleven percent of the British employees and 5% of the French did not respond to these questions, out of the total 126 women interviewed.

Where employees reported an increase in skill levels, training, use of initiative and increased responsibility this was associated with the development of up-skilling. Where employees reported an increase in the effort they made at work, an increase in the speed of their work and the tightness of supervision was associated with an intensification of work. Table 4.4 presents the condensed results of this analysis.

The development of functional flexibility raised the reported increase in skill by approximately 50% in both countries, when compared with those who were not functionally flexible. This, however, was not closely associated with an increase in training: only 44% of the British respondents and 47% of the French who could be considered to be functionally flexible, said that their training had increased. This could mean that less than half the sample could be considered to have been up-skilled. Approximately three-quarters of the functionally flexible workers reported an increase in initiative and responsibility, which was much higher than those workers who were not functionally flexible.

Table 4.4
The core concept of functional flexibility
compared with other aspects of work

% of respondents reporting an increase in	BRITAIN		FRANCE	
	flexible	not flexible	flexible	not flexible
skill level	82	31	81	38
training	44	19	47	13
use of initiative	77	38	74	13
responsibility	72	25	63	0
effort	80	38	36	0
speed	78	63	60	25
tightness of supervision	31	13	21	0
% of the sample	63	26	83	12
non response (%)	11		5	
total numbers (n)	62		64	

(Source: Employee questionnaire)

If we look at the aspects of work which could be associated with job intensification i.e. effort, speed and tightness of supervision, British respondents were more likely than French respondents to say these had increased. In Britain functional flexibility was associated with a substantial increase in effort: 80% of functionally flexible staff said the effort they put into their job had increased compared with only 36% in France. Even among non-flexible employees 38% of the British employees questioned said their effort had increased, whereas no French employees cited this change. An increase in the speed of work was cited by a large majority of respondents in Britain and by functionally flexible employees in France. Tightness of supervision was also higher amongst those who were functionally flexible and especially amongst those in Britain, although this was comparatively weaker compared with the other aspects of work.

These results confirm the developments outlined earlier to show how functional flexibility is more developed in France than in Britain. Secondly they provide some original material to address the debates on up-skilling and job intensification with regard to the development of functional flexibility. We have seen how the staff we have defined as being functionally flexible have experienced an increase in their skill, use of initiative and responsibility. This, however, has not been supported by a very extensive degree of training. With the evidence presented earlier a general conclusion would be that functional flexibility in banking has essentially involved a horizontal enlargement of tasks. There has been more enthusiasm for this policy in France than in Britain. However, attempts to reform the training system in the banks in France have only met with limited success, and more effort has been given to recruiting staff with higher qualifications. This has not become an issue in the British banks and in fact the most convincing arguments in terms of job intensification come from the British experience.

8. Conclusions

This chapter set out to examine the concept of functional flexibility by drawing on empirical evidence collected from the retail banking sector in Britain and France. The data presented here has shown how the concept has been used to refer to a diverse range of experiences. On an optimistic note, functional flexibility has been associated with a general improvement and up-skilling of work. At a more critical level, Pollert (1987 & 1991) has argued that task expansion is no more than a product of rationalisation and a form of task intensification. One of the problems with this concept is the need to make a clearer distinction between these two trends. Horizontal task enlargement has not been associated with the development of a "multi-skilled craftsman". In fact, for the majority of staff who were classified as being functionally flexible, increased task variety did not entail extra training. There is a significant difference between a deliberate strategy to up-skill staff, and one which inadvertently leads to an expansion of tasks, but this is poorly accounted for in these debates.

At a comparative level there were noticeable differences between the countries. Functional flexibility was more developed in France than in Britain. In France this was related to: the higher educational qualifications of available female labour; the development of a more extensive system of training; and the increase in recruitment standards to attract staff who would be more adaptable to future change. In Britain employers have been less concerned with introducing such a strategy, although this may well be changing. Branches and clearing operations in Britain are larger than they are in France and this encourages a more extensive division of labour and use of part-timers to meet fluctuations. British banks have segmented the services offered in the branches, and they have not made the same investment in cashier terminals. Questions of security are handled differently. In Britain, where it is easier to enter the branch and cashiers dealing with large sums of money are located behind glass screens towards the back of the branch, other staff offer advisory services and low level money transactions in the main lobby. Additionally, bank staff tend to be less well qualified with lower expectations of promotion, and a greater use of part-timers. There is evidence to show that the banks are restructuring their operations, but this is not fully accounted for by the rather amorphous and all encompassing category of functional flexiblity.

The neat prescriptions for a new form of functional flexibility were far from the untidy reality of current employment practices. Traditionally staff in the banking sector have been expected to perform a wide range of tasks and in the days of single port entry this experience was essential for promotion. The use of locational functional flexibility was a continuation of this practice. It served the bank's dual purpose of filling temporary staff shortages and giving low grade staff a broader experience of branch work. There did not appear to be a consistent strategy to develop functional flexibility in Britain, where the banks have opted for a strategy of service segmentation. An increase in tasks, for example in the case of the encoders, shows how this policy has developed in an ad-hoc way as a bi-product of re-structuring. Managerial strategy tends to develop in an incremental manner, adjusting to new developments, and in relation to existing practices and specific societal characteristics. These conditions are not fully appreciated in the literature on flexibility, and in the concept of functional flexibility.

From the evidence presented here we can see that the concept of functional flexibility needs to be more rigourously defined to identify where it refers to a genuine and deliberate strategy to increase skills, or else it needs to be rejected. A more accurate analysis needs to distinguish where task expansion has led to up-skilling, as distinct from ad-hoc, piecemeal change with the repercussions of intensifying work. Second, this research has shown how the use of functional flexibility varies between different countries. In order to explain this, employers' behaviour needs to be understood in relation to the social, economic and organisational constraints imposed on their capacity to develop a work force able to perform a wide range of skills.

Notes

1. See Lane (1989:168-181) for a discussion of the work of Kern and Schumann in Germany on this issue.

2. Alcorn E "The Bank Teller: His Job and Opportunities" Cambridge Mass: Bankers Publications Company 1950, cited in Strober and Arnold (1987: 126).

3. Attention needs to paid to this kind of data as it is drawn from different sources over a period of time, because the bias of the reporters could be quite different. It is intended to give an indication of how the job has been perceived, and how that perception has changed rather than a detailed analysis of work tasks.

4. This evidence was collected from examining the tracts kept by the union Force Ouvrière, in France. These tracts were published on a weekly basis since 1936.

5. The task of encoding involves typing the amount the cheque was written for onto the bottom right hand corner of the cheque so that it can be read by the electronic sorter. This is a very repetitive job requiring accuracy and speed. An encoder sits in front of a machine where she puts a "lot" of cheques into a compartment on her left hand side. Each cheque passes from the compartment into a space in the middle of the machine, where she can read it easily. She reads the amount written on

the cheque and types in the number, with her right hand. Once one cheque is done it passes automatically to a compartment on the right hand side and a new cheque appears in the central compartment. At the same time that she types in the amount, the adding machine keeps a record of all the cheques and produces a total at the end of each "lot". This total can be used to check the total supplied by the branch, and which will later be checked by the sorting machine.

6. For example cashiers can data entry "lots", of between 20-100 cheques or pieces of equivalent paper, into the computer via the keyboard terminal. If a cashier had some spare time and there was a "lot" ready to be inputted he/she could do this immediately. Specialisation at one task is currently disappearing, within limits, as all employees are taught how to use the terminals.

7. For example, within the Ile de France region there are four clearing houses: one in Paris and three in the surrounding départements of Versailles, Evry, and Pontoise. In France, the bank issuing the cheques has to mark on each cheque at which clearing house it is valid to exchange it. Within each region there is a head quarters which is responsible for the administration of cheques in their area. There are 22 regions in France and 96 departments.

8. Tuesday was the busiest day in the clearing centres because the money spent over the weekend is paid into the branches on a Monday and arrives in clearing on a Tuesday.

9. Rejected cheques are ones where the sorting machine could not read the magnetic code on the bottom of the cheque. The sorting machines can sort cheques on-line so that the information is entered directly onto the bank's computer. They can also sort cheques without this information being recorded.

10. To "meet the house" means to have all the work prepared for the exchange of cheques at the central clearing house.

11. Staff are expected to build up the skills of speed, accuracy and responsibility in the machine room. According to one branch manager, if they are sent to smaller branches they perform a wider range of tasks and are meant to develop a sense of responsibility and urgency.

12. Baccualauréat plus two or four years of post-18 education.

13. These jobs involved finding new business for the banks, and these staff were often paid on commission related to their sales. A cashier would typically pass through the categories of guichetier "débutant", "confirmé" and "polyvalent" ("Répertoire Opérationnel des Métiers et Emplois" (R.O.M.E) CEREQ 1975). In small branches a "guichetier" is expected to be polyvalent although in larger branches they are more specialised (CEREQ 1975).

14. In France poorly qualified employees were encouraged to take the CAP and the BP. This training was provided by the Centre de Formation de la Profession Bancaire (CFPB) together with the national education system. (The Crédit Agricole and the Caisses d'Epargne have their own equivalents to the CFPB, these are the Centre d'Etudes Techniques du Crédit Agricole (CETCA) and the CENCEP respectively.) The CFPB also prepares the exams offered by the Institut Technique de Banque (ITB). Management training is provided by the Centre d'Etudes Superieurs de Banques (CESB).

5 Temporary work

1. Introduction

In chapter four we saw that task flexibility was essentially about the range and level of tasks workers perform. In this chapter we turn to examine the external sources of flexibility available to employers. External flexibility is about employing outside workers on a temporary basis. It can also include externalising work, as in the case of subcontracting, which is discussed in chapter six. Employers are seeking to develop external flexibility, it has been argued, because work load fluctuations are becoming more volatile and unpredictable, together with an increase in the rate of technological change (Meager 1986:7; Atkinson and Meager 1986:14; Boyer 1986 and 1987). According to these arguments competitive pressure has forced companies to develop external sources of flexibility, and the cost of doing so has fallen. The advantage of using external flexibility is that staff can be dispensed with easily during slack periods, so that temporary workers provide a buffer against uncertainity for privledged, permanent staff. However, concern has been expressed over the rise in this form of employment as its buffer role has encouraged temporary work to be conceptualised in terms of secondary sector employment (Doeringer and Piore 1971). Büchtemann and Quack (1990) have examined the precariousness associated with atypical forms of employment, like temporary work, arguing that it is not temporary work per se, but the accumulation of disadvantage which makes this form of employment unattractive.

In order to examine these debates, we will look first at the evidence for a growth in temporary work. Second, an analysis of the reasons for using different types of temporary work in the banking sector is undertaken. This identifies distinct differences in the use of temporary work in each country. An explanation of these differences rests on the argument that the type of external flexibility employers can achieve is related to the nature of employment regulation, and the demand for this type of work, as well as the opportunities and constraints created by traditional organisational practices and competitive pressures. Such an approach emphasises how the options available to employers are constrained and embedded as a result of institutional practices outside the immediate boundaries of the firm. These factors shape the way employers adopt external forms of flexibility in different countries.

2. Has the use of temporary work increased?

2.1 Problems of defining and measuring temporary work

The paucity of long term, reliable and extensive data on temporary work makes it difficult to establish a widely accepted definition of the temporary work force. Surveys which have been used to examine temporary employment fall broadly into two categories. In employee based surveys the interviewee has been asked if their job is temporary. This, it is claimed by Casey (1988), can inflate the figure, because people who define themselves as temporary may not have a permanent commitment to the job, even if the job is for an indefinite period of time. The second type of survey which has been conducted asks employers about jobs which are recognized as temporary to both sides (Meager 1986; Wood & Smith 1992). However, this too over-estimates the figures, because the sample used in Meager's study encouraged responses from companies who were more likely to use temporary work. Casey (1988), in an Anglo-German study, identified 11 categories of workers who could be referred to as temporary.[1] Whilst this categorisation avoids an over simplified definition of temporary work, even Casey admits there is some overlap in the categories he presents.

The problem of definition is particularly acute when it comes to cross-national comparison. At a national level we can compare the use of temporary work in the case of Britain and France by using the data available in the British Labour Force Survey (LFS) and the French L'Enquête sur l'Emploi. Since 1983 the LFS has distinguished between "*seasonal, temporary or casual"* jobs and jobs *"done under contract or for a fixed period of time"* which were separate from *"permanent"* jobs. Figures from the L'Enquête sur l'Emploi are comparable since 1984, when the classification system was changed. These figures allow us to distinguish between agency temps, apprentices, work experience, short-term contracts and other employees who are taken to be working permanently. In France the separate classification of public sector employees makes it more difficult to identify temporary workers in the public sector.[2] These difficulties are not overcome using published Eurostat data, as this does not provide industry-specific figures. As a result the data presented here underestimates the level of temporary work in France because these figures exclude public sector workers; the British figures are based on total employment in the public and private sector.

A distinction is made here between *"agency staff/casual workers"* and *"fixed term contracts"* (FTCs). An "agency worker", is defined here as someone whose services are obtained through the intermediary of an agency. The client pays the agency directly, who then in turn pays the worker.[3] "Casual workers", as defined in the British Labour Force Survey, includes people employed through an agency or other means. In Britain it is common for casual staff to include "on call" temps (Wood and Smith 1992:27). This refers to informal lists of previous employees, especially young mothers who are willing to come back to work on an casual basis. This policy was much more popular in Britain than in France. In contrast fixed-term contracts are usually offered on a full-time basis for a specified period of time, although there was considerable variation in the length of contract. In this chapter the term "temporary work" refers to all forms of temporary employment; FTCs and agency/casual work are specified where necessary. Although these definitions allow us to interpret the data at one level, they do not, however, fully bring out the heterogenous nature of temporary employment in terms of age, skills and gender (Dale and Bamford 1988; King 1988; Lane 1989:284).

2.2 Size and growth of the temporary workforce

Given the difficulties in establishing a consensus on defining temporary work, there has been some debate over the size and growth of the temporary workforce. Meager (1986) and Hakim (1987) both, independently, calculated that the use of temporary

119

work in Britain was just over 7% of the total workforce, and growing. Casey (1988), in an analysis drawn from the 1984 Labour Force Survey, puts the figure for temporary work closer to 6%. More recent Labour Force data estimates that in 1990 temporary work in Britain accounted for 5.6% of total employment. In France, according to the Annuaire Statistiques, the use of temporary work, as a percentage of all workers, has nearly doubled: from 7.9% in 1985, to 14.2% in 1987 (Annuaire Statistiques de la France, INSEE Tableau C.01-19 p.113). However, in the L'Enquete sur l'emploi, agency workers and short-term contracts accounted for approximately 8% of all those employed in 1989 (This does not, however, include public sector employees). This highlights the disputes which emerge on interpreting the data. Nevertheless, data from the British Labour Force Survey and the French L'Enquête sur l'emploi can allow us to identify differences in the most popular forms of temporary work and its rate of growth in each country (Table 5.1).

In France, fixed term contracts were more popular than in Britain, where casual work has been a more common form of temporary employment. From 1984 to 1989, in both countries the use of agency/casual workers has increased, from different base levels, by just over 1% of total employment. The most convincing evidence for an increase in temporary work can be seen in France: at a national level, the use of fixed term contracts has more than doubled in this period; in Britain there has been little change.

The rate of growth in the financial services sector in both countries has been less rapid than at the national level (Table 5.2). The use of temporary work in the financial services sector has increased marginally and somewhat sporadically. Nevertheless, national differences are also visible at the sector level: British employers make greater use of casual staff, while French employers use more fixed-term contracts.

Whilst this national data can allow us to identify distinct trends in the use of temporary work, it does not provide us with explanations for these differences, and it does not tell us why employers use different forms of temporary work. In order to understand the rationale for employers' behaviour, we need to look in closer detail at data obtained from a case study approach. In the following section we will look at the reasons why employers use casual temps or FTCs in the banking sector in each country.

Table 5.1
Temporary work in Britain and France 1984-9
(as a % of total employment)

| | BRITAIN | FRANCE | BRITAIN | FRANCE |
	Agency/casual staff		Fixed-term contracts	
1984	3.0	0.8	1.4	2.1
1985	3.4	0.9	1.7	2.6
1986	4.0	1.1	1.6	3.2
1987	4.2	1.0	1.6	4.0
1988	4.1	1.4	1.5	4.5
1989	4.1	1.9	1.6	5.0

(Source: Enquête sur l'Emploi, 1984 to 1992,Table PA 09. For Britain LFS 1984 to 1992)

Table 5.2
Temporary work in financial institutions in Britain and France
(as a % of total employment in this sector)

| | BRITAIN | FRANCE | BRITAIN | FRANCE |
	Agency/casual staff		Fixed-term contracts	
1984	1.1	0.8	0.4	2.0
1985	1.9	0.5	0.3	1.9
1986	1.9	0.6	0.6	1.7
1987	1.9	0.4	0.7	2.4
1988	1.5	0.9	0.3	2.1
1989	1.6	1.0	0.8	3.5

(Source: Enquête sur l'Emploi de mars 1984 to 1992, Table PA 09. LFS 1984 to 1992).

3. Motivations for the use of temporary workers

Traditionally, employers have used temps to replace permanent staff on holiday, sickness and maternity leave; to meet seasonal fluctuations; for special 'one-off' projects; for staffing during the early stages of a new development; or to provide expertise lacking amongst permanent employees. However, Meager (1986:12) also claims that new strategies were being developed amongst a substantial minority (44%) of British employers he surveyed. He argues that they were seeking to avoid permanent staffing committments. The debate on temporary work has tended to be framed in terms of "traditional" versus "new" strategies (Meager 1986; Atkinson and Meager 1986; Hunter and MacInnes 1992; Hunter et al. 1993). However, it is not always clear where "traditional" reasons for using temps differ significantly from "new" reasons. One of the problems with this debate has been that, where researchers discover an increase in the use of temporary work, this has been for traditional, rather than "new" motives. Employers' motives are not always discernably discrete: a range of rationales can be identified behind a single employment practice. One of the advantages of a case study method is that it allows us not only to identify patterns of temporary work, but also to disentangle the reasons why employers used these. In this section we focus particularly on the use of FTCs and casual work.

3.1 Fixed-term contracts

FTCs are offered for a pre-determined period. However the length of contract can vary considerably,

> A fixed-term contract is more likely to be used for a minimum of one month, maybe six months or a year, but on the whole they are usually for about 3 months. It gives the bank a lot of flexibility. (Temporary Staff manager, France).

There are greater restrictions over the use of FTCs in France than in Britain, although they are more popular in France than in the UK. There are several reasons why employers are prepared to offer contracts for a pre-determined period. These include using FTCs: in the restructuring process, or as an initial screening device, or as a means to obtain specialised staff, as well as providing holiday relief. We examine each in turn.

3.1.1 Restructuring projects using FTCs has become more popular as the banks are increasingly concerned with cost cutting and competition. When employers plan to close down or automate a particular service, they use FTCs to maintain staff levels until the service is no longer necessary. Temporary staff are employed for the expected duration of the project without incurring the problems of redeployment when the project is finished.

> Short-term contract staff, I know they use quite often when they know an operation is either going to close down or relocate within say six months, a year or two years, something like that and they take out contracts for that time. (BIFU permanent rep, Britain).

> We usually keep fixed-term contracts for about six to eight months, usually for projects that are going to disappear. (Senior manager cheque clearing, France).

When operations are closing down, or being subcontracted, managers may redeploy their permanent staff to other departments, as vacancies become available.   Fixed-term contracts are used to meet the required staffing levels in order to maintain the operation until it closes down. At the end of the project, or when closure arrives, these staff are easily dismissed. Fixed-term contracts play an essential role in managing this strategy, this was particularly true for the French banks studied, although it was also happening in Britain.

In Britain restructuring has been used to reduce staff numbers;   during the early 1990s staff reductions were frequently revised upwardly. Staff planning has been quite erratic since the boom years of the mid 1980s, and in some banks compulsory redundancies have been announced (BIFU 1993). In France a reduction in staff numbers has been a long term objective. The banks have not been able to introduce a watershed reduction in staff numbers because of left-wing government policy committed to maintaining low levels of unemployment during the 1980s, and because the banks have been more directly under government control in France than in Britain (see chapter three).

3.1.2 Initial screening can be obtained using fixed-term contracts, before offering permanent employment. This is more popular in France than in Britain. For example, in the employee questionnaire full-timers were asked how they had found their current job. Nearly 12% of the French sample said they had initially been employed on a temporary contract, but none of the British respondents cited this. In France between 1980-89 the BNP recruited over a third of the FTC workers to permanent jobs (Table 5.3).[4]

Table 5.3
Fixed-term contracts converted into permanent jobs at the BNP, France
(as a % of all fixed-term contracts taken on during the year)

1980	28.7
1981	87.9
1982	35.6
1987	32.7
1988	51.4
1989	36.7

(Source: Bilan Social BNP 1980-9:4)

The tendency for French firms to make greater use of FTCs and use them as a method of vetting potential permanent employees is because employment protection is more restrictive in France than in Britain. Fixed-term contracts in France provide employers with flexibility that allows them to evade the restrictions which apply to permanent workers, despite attempts to regulate temporary employment (Liasons Sociales 1986, 1987, 1988 and 1990). In Britain employers are not faced with the same constraints (Lane 1989:284-5), and Casey (1987:72) argues that such contracts are viewed as unecessarily restrictive by British employers (see also Chapter 9).

3.1.3. Obtaining specialised staff can also be achieved through the use of FTCs. For example, specialised programmers, in computer services, are often employed on such contracts in order to set up specific programmes or develop new working systems. These specialised professional skills, for which the bank does not have a constant requirement, are skills which are not specific to the banking sector. This was a common practice, especially in

France. For example,

> In the study/research department, which is one of the more 'noble services', there are 650 permanent full-time employees of the bank, on top of this there are 100 people who work there permanently, but who are paid by an external company. This is known as "Travail en Regie". For example, if the bank was going to do a study and needed 50 computer engineers they could employ them from a specialist company for a month, two years or until the project was finished, or they could pay a company to do a specific task, for a set fee. (CGT Permanent delegate, France)

Using these types of contracts is a cheaper way of having computer staff without incurring the costs of training and the disruption to pay scales that these specialists can create. A computer systems expert requires expensive, specialist training to be kept up to date on new systems and methods, which makes them very expensive to recruit, without necessarily entailing the advantages of company loyalty. Companies are also unwilling to train staff who are likely to be poached by other companies which, not having invested in training, can offer higher salaries. Job mobility is seen as an advantage in the field of system design because it allows staff to gain a broader knowledge of contemporary developments in their field; it also avoids professional staleness which comes from working in the same organisation for too many years. The shortage of skilled staff in this area has made their market rate considerably higher than other clerical staff, and high turn-over rates make them unreliable and expensive. During the recession of the early 1990s a large number of staff with computing expertise have been made unemployed. For these reasons it is cheaper, and can prove to be less disruptive, for the bank to recruit these expert staff from the external labour market rather than develop them from within.

3.1.4 Holiday relief: 'Les stages' in France are when young people work for the bank on FTCs during the summer holidays. They are generally more popular in France than in Britain. The "convention collective" (collective agreement) specifies that these contracts can only be used to resolve the problems which arise from permanent staff going on holiday.[5] It was not unusual for these trainees ("stagiaires") to be the children of existing employees. Holiday auxiliaries, in France, can only be recruited from the school or student population over the age of 18, although for parents already working in the bank they can allow their children to work from the age of 16. Between 1981-9 there has been an increase in the number of "stagiaires" employed by the three leading banks (Table 5.4). The figures in brackets shows this as percentage of permanent employees. The British banks did not collect comparable data on the use of temporary work.

Table 5.4
Numbers employed on work experience
from schools or universities

	Crédit Lyonnais	Société Général	Crédit Agricole
1981	810 (1.8%)	825 (2.4%)	na (0.0%)
1987	2,571 (5.9%)	1,126 (3.3%)	160 (6.0%)
1989	2,264 (5.4%)	2,167 (6.5%)	263 (9.2%)

(Source: Bilan Social from each bank Box no.122)

This increase in the use of 'stagiaires' is partly a reflection of the more selective recruitment policy of the banks in France, as well as providing temporary cover. British banks do not use work experience programmes in a comparable manner to manage holiday fluctuations. In Britain managers impose greater restrictions on when staff can take their holidays. In France the national tradition of August being the holiday month makes it more difficult for the banks to stagger time off and, in general, stages are more developed in France than in the UK.

3.1.5. Overall, FTCs are used to facilitated restructuring, they allow for initial screening of future permanent employees, they also provide a means of obtaining specialist skills and cover for holiday periods. French banks have relied more on FTCs for these functions than have British banks. This is partly due to differences in the long term restructuring of French banks under the auspices of left wing governments during the 1980s, as well as higher levels of employment protection, as compared with the climate of liberal deregulation in Britain. The more extensive use of FTCs in France is also related to the practice of annual vacations occuring in the month of August and the generally widespread practice of encouraging 'stages'. In Britain employers find it easier to force their staff to stagger their holidays between June and September.

3.2 Casual temps

3.2.1 'On-call' former employees provide considerable temporary flexibility with company-specific experience. These are lists of ex-employees who have expressed a willingness to work temporarily for the bank. In an emergency these staff can be phoned up and asked to come in and work intermittently; "It's like an emergency bucket" (Regional recruiter, Britain). These lists were informal arrangements that the branches in Britain had developed incrementally, rather than being a formal senior management policy.

> The on-call staff don't have proper contracts, they're not really officially allowed, and they're used more to 'mop-up' any bits of work. The time and motion calculations say that you don't need them but the branches use them anyway... You have greater control over wage costs and wage rises if you use your own auxiliary staff than if you use temps. (Manager of the time and motion study team, Britain.)

This was a much cheaper form of temporary labour, with company-specific experience and attachment, than using agency staff. Staff were paid an hourly rate for the job which was transferred directly into their bank accounts, without any extra staff benefits like pension contributions.

> It's a totally casual arrangement, we have no commitment to them, and they can refuse to work if they don't want to. They have no contract they are totally casual. We maintain them on the staff computer and record the number of hours they work, and, "magically" they find their current account credited with the money. For the ease of administration we deduct PAYE directly.(Personnel Manager, Britain)

> Normally this staff panel list is sufficient so that we don't have to get in temps; agency staff are very expensive. We

only use an agency if we can find nothing else; always go first to known sources of employees. But each branch may have their own methods of handling these. (Branch Manager, Britain).

Other types of temporary staff were not needed, one senior cashier in the British bank explained, because they obtained sufficient flexibility from their part-time staff and the on-call list; these staff were readily available, were qualified, cheap and could be used without restriction. They were very flexible, with company-specific experience and were easier to control compared to agency temps.

In France, one personnel manager explained that it was illegal for employers to employ staff in a comparable way. This is because French employers are bound to conform to the Labour Code, and therefore do not have the same "freedom to contract" as British employers (these differences are discussed in greater detail in Chapter 9). There was no evidence of an on-call list being used on a permanent basis in the French banks. However, on one occasion fifty retired staff had been offered fixed-term contracts to work temporarily on the automation of the drafts department at the Crédit Lyonnais. These staff were given formal fixed-term contracts for the predicted duration of the project. This was a one-off job which required extremely specialised staff. In adopting this strategy the bank avoided incurring the costs of agency staff, or the futile effort of training their own staff; however this did appear to be an exceptional example. Overall, British firms make more use of former employees as casual temporary workers, than do French firms.

3.2.2 Agency staff are more likely to be found in clearing centres and credit card processing rather than in the branches. For example, in Britain, the Joint Credit Card company employed 14% of its work force on a temporary basis (IDS 1986). In some of the smaller banks, in both countries, agency temps are also employed as cashiers; however this tends not to be the case in the larger banks which can draw on internal reserves of experienced labour (BIFU 1988 & 1990).

We would never take temps on as cashiers because the responsibility of cashiering requires security and also they need specific training. It's better if we can get someone who knows how our branch works. It takes about 2 weeks to re-train someone who may have left 10 years ago. For security reasons we need continuity, and its better for the customers to get to know the staff. (First-cashier, Britain)

Continuity in customer contact was also cited as an obstacle to using temporary staff in France. A range of comments from a variety of managers and supervisors interviewed sum up some of the problems of using agency temps in the banks.

Temps can be used for specific tasks when there isn't enough staff, but these are fairly basic tasks with no training given or full-time supervision. (First-cashier, Britain)

If someone were ill I wouldn't get in an agency temp but just cover with the staff we already have, or if really pushed get someone in from the on-call list. (First-cashier, Britain).

Agency temps might be used when we get really behind in the research jobs, looking up old cheques and answering queries, but temporary staff tend not to be of the same professional quality as our own permanent staff. (Supervisor in clearing department, France).

It would be more common to turn to our relief staff first before we went to an agency. (Branch manager, France)

We're more likely to try and borrow staff from another section if we are short, rather than get in an agency temp. (Clearing Supervisor, France)

The problem with agency temps is that they don't have the specific training, and we don't have enough time to teach them, and anyway they are too expensive. (Senior manager cheque clearing, France).

In the banks agency temps are generally perceived as inferior to permanent staff because they lack company-specific experience and attachment. Agency staff are often less willing to do extra tasks, other than those for which they were employed, whereas permanent staff have a greater stake in being adaptable. The banks, especially in Britain, have built up their own pool of external labour with the on-call lists, and therefore do not need to rely on agency staff. In France the relief teams, although permanent staff, provide the functional equivalent to agency workers, except that they are controlled by the banks themselves. The British bank had tried to overcome these obstacles by working together with a temporary employment agency to produce a training pamphlet to be given to agency staff coming to work at the bank. This explained the basic language and procedures used at the bank; this strengthened the relationship between the bank and the agency. The banks interviewed in France did not appear to have developed a comparable training relationship with any temporary agencies. Some of the smaller banks in Britain and France employ temporary cashiers from employment agencies because they do not have recourse to an extensive network of staff as in the larger banks. These temporary cashiers are given two days' training by the agency to make them operational; however, this trend is rather limited.

The issue of control was another reason militating against the use of external temporary staff.

> The control you have over these staff alters compared to your own permanent staff. During a postal strike we had to get temps in but that was mainly for the secretarial jobs - you don't have the same kind of control over these staff as you do over your own. (First-cashier, Britain).

In France the director of an agency providing temporary staff to the banks admitted that temporary staff did not have the same attitude as permanent staff. He said that they saw themselves as "just passing through".

3.2.3. *Overall*, the use of casual temporary staff is more popular in Britain than in France. This is largely achieved through the use of an on-call list of former employees, rather than through an extensive use of agency staff. Despite the growth of temporary agencies, especially in France, this is not a popular form of flexible labour used by the banks. This is largely due to organisational constraints, and flexibility obtained through alternative channels. For example, in Britain predictable fluctuations are managed using varying shifts of part-timers (see chapter 7) and locational flexibility amongst full-time permanent staff (chapter 4). In France part-time work is less popular and greater emphasis has been given to developing task flexibility amongst all employees (see chapter 4), or subcontracting (chapter 6). Alternatives to temporary work suggest that the banks can rely on a variety of labour practices to manage work load fluctuations which undermines the strict division between core and peripheral workers. Although British employers make less use of temporary staff they are more likely to use casual contracts. In France temporary work is more popular, through the use of FTCs.

4. Accounting for these differences in terms of the societal context

The main argument developed in this book is that employers' ability to use flexibility is embedded in specific societal structures. This includes external factors like the way regulation shapes the conditions under which employers can use labour, as well as the characteristics and preferences of the available labour force. Together with internal constraints, deriving from traditional organisational practices, these factors impinge on employers' capacity to use particular types of labour. This model can be applied to the case of temporary work, as outlined below.

4.1 Employment regulation

Compared with British employers, French employers have been more restricted by legislation in their use of temporary workers. In France, temporary employment is clearly defined in legal statutes, whereas in Britain the maximum duration of temporary employment is not defined in labour law. In Britain, the length of service determines employment rights regardless of temporary or permanent status. In France after two years' employment with the same company, temporary staff automatically have permanent status (Casey 1988:5-6). In 1982 the French government attempted to curtail the use of temporary work by specifying a list of legitimate reasons for which employers could use temporary workers. In 1986, during the period of left and right wing "co-habitation", the Chirac government lifted many of the restrictions on the use of temporary employment (Liasons Sociales 1986). However, legislation in 1990 sought to correct some of the abuses that have arisen, and greater control on the use of temporary staff has, to some degree, been restored (Liasons Sociales 1990). In Britain, by contrast, the dominance of free market ideology has meant that little attempt has been made to regulate these agencies, or restrict the reasons for which employers can resort to this form of employment (BIFU 1990; Bronstein 1991). In France the legal restrictions surrounding the use of temporary work formalises rather than inhibits its use. This has meant a wider use of fixed-term contracts in France compared with a more casualised system in Britain.

4.2 Available labour force preferences

The differences between the two countries in the use of temporary staff is also related to the demand for this type of employment. In Britain the banks have found that there is a readily available source of former employees with company-specific skills, who are willing to return to work temporarily. Notably these former employees are often women who have left to have a family.

> The on-call lists are usually made up of women between 25-40 who have had previous experience in the bank and who have gone on to look after their family. A lot of them keep their foot in the door by doing temporary work, and as their responsibility for the family recedes they tend to come back on a more permanent basis. (Senior Personnel Manager, Britain).

The use of these on-call lists shows how employees move between different sectors, or types of employment, at different stages in their lives. For example, permanent full-time female employees leaving to have a family are often willing to work intermittently while their children are very young. When their children start school they are more likely to go back to work on a part-time basis. Wood and Smith (1992:27) suggest, from an analysis of establishments drawn from the WIRS, that it is a fairly common practice in Britain for employers to keep lists of regular casual workers, and that the majority of temporary workers in Britain are women. The literature on flexibility and labour market segmentation argues that there is a sharp distinction between core and secondary sector workers. However, the use of an on-call list suggests that in reality the distinctions change over time, especially for women.

In France the same reserve of labour does not appear to exist. French women are less likely than British women to leave paid employment for long periods of time after having a child. Temporary work is higher amongst British women than amongst British men, whereas in France the situation is reversed. The limited provision of childcare facilities in Britain encourages women to look for temporary work. In France, where childcare provision is more widely available, this may have the opposite effect, i.e. French women do not want temporary work (Dale and Glover 1989 and 1990; Desplanques and Saboulin 1986; see also chapter 8 where this is discussed in more detail).

4.3 Organisational constraints on the use of temporary workers

Despite competitive pressures to restructure, reduce costs and extend opening hours, the banks have made limited use of the flexibility provided by temporary workers to manage these changes. Part of the explanation lies in the constraints generated within the organisation. This relates in particular to the need for high quality staff, constraints imposed by security, and the costs related to using external temps when cheaper internal sources are available.

Traditionally the banks have offered permanent employment with attractive benefits and the possibility of internal promotion in exchange for reliable, honest and dedicated employees. The banks place great emphasis on the quality of their staff, not only in terms of skills or qualifications, but also on personal qualities i.e. responsibility, reliability and understanding. In the interviews conducted with managers, they expressed a preference for using existing staff, or in Britain for calling on former employees to cover for temporary labour shortages, rather than recruiting temps from the external market. By using known employees the bank can be more confident of the quality of staff they are employing. Security concerns reinforce the need for high quality, trustworthy, and loyal staff. These requirements can militate against the use of agency temps.

Alternative sources, like the on-call lists in Britain or the relief teams in France, are more likely to provide higher quality service than agency workers. In Britain the on-call staff are also considerably cheaper. The substitution of different forms of labour between the core and the secondary sector is not fully accounted for in the literature on flexibility. Locational functional flexibility conflicts with an extensive use of external temps. Chapter 4 examined how the banks in both countries have traditionally made use of this practice. This replacement possibility is facilitated by internal promotion: banking has traditionally been seen as a career where staff can "work their way up the ladder". Staff who have moved on to higher positions have the experience of lower grade jobs which means they can be temporarily moved about if needed. As one cashier explained,

> Take Paul, for example, he started on the tills and now he works on customer services and queries. A fair amount of swapping around is done especially if there is sickness on a Monday or Friday. Now Paul might be asked to go on the cashier desk for half an hour if there was a bit of a build up. Either way customers suffer delays, either in the bank, or in their query being dealt with. (First-cashier, Britain)

The possibility of developing locational flexibility allows the banks to meet temporary staff requirements in certain areas as well as claiming to provide these staff with the training they need to further their career. The cost of training external temporary staff was also a significantly prohibitive factor in the use of agency staff in the banks in both countries. By using former employees the bank can maximise on their company-specific knowledge and training, which makes them more reliable in terms of the quality of work they perform. Their familiarity with the corporate culture and their willingness to come back makes it easier to integrate them.

5. Conclusions

From the evidence presented in this chapter we have seen that the growth of temporary work was relatively feeble in Britain and slightly more significant in France. There were distinctive patterns in each country which emerged from the national level data and the case study evidence. In Britain in general, and in the banks in particular, employers were more likely to draw on former employees and known casual employees to furnish their temporary requirements. In France employers were more likely to recruit their staff from the external labour market, on fixed-term contracts, or use students on work experience programmes. The use of temporary staff was more formalised in France than in Britain. These differences were attributable to the nature of employment regulation, women's demand for temporary work, as well as traditional working practices generating constraints on the options open to managers.

In terms of flexibility, temporary work included a gamut of different employment experiences. Temporary work could be used for short or long term needs, high or low skilled tasks, and as a one-off arrangement or as a first step towards permanent employment. This makes the concept of numerical flexibilty too elastic. In terms of strategic practice, temporary workers were often employed in an ad hoc way to meet unforeseen changes. The British banks did not keep statistics on the use of these type of workers, which indicates the lack of senior managerial involvement in the decision to employ temps. Even though the French banks were more likely to use temporary work as a means of vetting potential employees, even here this was used in an inconsistent manner. There was limited evidence to suggest that temporary staff were used strategically, except for where fixed-term contracts were used to manage the closure of a particular operation. The capacity for employers to use temporary work or subcontracting in a strategic manner was related to their ability to predict long and short term fluctuations in the flow of work and labour planning.

The precariousness associated with temporary employment needs to be put into context, as suggested by Büchtemann and Quack (1990). In the banks there was evidence of high grade, well paid computer specialists, being employed on comparatively long contracts, as well as evidence of temporary work being used as a method of recruitment and vetting for permanent employment. The nature of precariousness in temporary employment should not be seen solely in terms of its legal status. The concept of precariousness is not a feature of atypical work alone, as can be seen from the increased redundancies amongst full-time permanent staff in this sector (BIFU 1991 and 1993; CNC 1989; Cossalter 1990). Added to this is the need to draw out gender distinctions in the use of temporary staff. Male workers tended to be on longer contracts and higher grades. These differences indicate the medley of experiences embraced by the concept of temporary employment or external flexibility.

The main argument developed in this chapter has been that numerical flexibility fails to draw attention to the diverse array of employment contracts covered by this term. It also fails to point out the various ways in which temporary work itself is stratified in relation to the qualifications of temporary employees, the length of their contract, and how gender segregation is experienced. By acknowledging this diversity we can begin to differentiate betweeen the use temporary work in different countries. In France temporary work is used in a formal way, compared to a more casual use in Britain. If we want to understand how employers develop and implement particular flexible labour policies, we need to take into account how societal and institutional factors shape the rules under which employers decide which labour options to avail themselves of, and also how these institutions shape the characteristics of those available to work in each country. These themes are developed in subsequent chapters and synthesised in chapter 10.

Notes

1. Categories of temporary workers defined by Casey (1988: 3-4).
- Consultants or freelancers - who are normally self-employed and who move from organisation to organisation performing one-off or short duration tasks.
- Labour only sub-contractors - who provide semi-skilled or skilled labour in the building industry.
- Casual workers - who are brought in to undertake tasks of very short duration, who work at the request of an organisation but are not obliged to accept any offer of work and for whom the organisation has no obligation to provide work.
- Seasonal workers - who are engaged to meet seasonal peaks in demand, particularly in such industries as distribution, tourism, agriculture and food processing.
- Fixed-term contract workers - who are employed for a pre-determined period of time.
- Workers with a contract dischargeable by performance - who are employed for the duration of a particular task.
- Workers on training contracts - who are employed only for the duration of their training. These include apprentices and certain categories of trainee.
- Temporary workers on indefinite contracts - who are employed to satisfy requirements for manpower which are recognised as temporary but the precise duration of which is uncertain, and who are informed in advance of their temporary status.
- Agency workers - who are placed on a temporary basis by employment agencies with user organisations which themselves do not employ them but which pay the agency for their services.
- Employees of works contractors - who are hired out by their

direct employer to other organisations to undertake specific tasks, provide certain services or to replace absent employees. - Participants in special programmes for the unemployed - such as the Community Programme offering temporary jobs on 'socially useful' work projects, or the Youth Training Scheme, offering temporary positions in enterprises.

2. Public sector workers are distinguished in terms of those who are "titularisé", i.e. permanent and those who are "non-titularisé". It is not possible to distinguish between those who are on fixed-term contracts and those who are casual or agency staff in the public sector in France. This latter category can refer to those on a temporary contract and those who are in a trial period of employment.

3. See Bronstein (1991) for a discussion of this, and Casey (1988:80-82) for the implications of legal definitions of temporary employment on employees' status.

4. The other French banks did not record this in the Bilan Social, and the British banks were unable to provide this data.

5. (Annexe XIII Convention Collective).

6 Subcontracting

1. Introduction

External sources of flexibility can be obtained through the use of subcontracting, as well as temporary work. In the early literature on dual and segmented labour markets the issue of subcontracting was discussed from the perspective of relations between large and small firms. One of the assumptions in this literature has been that smaller firms will be squeezed out of the market by larger firms, which have a broader market share and benefit from the advantages of advanced technology (Edwards 1979). However, small firms persist (Lui 1990). Piore and Sabel (1984) have argued that the relationship between large and small firms has been turned on its head and small firms, with greater flexibility, provide the dynamic for growth. Large firms manage fluctuations by externalising risk to these smaller firms, which are more adaptable to changes in production (Berger and Piore 1980).

In the model of the flexible firm, developed by Atkinson and Meager (1986), the concept of "distancing" is used to take account of the externalisation of work by the core company.

> What this generally involves is the displacement of an employment contract by a commercial one as a means of getting a job done. Or put another way, Why attempt to be more flexible to deal with these pressures (greater competition, market pressures, volatility, uncertainty) if its easier to pay some one else to deal with them? (Atkinson and Meager 1986:54).

However, arguments which emphasise the importance of cost reduction as the main criterion for subcontracting services and operations, are overly deterministic and simplified, as will become apparent from the cross-national data presented below. The regulatory environment, the nature of competition, the comparable strength of the various actors involved and the nature of the links between them can vary significantly between countries. The result is that in some countries it may be more profitable and easier to subcontract, whereas in others alternative sources of labour mean that companies use different methods of reducing costs. The emphasis on costs alone cannot fully encapsulate these factors, nor explain cross-national differences.

Defining subcontracting is not as clear cut as it may initially appear and as will become apparent from some of the case study examples cited below. The subcontracting relationship has to be understood as a continuum in terms of the degree and forms of control retained by the client company. Nishiguchi (1989) argues that the subcontracting relationship is more complex than these earlier theories have suggested. In examining the use of subcontracting in car manufacturing and electronics in Japan, Europe and the USA, he offers a critical perspective on these early theories. He shows that national and cultural factors significantly affect the quality of these relationships. For example, in Japan a more co-operative, problem-sharing approach has fostered close relations between the prime contractor and subcontractors. In contrast, in Europe and the US this relationship has been exploited: subcontractors are used to meet peaks in demand and are then dropped in periods of recession.

Nishiguchi identifies six possible rationales for the use of subcontracting: access to specialist technology, reduced indirect control costs, use of cheaper labour, dispersion of risk, the use of subcontractors as a buffer to core production and finally as a managerial strategy to divide the working class. These categories can provide us with a useful framework within which to examine the motivation for the use of subcontracting in the case of the banks in Britain and France. One of Nishiguchi's major criticisms is that previous theories have been too simplistic in identifying the motivations for the use of subcontracting. In his own study he found that there was little evidence to suggest that employers in Japan used subcontracting as a means to divide the working class (Edwards 1979), and he argues that the claims of Piore and Sabel (1984) give too much weight to the increased strategic importance of small companies. Product complexity needs to be taken into account in understanding motivations to use this strategy (Nishiguchi 1989). With simple labour intensive products, subcontracting is likely to be used as a buffer function with the advantages of providing cheap labour. Where production is more complex, a closer "symbiotic" relationship is likely to develop between the subcontractors and their customers. This is a valid distinction which can be applied to work in the banking sector.

Given the nature of the changes which have occurred in the banking sector related to the introduction of new technology, increased competition, falling profits and pressure to reduce overheads and re-orientate employees to commercial rather than administrative tasks, the banks have been looking for new ways to restructure operations, and in some cases this has led to a greater use of subcontracting. The three main areas in which the banks have developed subcontracting have been first, for low grade "non-bank" jobs which include catering, messengers and security staff; second, for jobs which are related to work flow fluctuations; and third, for jobs which are changing as a result of new technology. By examining these three areas we will be able to identify the motivations which have encouraged the banks to turn to subcontractors, and use these to assess the theories which account for externalising flexibility.

2. Non-bank jobs

With pressures to contain costs the banks have been reconsidering and redefining the services they offer, and distinguishing between jobs which are essential to the banks, and those which they can refer to as "non-bank" jobs.

> The bank used to employ its' own maintenance staff, electricians, telephonists, painters etc... Now it increasingly uses contract staff, and just keeps a few technical supervisory staff. This is a way of reducing the status of the salariat! (CGT representative, Crédit Lyonnais, France).

Traditionally bank employees in both countries have had a relatively privileged position, in terms of job status and non-pecuniary benefits. Due to commercial pressure, however, the banks have been re-assessing which staff are vital to their business interests and who will benefit from company perks. By subcontracting certain services they can reduce the number of staff who are covered by the banks' collective agreements, especially in relation to pay scales and employment protection. In this way subcontracting maintenance, cleaning, catering and courier services reduces the costs of managing these services as well as reducing the cost of benefits paid to these staff. It is often the case that employment terms and conditions in subcontracting companies, are far inferior to those of the bank employees. A good example of this strategy can be seen in France where a successful strike in the early 1970s, organised by the messengers and couriers at the Crédit Lyonnais, severely disrupted the transfer of funds between branches. Shortly after the strike the bank transferred these services to a private company called Brinks, thereby making this militant group of workers redundant.

There were several reasons why the bank decided to externalise these services. The bank had set up the subcontracting company and continued to have significant investments in Brinks, although it was legally an independent company. In using this company the bank was no longer responsible for the day to day management of these services. Furthermore, it did not need to be embroiled in industrial relations conflicts, and could exercise control over the company with the threat of withdrawing their contract or investments, thus jeopardising the jobs of the staff of Brinks. Unlike the previous full-time messengers, the staff of Brinks were covered only by the minimum protection of the "Code du Travail" and not by the superior benefits of the collective agreement applying to bank staff, which also reduced the cost of providing these services. Brinks has since diversified its operations and works for other banks, transferring securities, gold and cash as well as transporting money for supermarkets. Whilst the company was set up by the bank, the diversification of clients and jobs has given it greater independence from its initial client. In subcontracting these services the bank sought to break the unionised control of the couriers, as well as restructuring their investments and reducing costs. This shows how the rationales outlined by Nishiguchi are not exclusive and a variety of motivations can be attributed to the decision to subcontract.

Another example of banks subcontracting with the aim of reducing their indirect costs can be seen in the process of decentralisation. The re-organisation of the branches into clustered groups, as outlined in Chapter 3, has encouraged the local managers to develop new organisational initiatives in the provision of services, like inter-branch communications. The use of subcontractors for internal mail services at the Crédit Lyonnais displaced 150 people who were either redeployed, or, were offered redundancy payments, or cheap loans to set up a business. However, according to the CGT, "Attempts to get people to leave were not very successful, because of the fear of unemployment." (CGT representative, France).

In Britain, Barclays Bank also had plans to re-organise its non-bank jobs: it intended to phase out the messengers who were a well unionised group of workers within the bank. The bank had reduced their jobs by introducing a night shift with the future intention that permanent bank staff, or the employees of a private company, would do the work the messengers had previously done. The bank also wanted to reduce the allocation of management time to the administration of non-bank jobs as part of a rationalisation process. Another example of reorganisation was in 1987 when Barclays re-located its printing unit from Birkenhead to Bletchley, a green-field site in the south. This allowed the bank to re-assess jobs, and certain tasks which were not essential to the bank were contracted out.

Non-bank jobs have become a target for management restructuring, and rationalisation has taken the form of subcontracting or merging tasks and decentralising responsibility for them. The motivation for this has been a mixture of reducing indirect costs involved in administering these operations, replacing core employees with cheaper, poorly protected labour alternatives, as well as undermining unionised areas. This shows that managerial strategy is often developed by an amalgam of factors.

3. A buffer against fluctuations in work flow

Secondly, the development of flexibility is often attributed to the need to meet fluctuations in work flow. The secondary sector acts as a buffer for the core workforce: during peak periods secondary sector workers (Doeringer and Piore 1971), or numerical flexible workers (Atkinson and Meager 1986), absorb increased work loads, and are dispensed with when times are slack. In the banking sector fluctuations in cheque clearance tend to be fairly predictable but susceptible to dramatic differences during the week. These fluctuations are, however, mediated by the size of the operations.

In France, although weekly differences in the amount of cheques treated by the regional clearing centres were not as great as in Britain, encoding was either done in the branches, or excess work was subcontracted. Subcontracting was more popular in France because the decentralised system made the branches more vulnerable to change in business activity at the local level. For example, if a large store started trading in the local area, this would significantly increase the cheques handled by the local branch. In Britain these local changes made little difference because the system was centralised. In Britain, the fluctuation in cheques treated at the clearing centre was much greater than in France, however it was possible to predict these variations, and shifts of part-timers were employed at a central location to encode these cheques.

In France a variety of ad hoc subcontracting arrangements have been developed. One branch manager in France explained the situation in his own branch,

> You can use subcontracting a bit for encoding if you can't get it all done in the branch. Some days we may only send 70-80 cheques, another day a couple of hundred. One of our clients is Virgin Records, they pay their cheques in on Monday afternoon, this is mainly for the business they have done over the weekend. All these cheques are sent to the subcontractors. The permanent staff in accounts ride through at a basic level regardless if there are more or less cheques to deal with. (Branch manager, France)

> It depends on who your clients are. For example, in one branch I was in, we had the account of Amnesty International which meant handling a lot of cheques, but most of the encoding was done in the branch by the cashiers, the extra was subcontracted.(Branch manager, France)

Subcontracting is one way to manage fluctuations in work like encoding cheques, which is a labour intensive, low skill operation. In this way the subcontractors are used as a buffer to meet peaks in work flow, which is cheaper than employing permanent staff to process this work.

143

Subcontracting the encoding works out cheaper than employing someone extra to do the job, especially when you add up the social security charges, the problem of absence, the costs of training, office space and an extra machine. The bank also has a policy not to recruit any more purely administrative staff, they want to recruit people for the more commercial side. The use of cheques is also falling so it's not worth training someone and buying the machines. (Branch manager, France).

Subcontracting the encoding work gives us an enormous amount of flexibility: it costs 14 centimes for each cheque (approximately one and a half pence), if we have no cheques we don't pay. It's a big advantage at the end of the month when we pay salaries, or after bank holidays when we are very busy and there are a lot of cheques to encode. However one of the problems is guaranteeing no errors.(Branch manager, France)

Subcontractors are cheaper and avoid the extra responsibility and cost of employing someone to do this work in the branch.

One criterion for subcontracting was for simple bulk tasks. However one of the problems was maintaining quality control and reliability.

We have just changed the subcontractors we use because they were too unreliable. The only problem with subcontracting is that you don't have the same degree of control compared to when you do it yourself. We have to make sure that the cheques arrive here in time to send them to clearing and that all the totals are correct. The last subcontractor kept making too many mistakes, so we just went to a different company. (Branch manager, France).

In this case subcontractors are used as an interchangeable buffer to meet certain requirements, in the way suggested by Atkinson and Meager (1986) and the European model described by Nishiguchi (1989).

However this is only one type of subcontracting relationship. The externalisation of work can take diverse forms and result from ad hoc arrangements.

We came to another arrangement to deal with this type of

encoding work, although its not really subcontracting. One of our clients is an agriculture insurance company, and every month they have a lot subscriptions to pay into the bank. We made an arrangement to lend them one of our encoding machines so that they encode the cheques before they send them in to us, and they benefit by doing their own accounts at the same time. Any errors are found in the night sorting. (Branch manager, France)

In this case the externalisation of work had been negotiated as mutually beneficial. The agricultural origins of the bank and the insurance company helped them forge a common interest in contrast to the purely commercial example cited previously.

Decentralisation has made managerial strategy become more fragmented: individual managers are given a more significant role in finding alternative cost-effective ways to treat their work than they were in the past. Subcontracting is more developed in France than in Britain, (this case-study evidence is supported by Brunhes 1989). This cross-national difference is partly due to the more decentralised system in France, where branch banks are more vulnerable to changes in local business activity. Using subcontractors in this case relieves the bank of recruiting, training and paying for a full-time employee to do this extra work. The bank need not invest in modern equipment to encode cheques, given their predictions that this form of payment will decline as other direct forms of electronic transfers are adopted. Additionally, the bank did not want to employ people to do tasks they were later going to have to redeploy or make redundant.

4. New technology

The use of new technology has influenced subcontracting in two respects: there has been a strategy to draw on specialist skills, a rationale identified by Nishiguchi; but subcontracting has also been used to displace jobs which are expected to disappear with the introduction of advanced automated methods. The banks have been one of the major industries to take up the developments offered by advanced information technology systems. However the skills required to develop and set up these services are not specific to a traditional banking career, and the market for computer experts is highly competitive. The banks in both countries have found themselves in a position where it is more profitable to buy in specialist skills, rather than develop them "in-house". This avoids the problems of negotiating competitive salaries and the wage push effect this would have on other jobs in the bank. It also means that the banks do not have to invest in the expensive training these system developers require, with the risk of these staff being poached by other companies offering higher salaries. In France the system of "Travail en Regie" commonly refers to the use of computer specialists being used to work on a specific development project. This form of work crosses the lines of fixed-term contracts and subcontracting. Specialists are brought in to develop a new programme for the bank and to train permanent staff to maintain it (Khun 1989). These programmers are employed by the specialist company which is paid by the bank. During the project they may work on-site, but when it is finished they leave to work for another company.

Another way in which subcontracting has developed is where specialist services have been bought in by the banks. For example in France, the banks pay for the services provided by the interbank Groupe Intêret Economique (GIE) which controls credit card payments. In the past automatic distributors used to feed information directly into the banks' own computers. This information was then sorted and redistributed to the relevant branches where accounts would be debited. Now the information collected in the distributors is sent to the centre for the "carte bleue" credit card. This centre also received information from the banks about cards that have been refused or which are blocked. It then distributes the relevant information to the banks concerning clients' accounts, a service for which the bank pays them directly. This new system reduces the costs of managing the accounts and is a more effective way of controlling fraud. It reduces the costs of treating this type of work, as well as freeing considerable amounts of time on the banks' computers which had previously dealt with this work. Now the banks receive the information once a day, rather than throughout the day. The banks' computers are now used to treat the speculative market, for example the SIVAC,[1] or in extending their network. In both of these examples the banks, notably in France, have been prepared to pay for expert services because they are provided by a specialist organisation more cheaply and with less administrative cost to the banks than if they were to manage them themselves.

The third major use of subcontracting in relation to new technology comes closer to the motivation of reducing indirect costs and using cheaper labour. Technological change and automated payments have been aimed at reducing the administrative paper work processed by the banks and certain banks have been restructuring their operations with this in mind. At the CIC, in France, the job of tray agreement was being subcontracted to an external company. This specialist company already belonged to the same financial group as the CIC, and the bank owned approximately 15% of shares in the subcontracting company. By 1994 the bank plans to dispense with manual tray agreement and checking because this will have been replaced by transfers through magnetic bands. The subcontractors were given a two year contract to carry out the existing manual systems, on their own sites. By subcontracting this work to a subsidiary, the bank avoided future problems in redeploying these specialised staff. They could also replace them with cheaper staff who were not covered by the collective agreement for the banks,

> The bank avoids having to employ a night shift, with the extra bonuses that it entails. There are no disadvantages in using this outside company. (Senior manager cheque clearing, France)

At the Crédit Lyonnais the encoding, sorting and listing of cheques has been done by a specialist subcontractor which originally transported funds for the bank. The outside company collects the cheques at the end of the day from the branches and treats them at night, putting the information on to a magnetic band for the bank's computer. The next day they present the branch with a list, and the headquarters with the band and cheques to be transferred. One of the advantages of this is that an extra day has been gained in the exchange of cheques which works out more profitably for the bank, and the banks retain a degree of control over these companies because of their financial investment in the subcontractors. In this way there is greater co-operation and mutual development of service provision between the parent company and the subcontractors.

5. Conclusions

We have seen how the banks have re-defined and protected jobs which are central to their operations whilst moving towards externalising "non-bank" work. In this way the banks have been able to reduce their indirect labour costs, replace former employees with cheaper labour, and undermine areas where unionisation is well developed. In setting up subsidiaries to deal with courier services they have retained a degree of financial control over the externalisation of these tasks. There is also evidence to suggest that subcontractors are used as a buffer to meet variations in work load, as in the case of encoding in France.

However, strategic planning is more ad hoc as a result of decentralisation, and local managers are encouraged to find their own solutions to mundane administrative management. At this level the relationship between subcontractors and their clients can vary significantly, from one where market considerations of cost and quality are the main criteria on which to choose a subcontractor, to a closer mutually negotiated relationship as seen with the agricultural insurance company and system developers. Even at this level we can see the diversity of arrangements which can be used to externalise work.

In looking at the impact of new technology we have seen how the banks have bought in specialist services which they could not produce themselves as economically or as effectively. But at the same time technological developments will displace certain tasks which the banks, in some cases, have decided to subcontract. In this case the banks have exhibited long term strategic planning and a consistent plan to externalise their services. They have also secured control of these operations because of their financial investments in the organisations set up to treat this work. This allows the banks to reduce their indirect costs, replace their staff with cheaper, less well protected labour, and minimise on their staff performing low grade clerical work. These examples are particularly illustrative of the point made by Nishiguchi on the importance of taking into account product complexity and managerial strategy. From these examples we can see that, in the first instance there exists a variety of forms which can be referred to as subcontracting, and in the second that employers' motivation for using these strategies are equally diverse and complex. The subcontracting relationship should not be reduced to a simple formulae of large versus small firms.

Nor is cost the sole reason encouraging firms to subcontract. Instead it needs to be seen along a continum where the degree and forms of control retained by the client company can vary in strength and influence.

Whilst there was considerable overlap in the reasons for subcontracting in the two countries, this practice tended to be more developed in France than in Britain. Where French banks used subcontractors to handle particular changes in workload fluctuations, in Britain the banks made more use of part-timers for the same tasks. According to Brunhes (1989:29) this appears to be a common trait in France, even outside the banking sector. These results suggest that how the differences in the characteristics of available labour needs to be taken into account when explaining the labour strategies used by employers. In Britain, the banks found it easier to recruit casual staff and part-timers to meet changing work load fluctuations (Chapters 7 & 8). It was more difficult for French employers to employ women in a similar way, as there was less demand for this kind of work (Belloc 1986; Maruani and Nicole 1989; Bronstein 1991). French employers were also more constrained by labour regulation as to the type of temporary or part-time workers they could employ. As a result, an attractive option open to the French banks was to subcontract services to firms not covered by employment regulation or the collective agreement applied to banking staff. The way employers define and realise their needs for flexibility are embedded in societal differences, both in terms of the characteristics of the available labour supply and the nature of employment regulation.

The work presented here is intended to be illustrative of attempts to gain flexibility by externalising operations through the use of subcontracting in the banks in Britain and France during the 1980s and early 1990s. As suggested by Nishiguchi (1989), earlier theories about the relation between large and small firms and cost criteria have presented an over simplified thesis. Nishiguchi's work is more sophisticated, but the global nature of his analysis, based on constructing models contrasting Europe and the US with Japan, misses out on the differences which can be observed even between West European countries. This suggests that in order to understand the diverse rationales motivating employers to externalise we need to situate their action within the context of the given society in which they are operating. By adopting an approach which emphasises the embeddeness of economic action, a richer analysis and understanding of these practices can be obtained. This has the advantage of breaking away from dichotomised mono-causal explanations. It can identify the range of rationales which produce specific and varied forms of inter-firm relations and the institutions which hinder or facilitate these arrangements.

Notes

1. SIVACs are a form of investment savings accounts.

7 Part-time work

1. Introduction

The preceding chapters examined the use of temporary work and subcontracting, concluding that the concept of numerical flexibility gave a poor account of the diverse reasons employers resorted to these forms of employment. It also fails to account for differences between countries. The same criticism could be made with regard to the use of part-time work. The concept of numerical flexibility revolves around the management of time and numbers, and this has been tied to precarious forms of secondary employment. According to these theories, employers can hire and fire secondary sector workers, and change their working hours as required to meet work load variations.

This chapter sets out, first, to examine how part-time work has been used in the banks in each country, and to what extent this corresponds to the rationale associated with the concept of numerical flexibility. Second, if part-timers belong to a secondary sector, what criteria distinguish between core and peripheral staff, full and part-time employees? On the basis of this analysis it will be argued that the flexible labour options open to employers are severely constrained by, and embedded in, the institutional structures of a given society. In the case of part-time work this includes the role of labour regulation, the historical legacy of organisational culture and practices, as well as the characteristics and preferences of female workers, which are discussed in greater detail in chapter 8. As will be seen from the data presented here, part-time work offers different kinds of flexibility to French and British employers.

1.1 Problems in defining part-time work for comparative research

The study of part-time work from a comparative perspective raises several methodological difficulties (Dale and Glover 1989; Dex et al. 1993). One such problem is the lack of a standard definition of part-time work which could be applied to both Britain and France. According to the French Labour Code,

> Part-time workers are those whose hours of work are shorter by at least one fifth than the weekly or monthly statutory hours of work (currently 39 and 169 respectively), or than the hours of work fixed by collective agreements for full-time employment. Except for public servants, there is no legal provision for minimum part-time working hours other than those reached through collective agreements.[1]

Problems of comparability also arise due to the definitions used in national data sets. For the French Labour Force Survey the definition of a part-time worker is a person who worked "*less than 30 hours a week during the reference week, excluding those persons who do not have a regular job and persons on partial employment.*" In Britain the definition was less precise and was left up to the individual to decide if they were a part-timer or not (ILO 1989:40). The British definition is more inclusive than the French one and it makes no reference to the number of hours worked.

Some of the problems in making cross-national comparisons on the basis of national labour force surveys were raised in Chapter 1. To briefly summarise these problems, Beechey (1989:370) argues that activity rates are essentially social constructions developed in specific societies; this raises problems of comparability for cross-national research. The conceptual definitions structuring such data restrict the type of research questions which can be asked. Dale and Glover (1989) point out that categories which have developed historically affect the construction of the national data set. These categories are not always directly transferable between countries and this poses problems in terms of measurement of the same phenomenon. Substantive differences, for example, the existence of conscription, or the age of entering and leaving the labour force, affect employment and unemployment rates. These criticisms indicate the potential hazards involved in cross national comparisons using labour force data.

Nevertheless to reject such data outright would be to deny access to an important source of longitudinal material, which can provide us with an approximate measure of the pattern of labour force participation. According to an ILO report (1989),

> ...valid conclusions on the evolution of part-time work within countries can be drawn from the study of national time series, but ... international comparisons of levels of part-time work should be made with great caution. On the other hand, comparisons between countries of the distribution of part-time workers by industry, by sex or by age are less influenced by the concepts and methods of collection and are therefore reasonably reliable. (ILO 1989:33)

When looking at data on increases in employment absolute numbers can be misleading because the trend is for the work force to increase. What is important is the proportion of the increase between part-time and full-time work.

2. The growth in the use of part-time work

Britain has traditionally had a much higher level of part-time work than France. For example, over 27% of the work force in Britain worked part-time in 1991, compared to just under 12% in France. In both countries part-time work is predominantly performed by women, although in Britain nearly twice as many women work part-time as in France. This can be seen in Table 7.1. In Britain the use of part-time work remains nearly double the French figures, despite the increase in part-time work in France between 1982-9.

The service sector usually has a high level of part-time employment. However, the overall use of part-time work in financial services is lower than the national rate in both countries. The reasons for this are related to the quality of products and services, the nature of security arrangements and the 'diamond' hierarchical structure. First, where the emphasis is on high quality, the staff employed will be expected to have higher qualifications, experience, or skill. For example, although the work of a supermarket check-out cashier and a bank cashier are fairly similar, especially in Britain, part-time work is more popular in the retail food sector than in the retail banking sector

(Gregory 1989). Second, security questions are more prominent in a bank which emphasises the need for reliable and trusted staff.[2] Third, there are a limited number of staff in the banks employed in the very low grades, where part-time work is usually found. Crompton (1989) has pointed out that the grading structure of the British banks is like a 'diamond': the base of the grading pyramid is very narrow, compared to the swollen ranks of middle management. A similar picture is also true for France (CNC 1989; Cossalter 1990)

Table 7.1
Part-time work in Britain and France
(as percentage of total employment)

	BRITAIN			FRANCE		
	Male	Female	Total	Male	Female	Total
1982	na	42.1	18.1	2.5	18.9	9.2
1983	na	42.4	18.3	2.6	20.0	9.7
1984	na	42.6	18.7	2.7	21.0	10.3
1985	7.0	42.8	22.9	3.2	21.8	10.9
1986	7.4	43.3	23.6	3.5	23.1	11.7
1987	7.7	43.2	24.0	3.6	23.1	11.8
1988	7.8	42.1	23.6	3.4	23.8	12.0
1989	7.8	41.7	23.8	3.5	23.7	12.0
1990	8.1	42.2	24.6	3.3	23.6	11.8
1991	9.6	44.7	26.4	3.3	23.5	11.9
1992	10.5	45.3	27.3	na	na	na

(Source: Annuaire Statistique de la France 1982-3 to 1991-2, Tableau C.02-5 and C.01-8 A, INSEE. Employment Gazette 1982-92 June. Figures for male part-timers were not kept until 1985.)

The use of part-time work has increased in the financial services in both countries, between 1982-92. In 1982 part-time work accounted for 12.0% of the workforce in the British financial services. This rose to 18.0% by 1992. In France over a similar period, part-time work as a percentage of employees in this sector rose from 7.3% in 1982 to 9.6% in 1991 (Table 7.2).

Table 7.2
Percentage of part-timers in Britain and France
in the financial services
(as a percentage of employment in this sector)

| | BRITAIN | | | FRANCE | | |
	Male	Female	Total	Male	Female	Total
1982	na	25.0	12.0	1.3	13.3	7.3
1983	na	24.9	12.0	0.9	13.0	7.1
1984	na	25.2	12.3	1.2	13.7	7.7
1985	6.0	25.0	15.3	1.7	15.4	8.9
1986	6.1	25.7	15.8	2.0	14.6	8.6
1987	6.1	24.4	15.2	1.9	15.2	8.8
1988	4.7	22.8	13.9	1.2	17.4	9.6
1989	4.4	22.7	13.9	1.4	15.9	9.2
1990	4.9	24.2	14.7	1.4	14.7	8.4
1991	7.8	25.1	16.6	1.6	16.9	9.6
1992	9.9	26.0	18.0	na	na	na

(Source: Annuaire Statistique de la France 1982-3 to 1991-2, Tableau C.02-5, cat. U11-13; INSEE. Employment Gazette 1982-92 June.)

Part-time work in the banks has been growing slowly and relatively consistently. In Britain, since the increase in 1985, levels of use have fallen off slightly, rising again during the 1990s. In France, part-time work has crept up slowly over the past decade. However, we need to note that this aggregate data includes organisations other than banks.

If we look at the data available from individual banks we can see that the use of part-time work varies quite considerably between the banks (Table 7.3). The use of part-timers at the BNP in France is equivalent to the leading British banks. The Société Générale and the Midland have the lowest levels. Although there is considerable variation between the banks, there has been a continued increase in the use of part-time work. Lloyds Bank said that, between 1979-1987, they had increased their clerical staff by 25% of which their increase in part-time staff amounted to a rise of 275%.[3] However, part-time staff, as a proportion of full-time staff, remained relatively low, even though it has risen from 3% to 9% in this period. The banks in France had also experienced an increase in part-time work. At the Crédit Lyonnais the use of part-time work had increased from 3% in 1983 to 6.7% in 1988, and personnel managers expected this to increase further. The Crédit Agricole had also experienced a similar increase. The Société Générale kept no record of the use of part-time work in the early 1980s and since 1987 its use has increased only marginally. At the BNP, after an experiment following the 1981 legislation on part-time work, its use had risen from 3% in 1982 to 10% in 1988. Does this evidence of a growth in the use of part-time work suggest that employers in both countries have been developing a policy of numerical flexibility? In order to assess these developments we need to take a closer examination of how part-time work is used in the banks in each country.

Table 7.3
A comparison of the level of part-time work
in the main banks in Britain and France in 1988
(% of the total workforce)

FRANCE
BNP	10.4
Crédit Lyonnais	6.7
Crédit Agricole	5.9
Société Générale	4.4

BRITAIN
Barclays	13.6
Natwest	10.2
Lloyds	9.0
Midland	1.2

(Source: British figures supplied by the companies themselves, French figures published in Bilan Social.)

3. Motivations for the use of part-time workers

On the basis of interviews and observations conducted in the banks in each country there appeared to be three main reasons why the banks used part-timers: for mananging workload fluctuations (especially in Britain), in response to staff demands for reduced working time (particularly in France), and to resolve recruitment problems or reduce FTE staff numbers. There were cases where more than one reason could be identified behind the use of a particular type of part-time work.

3.1 Managing fluctuations

This is one of the most important reasons why employers use part-work, although the nature of these fluctuations varied in each country. In the branches work load variability was dictated by the flow of customers, so the busiest days were before and after the weekend, usually Mondays and Fridays, or Tuesdays and Saturdays depending on opening hours in each country.

In a typical British branch bank part-timers were frequently employed as cashiers on either the quick service tills, staffed ATMs, or behind the traditional counters. They usually worked on two day a week contracts (Mondays and Fridays), an average of 14 hours a week. When there was a Bank Holiday, if they normally worked on a Monday they were expected to come in on the Tuesday. Part-timers were also employed to cover for busy lunch periods, so that a typical work schedule could involve working from 11.30 to 2pm or 3pm, three or four days a week. A myriad of part-time contracts were used in Britain, compared to more formalised practices in France. In the branches in France half-time contracts, of two and a half days a week, were the standard part-time contract. Half time contracts were given for a year at a time, and the days worked were determined according to local needs.

In the clearing centres the main fluctuations in work loads were on a daily and weekly basis. In Britain there were daily pressures to meet the central clearing house deadline for the exchange of cheques. These pressures were less intense in France (see chapter 3). On a weekly basis the flow of cheques was at its highest on Tuesdays, and tailed off at the end of the week. There were also seasonal variations during the Christmas and holiday periods. In the clearing centres in Britain a diverse range of part-time contracts were offered. These included morning and afternoon shifts, "week-on-week-off" contracts and two or three day a week contracts. In France 50% or 80% contracts were more popular.

In Britain the morning shifts of part-timers were employed in encoding, where they had to meet the 11am exchange of cheques at the central clearing house (11.30am on Tuesdays). Chapter 4 discussed how the task variety of these encoders had recently increased because the levels of encoding work had fallen off. Afternoon-only part-timers were employed as manual sorters in the correspondence sorting room.[4] This all female shift lasted from 2pm to 6.30pm and the heavy lifting work was done by the full-time male messengers. These jobs were organised on a part-time basis, the bank explained, because they had found it difficult to recruit full-timers to these low grade jobs in the centre of London. The two and three day a week contracts had reduced the number of staff needed by matching employees to fluctuations and thereby reducing overall labour costs.

The extension of regular hours can also be seen as a means of achieving numerical flexibility. Approximately half of all the interviewees, in both countries, said they had worked more hours than normal in the past month. British part-timers (53%) were more likely to say they had worked extra hours compared to British full-timers (41%); in France the pattern was reversed. Part-timers in Britain, were more likely to be used to meet fluctuations in work load, and were also more likely to have their hours increased compared to part-timers in France. At the same time the majority of part-timers worked regular hours and had not experienced any radical change in the hours and days they worked. In the British bank a new employment contract for full and part-time employees had been introduced gradually since 1987. This contract stipulated that employees had to "work to finish", which meant that staff had to stay on until their work was completed. If, for example, the computer system broke down the staff would have to remain until it was repaired. They were paid at the normal hourly rate without overtime. This contract was offered to all new recruits. This stated that,

> staff working set hours daily are obliged to work up to an extra one hour per day. Any additional hours may be worked at the request of the bank on a voluntary basis. The bank will endeavour to give reasonable notice where possible. Payment for these extra hours will be on normal rates unless they work more than 7 hours in one day. (From work contract provided by BGSU)

Those employed before February 1987 worked set daily hours and were not obliged to work extra hours.[5] All new employees had to sign these contracts. As the average turnover of labour was between 8-12% per annum, this process of change was occurring gradually and in a piecemeal fashion.

Essential to the concept of numerical flexibility is the idea that such staff can have their days and hours altered to meet changing fluctuations in the work load. However when interviewees were asked if they were ever expected to change the days they worked, the vast majority said no (O'Reilly 1992:171-2). Only 7% of the British part-timers said they were expected to change often; 17% of French part-timers sometimes had to change the days they worked. The vast majority of part-timers worked regular days, although they were more likely than full-timers to be asked to change their days, especially in France.

Overall, the British banks were more likely to use part-timers to meet particular work load fluctuations, whereas French employers were more likely to be trying to develop functional flexibility amongst their staff, or else would be seeking to subcontract out particular services.

3.2 Responding to Employee demands

Part-time work in France had originally developed in the 1970s to meet employees' special needs for shorter working time. As a result, in the French banks part-time work was tolerated rather than being used by employers to achieve numerical flexibility. These part-time employees in France retained the benefits of full-time employment which in some cases created resentment from the full-timers:

> Part-time work is sometimes the source of internal conflicts. In certain administrations, for example, where part-time work has been introduced with full legal protection for women working on these contracts, those employees who work full-time consider - not without reason - that there has been a sort of injustice towards them. (cited from FO's journal Employees et Cadres 22nd May 1978.)

The use of part-time work in France differs significantly from the British experience. In France part-time work has developed slowly, with full legal protection, and in the banks it has been offered as a concession to employees' needs. Part-timers in the banks were put into positions where there was less pressure to meet daily deadlines, or in low grade administrative work, or as tray agreers.

> Part-time work is still not all that developed in France. It is easier to integrate part-timers into a larger organisation like

the administrative headquarters where the work is mainly administrative, rather than to have a lot of part-timers in a branch bank. (Chief Personnel Manager, France)

Although there were also higher grade part-timers in the computer systems department.

It's easier to work part-time in this department because there are no daily deadlines. We work on long term projects and it's up to us to get the work done on time. Even though you're part-time you're still expected to do as much work as a full-timer. (Part-timer in the computer systems department, France)

The banks in France did not use part-time work to meet daily deadlines in the way the British banks did. Instead part-timers in France were tolerated, and segregated to an area where their absence would not be too disruptive to an organisation centred on full-time employment. French employers rarely perceived any strategic advantage for the company in the use of part-time work. Managers at the Crédit Lyonnais said that it was too difficult to organise part-timers to work for just half a day. When I asked managers and supervisors what they thought were the advantages of part-time work, a lot of them would typically say *"It allows women to combine their work and family life more easily"* rather than perceiving the interests of the company first, as was the case in Britain.

Part-time work is always at the demand of the staff we never take anyone on a part-time basis (Senior Personnel Manager, France)

In France bank employees could ask to work on a part-time basis because of government legislation and negotiations accepting this between the banks and the unions (see chapter 9). In Britain, employees did not have the same rights, but employers were attempting to design part-time jobs they knew they could fill with the available labour in Britain. For example, attempts were being made to introduce "term-time" contracts which would allow women to work while their children were at school and then take the holiday periods off. However, these were largely experimental projects initiated by managers rather than employees. The major difference between the two countries is that in the banking sector in France part-time work was seen as a selective policy to allow reintegration into work, after a period of illness, or exceptional difficulty; in Britain, due to limited childcare, part-time work represented a much larger demand allowing women to combine family and professional life.

3.3 Managing Personnel

In France, in certain companies, part-time work was being used as a means to reduce the FTE number of staff in the banks. For example, in September 1986 the Crédit Lyonnais announced that they wanted to reduce their staff by 1% a year. A range of possibilities were offered to existing employees, for example: unpaid holidays taken 5 days at a time; 2 year sabbaticals with the possibility of renewal once only; early retirement and retirement on a part-time basis; and the further development of part-time work in general. The Crédit Lyonnais offered attractive part-time contracts: those who agreed to work half-time, for four years were paid 60% of their full-time salary, and those agreeing to do it for 8 years received 70% of their full-time salary. By persuading two people to accept this they could halve their staff numbers and reduce their wage bill by nearly a third. These terms did not apply to those already working part-time. Only staff between the age of 30 and 45 who had worked for the banks for 10 years or more and who had been working at the bank in the past 12 months, were eligible to transfer to this type of part-time work. This was specifically aimed at the "problem" of the age pyramid and low grade administrative workers. The Association Français de Banques (AFB) felt that only a few French banks were exploiting the flexibility offered by part-time work.

> It is well understood that part-time work responds to the aspirations of employees but it also allows a more intense use of expensive investments like branch banks and computers, and it permits a certain flexibility in the functioning of companies which fully understand its possibilities. ("L'Actualité Bancaire" 6/4/87.)

Staff reductions, using part-time work, sustained the credibility of the bank as a 'good' employer, and allowed it to recruit higher qualified staff in line with the trend to develop polyvalence in France. Part-time work was not used to manage short-term fluctuations.

Part-time work in Britain was also being used to manage changes in personnel. For example, during times of labour shortages, the banks were going out to attract mothers back to work via the part-time route. This policy was evidenced with the establishment of creches and Career Break schemes by a number of institutions.[6] In this way the banks sought to retain the skills of these former employees and to protect themselves against the impact of a tight labour market. With the recession in the 1990s these concerns have been less vocalised as the banks have been more concerned to protect themselves against bad investments and radically reduce the size of their labour force (BIFU 1991 & 1993).

The "week on week off" contracts used in clearing in Britain had traditionally been offered because it had been difficult to employ and retain full-time staff at the central London clearing department. Part-timers on these contracts worked a full 35 hour week, 26 weeks of the year, and received a pro-rata London weighting to cover for travelling. These contracts effectively provided the bank with full-time cover. The recommendations of a management consultant had led to these contracts being replaced by 2 or 3 day a week contracts. These new contracts were designed to match the changing weekly flows of work more closely. The new contracts involved working on a Tuesday, the busiest day, and on one or two other days. Full-time staff were used to meet the minimum levels of work; part-timers on 2 or 3 day a week contracts were used to "top up" on the core staffing in order to meet the weekly flows. These two or three day a week contracts came closest to the idea of using part-timers to meet peaks and to supplement the full-time staff in the way described by numerical flexibility, whereas the "week on week off" contracts had been used because of the difficulty of recruiting full-timers.

Overall, we can see that in Britain part-timers are used to achieve numerical flexibility in the sense that staff numbers are matched to peaks in the work load in a way that does not occur in France. In France there is more of a trade-off between employees' and employers' need for flexibility than is the case in Britain. Part-timers in Britain are used to meet regular and predictable changes in the work load, whereas in France employers are only beginning to see the potential flexibility these contracts can offer, namely in reducing the overall size of their work force and in meeting staffing needs in changing shape of their branch network. This case-study evidence, unlike aggregate data, indicates that the motives for using part-timers varies between the two countries. In order to account for these differences we need to take a societal approach which can allow us to situate the actors in the banking sector within a broader context.

4. A societal explanation

In previous chapters we have seen how the relationship between legal regulation, organisational practices and the characteristics of available labour have shaped the way employers develop functional flexibility, employ temporary workers, or resort to subcontractors. It is the interplay of these factors which accounts for the differences observed in each country. This model can also be applied to the use of part-time work, as outlined below.

4.1 Legal regulations on the use of part-time work

One of the main reasons for the distinctive use of part-time work in each country has been related to the differences in labour regulation. In France, in 1981, the Mitterrand government legislated to protect the rights of part-time workers. At this time part-time work was strictly defined as "mi-temps" or half time; in 1982 this was amended to include part-time work as 80% of a full-time job, and subsequently a range of modules 80%, 70%, 60% or 50% have been developed. In Britain employers have had more freedom to contract part-timers as they needed them: contracts can include anything below 30 hours a week.

The French Labour Code specifies the principle that there should be no discrimination between full-timers and part-timers,[7] in Britain there is no equivalent statutory provision. Employment protection in Britain has been accorded on the basis of the number of hours part-timers work.[8] Up until the law courts decision to grant equality between part-timers and full-timers in March 1994 part-timers entitlement to employment protection was based on thresholds of working 8 or 16 hours a week (see chapter 9; Financial Times 4/3/94). As of 1994 part-timers, like full-timers, will be entitled to benefits after 2 years' continuous service. Before this decision part-timers working less than 16 hours a week had to work for the same employer for 5 years continuously, before they received entitlement.

Part-time work and issues related to working time have developed differently in each country (Gregory 1991:501-2; Daune-Richard 1993). In France the use of part-time work has been associated with the concept of 'temps choisi'. This means that people chose their working time to fit in with their own needs, although during the recession of the 1990s more concern has been given to economic needs. Concerns with working time in France stem from the Popular Front government of the 1930s. In the 1970s the unions tried to revive interest in these issues, and the election of a left-wing government in 1981 this became a possibility. Whilst a reduction in working time was linked to 'temps choisi' it was also seen as a partial means to solve the problems of unemployment.

Various active labour market policies have been introduced in France with these goals in mind. For example a range of solidarity contracts was introduced by the Socialist government to create jobs for the unemployed. For example, phased retirement, introduced in France on a part-time basis in 1982,[9] legislated that an employee accepting part-time early retirement had to be replaced by a new permanent member of staff, for which the company received a state subsidy. A similar scheme was set up in 1987 with solidarity agreements for half-time work for those threatened with redundancy.[10] Other legislation was also introduced to encourage phased retirement, extended use of part-time work in the public sector (ILO 1989:166), and the option introduced in 1984 of half-time work to enable employees to care for a child (ILO 1989:165).

Despite these initiatives, the development of part-time work in France during the early 1980s was fairly limited. When the Chirac government came to power in 1986 it introduced legislation to reduce the social security costs paid for part-timers as a financial incentive to employers.[11] This reduced payments for accident insurance, family allowance, pensions and unemployment insurance; however sick pay, maternity, sickness and invalidity insurances were paid at the same rate as for full-timers. The re-election of the right has led to further attempts to 'compensate' employers using part-timers with legislation passed in 1993 (MISEP 1993:15).[12]

Decrees on working time have also had a direct impact on the banking sector in France. For example, the 1937 decree stipulated that bank employees were entitled to two consecutive days holiday, one of which must be a Sunday. This continues to operate today, despite attempts by the AFB to have this decree abolished. The banks in France are more restricted in extending the opening hours of the branches: a branch open on Saturday had to close on Monday. In Britain the same restrictions did not exist and Saturday opening has for the most part been restored.

Overall, the use of part-time work has been more restricted in France than in Britain, despite attempts to encourage its use. Where companies are under state control the government has been able to play a more interventionist role, as in the case of the banks (Green 1989). Many of the senior personnel managers interviewed in this research cited the importance of the government policy encouraging the use of part-time work in France.

> The CIC is not in a position to refuse requests for part-time work because the government are in favour of it. (Chief Personnel Manager CIC, France)

> The improved flexibility in working time is a positive result of the social climate (Senior Personnel Manager Crédit Lyonnais, France)

In Britain it is easier for employers to use their freedom to contract, in creating a diverse range of part-time contracts. In France employers can only contract on the basis of what is permitted in the Code du Travail. This difference highlights the long-term effect of labour law based on Common law traditions as in the UK, as opposed to Roman law as in France. The social and political climate have shaped the terms on which employers can use part-time work in significantly different ways in each country: during the 1980s the Socialists government sustained the *dirigist* tradition in France, whilst in Britain the Conservative party set out to purge the economy of regulatory interference. These factors indicate how embedded societal features can continue to impinge on employers' behaviour, creating a framework in which they operate.

4.2 Organisational practices

4.2.1 An Integrated service policy tends to deter the use of part-timers. Where staff were expected to provide a range of services, as in France, it was more difficult to use part-time workers; where services were more segmented, as in Britain, it was easier to incorporate the use of part-time workers as could be seen in the organisation of tills.

In the British bank there had been several changes in control of the tills. Under the old system the cashiers had been responsible for their own tills, as was currently the practice in France. This meant when one cashier came to take over from another the till had to be totalled up, a process which involved nearly 15-20 minutes, before the next cashier could start serving. If a queue suddenly built up in the bank it would have gone, or be even longer, by the time a new cashier had cashed up and was ready to deal with customers. As a result a "pool" till system, where all the tills were accounted for together, was introduced in the British bank to meet fluctuations in customer demand.

However the "pool" system made it more difficult to trace mistakes in totalling up at the end of the day. Although this pool system was still being used in smaller branches of the bank in Britain, larger branches had moved to a "batch pool" system where a team of cashiers were responsible for each till, rather than each cashier having their own till. This "batch pool" system made it easier to check mistakes, whilst also being responsive to fluctuations in customer demands. Also the quick service tills in the British bank facilitated the use of part-timers because book keeping was done automatically by the machine and it was easy to interchange full and part-time staff, especially over the lunch period.

In France greater emphasis was placed on providing an integrated service and developing polyvalence. French cashiers were individually responsible for their own tills throughout the day and expected to perform a wider range of tasks than their British equivalents.[13] Every month, in the French bank studied, a different cashier was expected to take responsibility for the main till which distributed the money to the other tills; in this way they broadened their skills. In Britain the position of chief cashier was performed by one person on a continuous basis; this position was seen as promotion and was a higher grade than the normal cashiers. The technology used fitted in with, and encouraged, the use of part-time work in Britain and functional flexibility in France. This was related to the service policy and employment strategy being pursued by the banks in each country.

4.2.2 *Staff allocation methods* also encouraged the use of part-timers in Britain. In Britain a highly developed time and motion study, called the Clerical Work Improvement Programme (CWIP), analysed work flow rates, hour by hour, to assess the staffing levels required for each branch.[14] This study established the number of FTE jobs required in each branch, but it would then be up to the local branch manager to decide how to staff these jobs, with full or part-timers. For example, there could be a core of five permanent full-time cashiers during the week. On busy days this could be supplemented with the use of auxiliary part-timers, increasing the number of cashiers to nine. Regular fluctuations for example in special monthly, quarterly or annual jobs in Britain were also accounted for in the staffing levels set by the time and motion study. One branch manager explained that "auxiliaries[15] are used where there is not a full-time requirement or where the nature of the work would be best served by using part-timers." Another branch manager explained the decision to use part-timers or full-timers as follows:

> If the time and motion study said you needed 23.1 staff in the machine room that 0.1 may be sending out statements so you might employ an auxiliary in the mornings to do this. They might only work the first Monday of the month or the first three days of the month it depends on the demand. (Branch Manager, Britain).

In France branch staff were allocated by the regional office depending on the number of client accounts held at the branch. Staffing requirements were assessed on an annual basis, whereas in Britain CWIP assessment took place every four years.[16] If a branch in France had increased the number of accounts held, it could request a new full-time member of staff. However part-timers were increasingly being sent to branches which had not sufficiently increased their number of clients, or where the number of accounts had fallen. These different forms of measurement influenced the way staff were used in each country. In France a simpler and looser system of staff allocation was tied to clients accounts, whereas in Britain staff requirements were minutely measured in a Taylorist manner.

4.2.3 Managerial hostility to part-time work is higher in France than in Britain. This resistance on the part of employers is related to the problems of incorporating part-timers into an organisation where the paradigm is based on full-time work (Dex et al. 1993:112). This is illustrated by the various comments made by Personnel Managers in the different banks in France.

> Above all, the major problem is organisation, for companies and for the hierarchy to accept such a system of part-time working by a section of their personnel. Without doubt there exists, for a given type of organisation, a maximum level of "tolerance" for part-time work, 15 to 20% of all employees for example. (Senior Personnel Manager, France)

> It is unusual to find part-timers in smaller branches because they make it too difficult to organise the work. (Chief Personnel Manager, France)

> Those who work part-time are more difficult to organise especially in posts which require a daily presence or in jobs where the orders are given in the morning and executed in the afternoon, for example those working on the stock market. (Personnel Manager, France).

In France having a part-timer was seen as having a handicap: the French held closely to the model of permanent full-time employment.

> For the company it is more difficult to have part-timers because they have to get someone to replace them when they are off.(Manager Cheque clearance, France)

Even in the British clearing department the managerial staff also complained of the difficulty in organisation,

> We have so many people working on so many different days it's nightmare trying to manage it all. (Senior Manager, Clearing, Britain).

The two or three day a week contracts had been established, on the advice of a management consultant, to meet peaks on busy days like Tuesdays and to a lesser extent Wednesdays. These contracts became a standard method of labour management and once enough people were recruited for the busy days new employees could choose which ever days they wanted. Although the original purpose of the contracts had been achieved it continued to be used, even though managers complained of the administrative difficulties created by having so many staff working on different days. Overall, the hostility to part-time work was higher in France where managers saw few advantages of this type of contract accruing to them.

4.3 Demand for part-time work

The basis of French employers' prejudice against part-time work was due to the incompatibility between part-timers wanting to have Wednesdays off and employers who had daily deadlines through the week.[17] Part-time employees' overwhelming preference for 80% contracts may explain the hostility expressed by employers to the use of part-time work in France.

> It's OK for the part-timers but when they are having their day off the rest have to work harder to cover for them. One of the disadvantages with part-time work is that if it was extensive nobody would work on Wednesdays. There are no advantages for the company, only for the women who work part-time. (Supervisor, France)

> If I had to have a part-timer I would rather they worked five days a week on shorter days, rather than having a complete day off. We have daily deadlines which makes it very inconvenient if we are one short every week. (Manager Clearing, France)

French part-timers did not appear to be as flexible as British part-timers. For example when asked if they were prepared to work more hours if their employer asked them to do so: in Britain 67% of all part-timers questioned said they would, compared to only 27% of French part-timers. This can be explained by the fact that French part-timers already work longer hours than part-timers in Britain (Barrere-Maurisson et al. 1989; Letablier 1986). There was less difference amongst full-timers: in Britain 75% of full-timers said they would be prepared to work longer hours compared to 68% in France. In France the use of part-time work is not directly linked with the idea of flexibility, as in Britain. Women's demands for part-time work also vary (see chapter 8).

Overall, the limited use of part-time work in France can be explained in terms of the tighter and more costly regulation covering employers' use of part-time contracts. In Britain, part-time work has been a cheap, poorly protected source of labour for employers. Organisational practices also constrain the use of this type of labour strategy in France. For example with the development of an integrated service policy, the methods of staff allocation, and managerial hostility are all factors which militate against an extensive use of part-time work in France, compared to Britain. Finally, there is also the question of demand for this form of work. In Britain the demand appears to be more extensive and flexible; in France, whilst there is a demand, this is more limited. This is discussed in more detail in chapter 8.

5. Part-time work and the secondary labour market

Part-time work has usually been associated with disadvantaged, secondary forms of employment. Employers' labour strategies and the behavioural characteristics of secondary sector employees made it impossible for them ever to move out of poor quality employment, according to the early literature on dual labour markets (Doeringer and Piore 1971). But how distinct are part-time workers in the banks from core employees, and on what grounds is this distinction based? Secondary sector work encompasses a variety of precarious forms of employment defined in terms of their access to training, internal labour markets and employment protection, but how vulnerable or secure are part-timers, and is the situation the same in both countries?

5.1 Training and promotion

Employers maximise on their investment in training by developing internal labour markets for core, permanent staff (Osterman 1984). Secondary sector employment is characterised by limited training opportunities and an absence of a career structure or internal labour market. When asked about training provision, part-timers in both countries did less well than full-timers (Table 7.4).

Very few British part-timers (17%) said their training had increased. In France, part-timers were more likely to say that their training had decreased, compared to full-timers. This could be because the French part-timers were used to higher levels of training compared to the British employees. Dex et al.

(1993:118) argue that French women are involved in longer periods of training, compared to British women. However, in both countries part-timers tend to do less well.

This pattern was also seen in relation to perception of promotion opportunities. From a nationally representative survey of French and British women Dex et al. (1993:113) argue that in both countries more full-timers thought they had 'some' promotion opportunities compared to part-timers. In their sample, across several sectors, they discovered that French women were more likely to think they had more career opportunities than women in Britian. Responses collected in the employee questionnaires used in the case-study banks support some of these conclusions (Table 7.5).

Table 7.4
Perceptions of training provision

	BRITAIN		FRANCE	
	part-time	full-time	part-time	full-time
	%	%	%	%
increased	17	47	40	44
stayed the same	40	34	37	44
decreased	10	13	20	3
don't know	33	6	3	9
Total %	100	100	100	100
Total (n)	30	32	30	34

(Source: Employee questionnaire)

Table 7.5
Perception of promotion opportunities

	BRITAIN		FRANCE	
	part-time	full-time	part-time	full-time
	%	%	%	%
increased	7	47	17	27
stayed the same	33	34	7	27
decreased	33	16	73	38
don't know	27	3	3	8
Total %	100	100	100	100
Total (n)	30	32	30	34

(Source: Employee questionnaire)

In the French banks fewer full-timers thought their promotion opportunities had increased, compared to full-timers in Britain. This may in part be due to when this survey was conducted: British banks had not yet started to make the drastic announcements of job losses, whereas the aim of reducing FTE staff numbers had been a long term strategy in the French banks. Nevertheless, this smaller survey indicates that part-timers are less likely to think about their promotion opportunities, compared to full-timers.

In France nearly three-quarters of all part-timers interviewed said their promotion opportunities had decreased. These findings were supported by the comments respondents made during the interviews in Britain and France,

> If you want to get on you have to work full-time. (Part-time cashier, France)
> None of the supervisors or managers are part-time, I think you need to work full-time if you want to get promoted. (Part-time tray agreer clearing, France)
> If you go part-time you can forget about promotion! (Part-time cashier, Britain)
> We're never going to get promoted in this place! (Part-time encoder clearing, Britain)

Part-timers clearly realised that in working part-time they were reducing their chances of being promoted. Part-timers also felt they were outside the company career paths. An example of this could be seen from attendance of part-timers in France at the weekly training/briefing meetings to develop a quality, integrated service. These hour long meetings were held in each branch for the manager to explain new products and discuss team goals, and for the staff to raise any problems they had. Part-timers rarely attended these meetings which were often held on a morning when business was quiet, and usually on a day when part-timers were not working. Information from these meetings was passed on in an ad hoc way to part-timers when they were present.

> You feel a bit left out, you don't get all the information from the meetings because people forget to tell you things. And the manager here hasn't given me any goals to achieve, like the full-timers have. You're not really part of the team when you're part-time. (Part-time cashier, France)

In France employee perceptions of being left out were matched by managers' opinions that part-timers would be less well trained and have less commitment to wanting a career in the bank.

5.2 A source of cheap labour: wages and benefits

One of the advantages often cited for employers using part-time work is that it provides cheaper, poorly protected labour (Hurstfield 1978). However, for the banks in both countries, part-timers were paid pro-rata, according to the number of hours they worked, on the same scale as full-timers. However, in the British bank studied there were examples of wage savings being made by re-organising the tasks included in a job. For example, if the more responsible tasks of a cashier were removed, part-timers could be put on lower grades and lower rates of pay. This was more likely to be the case in Britain where employers had greater flexibility than French employers in offering a diverse range of part-time contracts. So whilst the banks did not have a formal structure to pay part-timers less than full-timers, in Britain job reorganisation allowed them to make savings, which was not the case in France.

The really important area where employers could make savings by using part-timers was in the entitlement to extra wage benefits. British part-timers were the worst off, whereas French part-timers received benefits on equal terms with full-timers, in accordance with the legislative principle of equal treatment. Part-time and full-time employees interviewed for this research were asked which benefits they received,[18] these results are presented in Table 7.6.

British part-timers receive far fewer benefits than any other group of workers in this sample. For example, according to these responses only 30% of the part-time employees interviewed in Britain said they received help with travel costs, compared to 66% of full-timers in Britain. In France the response rate was much higher: 83% of part-timers and 94% of full-timers said they received this benefit. The penultimate set of figures in Table 7.6 give the average percentage score for all benefits received by each group of employees. In Britain part-timers are a much cheaper alternative source of labour than in France, in terms of extra wage benefits. For French employers there is no equivalent financial incentive to encourage them to use part-timers, although government measures have tried to reduce the employers' social insurance costs entailed in employment part-timers.

However, as part-timers' benefits improved during the 1980s in the British banks, the advantages of part-timers providing cheap labour diminished. This happened for a variety of reasons. The banks in Britain, at the end of the 1980s were keen to encourage women to return to work because of the predicted demographic fall in the number of school leavers entering the labour market. Improving benefits offered to these potential employees was seen as a means to improve the banks' public relations image.

Table 7.6
A comparison of the extra wage benefits received by part-timers and full-timers in the banking sector in Britain and France

The type of benefit	BRITAIN part-time %	full-time %	FRANCE part-time %	full-time %
holiday pay	83	97	100	100
pensions rights	73	91	100	94
sick pay	83	100	97	97
profit sharing	77	98	97	91
discount mortgage	53	94	97	97
discount loan	30	72	53	56
health insurance	0	25	93	91
maternity leave	40	97	97	88
subsidised travel	30	66	83	94
subsidised meals	27	34	100	100
sports/social club	37	82	100	97
bonus	63	94	83	71
merit pay	27	38	40	42
overtime	53	100	20	32
Average receipt of all Benefits	48	78	84	82
Total (n)	30	32	30	34

(Source: Employee questionnaire)

Secondly, the banks in Britain recognised the future impact of the European Court decision on Bilka Kaufhaus v. Karen von Weber (IRLR [1986] 317). The implications of this decision for British law was to extend the interpretation of the Equal Pay Act to include indirect sexual discrimination. Part-time workers are predominantly women and therefore any inferior terms and conditions operating systematically could be interpreted as indirect sex discrimination. In order to save the expense and the publicity of being taken to the European Courts, many British banks had decided to take the "initiative" in improving the terms and conditions of part-time employment. According to the union it was a mixture of "union pressure, legal and market pressures" which forced the Bank to change; the Bank, however, considered the union the least important reason.

Although part-timers are cheaper in Britain this is not the main criterion for their use, as one British trade unionist explained:

> Employers don't manipulate contracts to avoid National Insurance payments. When all part-timers were excluded from benefits it made them very cheap. Now anyone over 14 hours a week in the bank is entitled to pro-rata benefits. There has not been an obvious rise in contracts less than 14 hours a week. Part-time work is demand led and customer sensitive. The range of possible schedules is vast. (BGSU, Britain)

So whilst we can draw distinctions between the comparatively disadvantaged British part-timers and the rest, we have to recognise that the reason for using part-timers in the case of the banks is not based solely on cost criteria.

5.3 Job security and mobility

The literature on flexibility suggests that the key distinction between core and secondary sector workers is their difference in employment security. However, Büchtemann and Quack (1990) and Quack (1993) have argued that it is not part-time work per se which affects employment security, but rather the accumulation of various forms of disadvantage. Secondary sector employment has been associated with numerical flexibility because employers can hire and fire these staff as needed. If employers have been looking to develop numerical flexibility we

175

could expect part-time employees to have experienced a heightened sense of insecurity. As British part-timers are less well protected we might also expect this experience of insecurity to be more widespread in Britain than in France. To measure these changes respondents were asked if their job security had increased, decreased or stayed the same since they first came to the company (Table 7.7).

In both countries the majority of respondents felt no change in their job security. Less than a quarter of the part-timers in both countries (13% in Britain and 17% in France) felt that their job security had decreased. This is comparatively low given the conditions set out in the flexibility debates. One surprising feature was the high number of full-timers in France (35%) who felt their job security had decreased. This may be a product of the greater concern in France to reduce the number of low grade bank employees, like those interviewed for this research. At the time this survey was conducted,[19] British employees were, in general, more optimistic about their job prospects compared to their French colleagues, although their attitudes may have changed with recent job losses in Britain (BIFU 1991 & 1993). The level of job insecurity was lower than anticipated for French part-timers, and higher amongst the full-timers in France. These results show how perceptions of job security are not directly correlated to legal employment status, but that they are more sensitive to policies being developed within the firm, sector or economy in general. They also suggest that employment security is not a static concept which puts into question the strict dichotomy between core and secondary employment status.

Table 7.7
Perceptions of job security

	BRITAIN part-time	full-time	FRANCE part-time	full-time
	%	%	%	%
increased	7	38	3	15
stayed the same	57	59	77	50
decreased	13	3	17	35
don't know	23	0	3	0
Total %	100	100	100	100
n	30	32	30	34

(Source: Employee questionnaire)

Dual labour market theory conceptualised secondary sector employment as a confined enclave (Doeringer and Piore 1971, Edwards 1979). As a result little attention has been given to examining where, if at all, mobility between sectors takes place. With this in mind respondents were asked how they found out about their existing job, to see how confined part-timers in the banking sector actually were. Table 7.8 presents these results for part-timers in both countries. Respondents were allowed to give more than one response to the various alternatives presented to them, in recognition that people pursue diverse means of job search at the same time. (These figures should be read as a percentage for each type of job search, and not as a column percentage.)

Table 7.8
How part-timers found their present jobs
(as a % of all part-timers in the sample)

	BRITAIN	FRANCE
Internal labour market		
Worked here before		
as a full-timer	60%	83%
as a temp	0%	3%
External labour market		
Advert in the paper	17%	20%
Job centre/ANPE	0	0
Private employment agency	0	0
Personal contacts		
(family or friends)	20%	37%
non response	23%	7%
Total (n)	30	30

(Source: Employee questionnaire)

The vast majority of part-timers in both countries had previously worked for the bank on a full-time basis. There exists a significant degree of internal mobility between full and part-time work in the banks in Britain and France. Part-timers are more likely to come from within the firm rather than from the external labour market. Temporary work as a means for recruiting permanent part-timers is negligible in France and non-existent in Britain. Personal contacts of family or friends are important in both countries. Data on job mobility was also collected from full-timers (Table 7.9).[20]

Table 7.9
How full-timers found their present jobs
(as a % of all full-timers in the sample)

	BRITAIN	FRANCE
Internal labour market		
Worked here before		
as a part-timer	3%	3%
as a temp	0%	12%
External labour market		
Advert in the paper	22%	26%
Job centre/ANPE	0	0
private employment agency	0	8%
School contacts	34%	0
Personal contacts	22%	38%
(family or friends)		
non response	3%	0
Total (n)	32	34

(Source: Employee questionnaire)

    Mobility between full and part-time work appears to be taking place in a one way direction. Hardly any full-time staff, in this particular sample, used part-time work as a channel back into full-time employment. Although it is often suggested that part-time work is a way for mothers to re-enter the labour market, it is not clear that this marks a step towards full-time, permanent employment. In France temporary work represents an important way to recruit full-time permanent staff, but it is not used at all in Britain, which supports the evidence presented in Chapter 5. Recruitment from the external labour market, using newspaper adverts, is fairly similar for both countries. The importance of school contacts in Britain, reflects the traditional recruitment strategy of the banks. Personal contacts are important in both countries, especially in France.

    From reviewing this evidence we can see that part-time work

can be considered a secondary form of employment in terms of limited training and promotion opportunites. In terms of benefits received, however, French part-timers were more likely to receive equal treatment with full-timers, compared to the part-timers in Britain. Perceptions of job security were not a reliable indicator of secondary status: the majority of part-timers in both countries felt reasonably secure; feelings of insecurity were higher amongst full-timers, espcially in France. This suggests, as Büchtemann and Quack (1990:321-328) argue, that part-time work per se is not a form of secondary precarious employment. Instead it is the process of accumulating disadvantage, i.e. in missing out on training and promotion opportunities over the years, which makes people in these jobs less secure.

6. Conclusions

From the evidence presented in this chapter we have seen how the use of part-time work in Britain and France has increased during the 1980s. In the financial services in Britain 18% worked part-time in 1992, compared to just under 10% in France in 1991. Part-time work was used less in the banks than in the service sector as a whole. This was related to the status and quality of services provided by the banks, the constraints imposed by security considerations and confidentiality, and finally because of the 'diamond' shaped grading structure prevalent in the banks in both countries. Nevertheless, the use of part-time work at the sectoral level resembled the differences observed at the national level: part-time work was more popular in Britain than in France.

Part-timers in Britain were employed on a regular basis to meet peaks in customer demand in the branches on Mondays and Fridays and during the lunch period. In clearing, two or three day a week part-time shifts were designed to meet peaks on a Tuesday. These uses of part-time work come closest to the concept of numerical flexibility. Part-time work as an auxiliary work force was a conscious management strategy in Britain, and the CWIP time and motion study encouraged its use. Nevertheless, meeting peaks in the work load was only one of the reasons for using part-timers.

Part-time work was used for different reasons in each country. In Britain, it provided a solution to a tight labour market. For example, when employers found it difficult to recruit full-timers, they could re-design the job to attract part-timers as seen in the use of "week on week off" contracts in the clearing department. The predicted fall in the number of school leavers also encouraged the banks to offer part-time jobs as a way to retain skills and overcome labour shortages. In France, part-time work initially developed in response to employees' demands for shorter working hours. Recently, however, the banks started to use these contracts more strategically. For example, part-time work provided a way of gradually reducing the size of the FTE labour force at the Crédit Lyonnais; and in the branches at the Crédit Agricole part-timers are been deployed to meet limited business growth which does not merit a new full-time member of staff. There was limited evidence to show that employers were frequently changing the hours and days a part-timer worked so as to meet fluctuations. The concept of numerical flexibility is misleading because it categorises part-time work in the same terms as temporary workers or subcontracting, which offer a different kind of flexibility, as discussed in Chapter 5. Part-timers in the banks were used on the whole to meet long-term, predictable and regular peaks in work load.

With regard to secondary employment, part-time work is clearly distinct from full-time employment, especially in Britain. French part-timers had more benefits and felt comparatively more secure in their jobs than British part-timers. However, both groups were clearly aware of the limited training and promotion opportunities open to them while they worked part-time. On these terms it is possible to argue that part-timers have secondary sector status. However, as Table 7.8 indicated, the greatest sense of insecurity came from French full-timers, rather than from part-timers in either country. This calls into question the nature of job security amongst 'core' employees, especially under the circumstances of increasing job losses. The evidence of mobility between sectors also showed how most part-timers had previously worked for the bank as full-timers. In France half-time work was used as a "legitimate" means to effectively reduce the numbers of full-time staff, whereas in Britain at the end of the 1980s it was being used to bring in qualified staff; and in the 1990s it facilitated cost cutting.

Previous debates on labour flexibility have paid scant attention to the differences between long and short-term needs, the nature of fluctuations in work loads, the relationship between product or service policy and employment policy, as well as issues of gender and the quality of available labour. No account is given of the societal differences in terms of labour regulation and organisational culture, which shape employers' views of flexibility. The use of part-time work needs to be more firmly situated within the societal context, in which we can identify the influence of both employee characteristics on employers' ability to use part-time work as a flexibile form of employment.

Notes

1. Cited in the ILO Report (1989:79), from the French Labour Code, as amended by Act No 81-64 on part-time work, dated 28 January 1981 in Journal Officiel No 24 Jan 1981 page 370, Article L.212.4.2 Legislative Series 1981 Fr 1.

2. The implications of security arrangements on the organisation of work were discussed in Chapter 4.

3. This data was provided by individual requests to the research departments of each bank, and is not publicly available.

4. This work involved opening and filling bags for branch banks which would be delivered that night ready for the branch manager the next morning.

5. Detailed documents between management and unions concerning the introduction of these contracts and changes in part-time benefits were confidential and could not be accessed.

6. This is where an employee can take between three to five years break and return to their former job, or take less time off and work part-time. Career Break Schemes are usually only available to grade 4 and higher, which would be equivalent to a Senior First Cashier.

7. L'Ordonnance on part-time work No. 82-271 26 mars 1982, "assure aux salariés qui la pratiquent des guaranties collectives et individuelles comparables à celles des salariés à temps complet, à fin de mieux les insérer dans la collectivité du travail." (Journal Officiel No 74 28 March 1982 p953 Article L.212.4.2 in Legislative Series 1982 Fr 1E.

8. See Employment Protection (Consolidation) Act 1978 dated 31 July 1978 (The General Acts and Measures, vol II 1978) Chapter 44 Part I Section 3 Legislative Series 1984 UK 1.

9. Article L.322-4 of the French Labour Code as amended by Ordinance No 84-198, dated 21 March 1984 (Journal Officiel, No 69, 22 March 1984 page 896.). See also Circular No 8/85 of the Employment Delegation defining rights and obligations of employers with regard to solidarity contracts for phased retirement, dated 5 February 1985. (Legislation sociale, D.4, No 5646, 20 May 1985, as cited in "Travail à temps partiel - travail intermittent", in Liaisons Sociales, No 10369, 30 December 1988, page 55).

10. Decree No 87-269 and Decree No 87-270 on half time work for threatened redundancy, dated 15th April 1987 (Journal Officiel, No 91, 17 April 1987, page 4379; and Journal Officiel, No 227, 1 October 1987, page 11,466) (ILO Report 1989).

11. Act No 86-75 on social security contributions for part-time work, dated 17th January 1986 (Journal Officiel, No 15, 18th January 1986, page 888).

12. These reductions do not apply to part-timers on fixed-term contracts. Decree no. 93.238, of the 22nd February 1993 allows for a 50% reduction in social insurance pyaments, accidents at work and family support.

13. In some tills in France the separation between caissier the person who pays out, and guichetier the person who performs the administrative transactions, still persists but this is declining (Cosslater 1990).

14. These month long studies were conducted on a four year rota basis at each branch; the staffing allocation could be reviewed earlier if the bank had a massive growth in business. These studies were extremely detailed, for example the average number of lines typed on a standard letter would be counted; in one branch studied in Britain this exceeded the national average for the bank by 3.5 lines which meant that the CWIP team gave a higher staff allocation for this job.

15. Auxiliaries refers to both part-timers and other forms of non-full-time labour, for example the on-call teams.

16. If the work of a branch increased substantially in this four year period, a request could me made for extra staffing. Branch managers were often very hostile to the decisions made by the CWIP team, as they thought it was very restrictive.

17. In France children do not go to school on Wednesdays, instead they have to attend school on Saturday mornings. This is a historical residue from the time when the Catholic Church insisted that children attend catechism classes on Wednesdays. Although this is less popular today, the practice of Wednesdays, or half day Wednesdays continues. The possibility of changing this is currently under discussion.

18. For each benefit where a respondent said yes they received a specific benefit, they were given a mark. Where some of these figures are incomplete is because of non-response, or because respondents said they did not know. The non-responses for every benefit are not recorded here because they vary for each question, and they are not significant.

19. January-March 1989, and January 1990 in Britain; June, July and September 1989 and February 1990 in France.

20. These figures need to be interpreted with caution because of the limited numbers in the sample. Unfortunately the individual banks could not provide figures at a corporate level for the numbers of staff who changed their status from part-time to full-time.

8 The societal construction of female labour supply

1. Introduction

Up until this point we have examined flexibility purely from the perspective of employers' policy and organisational needs, which has been characteristic of much of the research conducted on the use of part-time work (Robinson & Wallace 1984; Blanchflower & Corry 1986; Beechey & Perkins 1987; Atkinson & Meager 1986). Much of the research on changing working practices tends to focus on employers as the instigators of change. This project aimed to redress this imbalance in recent debates by including the attitudes and preferences of employers and employees. This chapter sets out to examine the characteristics and attitudes of a comparable sample of full- and part-time female employees from Britain and France. It aims to draw together some of the elements of a gendered societal model which has been developed throughout this book. This revolves around the question of how the attitudes and characteristics of available female workers influence the way employers develop flexible workers. For this purpose we will concentrate on the effects of the system of education and training and the provision of childcare, in structuring opportunities and imposing constraints on women's ability and preferences for paid employment.

2. Women's employment: choices and constraints

A number of useful studies have recently been published looking specifically at the differences and similarities in women's labour force participation in Britain and France (Dex et al. 1993; Daune-Richard 1993; Hantrais 1990; Dale & Glover 1990; Beechey 1989; Benoit-Guilbot 1987; Gregory 1987). In general these studies have shown how French women have a continuous pattern of full-time, permanent employment. British women, in contrast, are more likely to work part-time, and take longer periods out of paid employment at the time of child rearing (OECD 1984), using part-time work at a later stage to re-enter paid employment.

Discussions on part-time work have been broadly divided into two camps. On one hand part-time work has been seen as a form of chosen working time, i.e. people work the hours which suit them. On the other hand, it is argued that women are forced to accept part-time work because of their domestic responsibilities, and because of the way employers design jobs. The idea of constraint suggests that part-time women workers are the victims of social structures beyond their control. The idea of choice, alternatively, focuses on the extremely atomistic behaviour of individuals, who are presented as if the decisions they make are independent of the social structure in which they act.

The propensity of British women to work part-time, compared to French women, has been explained in terms of structural factors which constrain women's choices. For example, the lack of adequate childcare in Britain makes it difficult for women to work full-time (Garnsey 1984; Dale & Glover 1990; Hantrais 1990; Dex et al. 1993). Labour market participation is thus explained in terms of the structural provision of childcare. Maruani & Nicole (1989), however, have placed greater emphasis on attitudes, arguing that French women do not want to work part-time, which is why this form of employment is substantially lower in France than in Britain.

The idea of choice has been associated with the concept of strategy, in the sense that subjects can chose between different sets of behaviour in order to reach desired goals. However, the debate around the concept of strategy has brought to attention the often casual way in which this term has been used in the past (Crow 1989; Morgan 1989; Knights & Morgan 1990b; Edwards and Ribbens 1991). Referring to behaviour in terms of "choice" or "strategy" is problematic because it is implicitly based on a model of "economic man": the rationally calculating individual who is out to maximise their interests in the most cost effective way as assumed by Human Capital theorists.[1]

The concept of strategy has become popular in recent years, with regard to women's management of domestic responsibilities and paid employment, because it describes women as active, rather than passive subjects, who have some choice over the way in which they govern their lives (Yeandle 1984). Edwards and Ribbens (1991) however, are critical of the use of strategy to describe women's behaviour between the domestic and public realm. They found in their research of a) mature women students and b) child rearing, that the women they studied never used the term strategy themselves. Edwards and Ribbens (1991:481) argue that the women in their studies *"were acting on an emotional, unconscious level and on a reasoned, conscious level at the same time."* These women did not see themselves as doing anything out of the ordinary, they were *"just 'being' mothers/partners and students as they felt they should"* (loc.cite.). Thus they pin-point the problem of conscious and unconscious behaviour: in order to have a strategy there needs to be a self-conscious, publicly defined end goal, with a recognised means of achieving it. If people are unconscious of the implications of their actions, and they do not have an identifiable "end goal" we cannot say they are behaving strategically. Debates on the issue of part-time work have speculated on attitudes or the effect of structural factors, and clearly there is a strong relationship between the two.

Rather than formulating simplistic dichotomies between strategy or structure, choice or constraint, Granovetter has offered a position which takes account of the on-going social relations in a specific society. Granovetter argues that,

> Actors do not behave or decide as atoms outside a social context, nor do they adhere slavishly to a script written for them by the particular intersection of social categories that they happen to occupy. Their attempts at purposive action are instead embedded in concrete, on-going systems of social relations. (Granovetter 1985:487)

This indicates a useful perspective concerning the relationship between structural variables and individual attitudes which is pertinent to discussions on part-time work. One way of understanding these "on-going systems of social relations" is to identify the norms and practices of specific, comparable groups of people.

By norms we mean the common expectations or values held

by the groups we are interested in. Practice is the way norms are translated into daily life: repeatedly they are made and re-made, altered and re-made. Such a perspective allows for the possibility of social change and diversity: practice can be directed against particular social structures, at the same time, specific historical and societal structures limit practice (Connell 1987:95; Hantrais 1990: 173-4).[2] Normative gender relations, Connell (1987) argues, are made through the inter-relationship of the 'gender order' and different 'gender regimes'. By 'gender order' Connell refers to the way power relations, and the definitions of femininity and masculinity, have been historically developed in society in general. By 'gender regimes' he refers to the way these power relations and identities are shaped in specific institutions namely the family, the state, and the street, i.e. peer group encounters. He also tries to account for the relationship between state social policy, labour demands and the emotional sphere. By pointing out that there is not necessarily a functionalist fit between these institutions, he can identify the arena through which change comes about.

There are several ways to conduct a study of group norms, ranging from qualitative ethno-methodological approaches to quantitative attitude surveys. The decision about which method to adopt is epistomological as well as practical, i.e. what resources, time and access are available to study a given group. In this research we wanted to find out if there were important differences in the hours women wanted to work, and if so why. It was felt important to examine the role of women's attitudes because it is an aspect which is often ignored in the debates on labour market segmentation and flexibility (see Dex 1988; Watson & Fothergil 1992; and Alwin et al. 1992 as exceptions to this). Where possible the results have been compared to large scale data available from single country studies. The advantage of this approach is that it was directly comparative, and that it can attempt to probe at the relationship between structural factors and attitudes, and how these affect employers' behaviour.

3. Attitudes to work

From an analysis of the Women and Employment Survey Dex (1988) found that women working longer hours had less traditional attitudes to the role of women in the family and at work compared to part-timers, who were inclined to have more traditional attitudes. Dex tries to understand the nature of causality in this relationship - is it because these women have more traditional attitudes that they decide to work part-time, or, is it because they find themselves in part-time jobs, where their paid work is given less value, that traditional attitudes to women's domestic role are reinforced? From an analysis of the Women and Employment Survey Dex argues that "...*attitudes have a significant but extremely small effect on women's choice of hours of work.*" (Dex 1988a:147). In her conclusion she gives greatest weight to structural factors:

> ... a woman's decision to work fewer hours is heavily constrained most notably by the presence of children and the child-care problems which this raises. These constraints far outweigh the direct effect of traditional attitudes. (Dex 1988a:146)

Given the possibility of identifying differences in attitudes to work between British women, it was decided to apply a similar approach to identify attitudes between British and French women. For the purposes of this research an interview survey was conducted with 126 full- and part-time female employees, in comparable jobs from the two countries. This method was adopted for two reasons. First, it allowed the respondents to be directly comparable; and second, it allowed the researcher to draw links between managerial behaviour and employees' attitudes. This survey is clearly not as representative as the Women and Employment Survey. Nevertheless, the sample chosen aimed to achieve comparability by carefully controlling for job type and location, i.e. all the women interviewed were in low grade cashier or administrative jobs in the branches or clearing centres. The sample also controlled for the number of full- and part-time employees.[3] Where national surveys were available, these results were compared with the case-study results to test for reliability. In the following section we will examine the demand for part-time work, the reasons for working, and employees' satisfaction with a range of work related factors.

3.1 Demand for part-time work

Part-time work is commonly considered "suitable" employment for women with young children. This assumption, however, does not necessarily explain why British women are more likely than

French women to work part-time. Although superior childcare provision is often cited as the main reason for the difference in the two countries, Maruani and Nicole (1989) argue that French women do not want part-time work. With the aim of providing comparable cross-national data, interviewees in Britain and France were asked if, in the near future, they would prefer to change to full or part-time work, or, if they wanted to continue as they were (Table 8.1).

Table 8.1
Future plans for paid employment

	BRITAIN part-time %	full-time %	FRANCE part-time %	full-time %
continue full-time		63		76
continue part-time	53		63	
change from full-to part-time		34		18
change from part-to full-time	17		10	
other/don't know	30	3	26	6
Total %	100	100	99	100
(n)	30	32	30	34

(Source: Employee questionnaire)

There is a much higher expectation of moving between part-time and full-time employment in Britain than in France: approximately 18% of the French sample, compared to 34% of the British full-timers, said they would like to change to part-time work in the future. These results for France are supported by the work of Belloc (1986). Drawing on ANPE[4] records Belloc (1986:50) estimated that the demand for part-time work, amongst unemployed women actively seeking this, was approximately 17%. However, we have to be cautious in interpreting this data because as Dex et al.(1993:101-2) point out, there is a difference between those who would like to work part-time, and those who actually do. Maruani and Nicole (1989) have argued that the growth in part-time work is not related to women wanting this form of employment: whilst 17% of women in France were actively looking for part-time work, 23% of women were actually working part-time. On the basis of these statistics Maruani and Nicole argue that part-time work has been imposed on French women.

In France most of the women interviewed did not expect to work part-time whilst their children were young. However, women with three children were more likely to work part-time. British women, were more likely to consider part-time work as "normal" for most mothers. An example of this can be seen in the comments of one young woman when asked if she would like to work part-time in the future,

> Yeh, I suppose so. That's what most of the other women here do. I guess I'll do the same when I have a baby. (18 years old, full-timer, Clearing Britain).

Hantrais (1990) argues that part-time work forms part of the life cycle of employment pattern of British women, in the early years of childrearing. French women are more likely to chose part-time work at a later stage in their lives.

Despite this trend some British women were critical of this pattern of working. One young woman working in the same department said,

> The problem here is that a lot of women just don't want a career. They are happy enough to do their job and go home. I don't want that though, I want to have a career. (20 year old supervisor, Clearing, Britain)

This indicates that there is a space in which individual action attempts to resist the constraints of social structures, and particular gender regimes (Connell 1987). However, as Hantrais (1990:173-4) points out, these structural factors impose considerable restraints on the desires of individual actors.

When French women working full-time were asked about working part-time a common response was, "Yes, I would love part-time hours, but not the pay." (Full-timer Clearing France). French women were more likely to say that less pay was the major deterrent to working part-time. This rationale can be more fully understood when we look at the reasons why these women were said they went out to work.

There are a vast array of reasons why people go to work. At one level we can identify purely instrumentalist, or economistic rationales where the wages earned are the sole, or principal, reason for working. But work is a social, as well as an economic, experience. A wider range of intrinsic motives including the sense of feeling valued, doing something worthwhile, or establishing friends and one's self identity, are some of the other reasons people work (Dex 1988).

To examine women's reasons for working, interviewees were asked which of the following four reasons explained why they went out to work: for essentials, for luxuries, mainly for social reasons, for both social reasons and for the money. These categories can be divided between those which are instrumental, emphasising purely economic motives, and those which are intrinsic, emphasising social as well as monetary reasons. Although much criticism has been made of trying to reduce people's motivations to pre-coded categories, it was nevertheless felt that this would systematically distinguish between those whose orientation was purely economic and instrumentalist, and those who associated work as important for their social relations as well as providing them with a wage (Table 8.2).[5]

Table 8.2
Reasons why women go to work

	BRITAIN		FRANCE	
	part-time	full-time	part-time	full-time
	%	%	%	%
For essentials	13	31	21	32
For luxuries	23	3	3	0
Social contact is the most important, the money is less important	20	31	13	9
Social contact and money are both very important	37	35	53	59
not answered	7	0	10	0
Total %	100	100	100	100
Total (n)	30	32	30	34

(Source: Employee questionnaire)

The differences between part-timers' and full-timers' reasons for working were more distinct in Britain than in France. Nearly a quarter of the sample of British part-timers (23%) said they worked because "*the money I earn gives me a little extra for luxuries, holidays and going out*", i.e. instrumental reasons. This suggests that their wages were not perceived of as being essential to their household income. These results were supported by similar findings for British part-timers in the Women and Employment Survey (Martin and Roberts 1984). There was less difference between the French part-timers and full-timers, both of whom gave more importance to both the social contacts and the wages they earned. The orientation of British part-timers appeared quite different from all the other groups of women.

There were observable differences between the British and French women. For example, French women, both full- and part-time, were more likely to emphasis the equal importance of monetary and social aspects of their job. British women were divided: just over half held similar views to the French women; approximately a third gave greater importance to the social aspects. Whilst we have to be cautious in generalising from this data sample, clear distinctions in the motivations and attitudes to work could easily be identified in each country and between different categories of employment.[6]

The women interviewed were also asked for the specific reasons they had accepted their current job (Table 8.3). Overall, French women and full-timers in Britain were more likely to cite the work itself as the most important reason for taking their current job. Nearly half the British part-timers interviewed said the hours of work was their main reason for accepting their present job; only 17% of the French part-timers cited this. The limited importance the French part-timers gave to their hours could reflect the fact that they were less constrained to take this type of work, compared to the British part-timers for whom it was a more significant reason. Very few respondents cited wages as the main reason for taking their current job. This may be either because the wages they earned in the bank were not much higher than those they could expect to earn in other jobs, or because it was not their main orientation to work. Clearly there are identifiable differences in attitudes to work which are tied, not only to employment status, but mediated by different national cultures.

Table 8.3
Reasons for accepting their present job

	BRITAIN		FRANCE	
	part-time	full-time	part-time	full-time
	%	%	%	%
I liked the work	27	41	37	56
I liked the hours	43	0	17	0
Good wages	10	6	0	6
There's job security	0	19	0	0
There's job prospects	0	12	3	0
My friends work here	17	19	40	29
It's convenient to home	0	0	0	6
Don't know	3	3	3	3
Total %	100	100	100	100
(n)	30	32	30	34

(Source: Employee questionnaire)

3.3 Satisfaction at work

In Britain, part-timers have expressed a higher degree of satisfaction with their work than full-timers (Martin and Roberts 1984a). In France, however, Belloc (1986) has shown that the reverse was true: part-timers were more dissatisfied with work than full-timers. A similar pattern emerged from the sample interviewed in this research. Respondents were asked for an overall assessment of their job satisfaction (Table 8.4). This overall measure indicates that in Britain part-timers and in France full-timers expressed more satisfaction than other groups of women employees. However, when asked about their satisfaction with specific aspects of their job, a different picture emerges (Table 8.5). Nearly three-quarters of the part-timers in Britain were in general happy with their current job, although this satisfaction was largely based on their hours. There was much less satisfaction amongst part-timers in Britain with promotion prospects, bonuses, or job security. Overall, full-timers in Britain were the most content with their situation, although on the question of hours they were less satisfied than the British part-timers. Hours of work appears to be a central feature around which employee attitudes differ in the two countries.

Table 8.4
Overall job satisfaction

	BRITAIN part-time %	full-time %	FRANCE part-time %	full-time %
unhappy/very unhappy		13	31	33 24
happy/very happy	77	69	64	71
not answered	10	0	3	5
Total %	100	100	100	100
Total (n)	30	32	30	34

(Source: Employee questionnaire)

Table 8.5
Job satisfaction on a range of aspects

	BRITAIN part-time %	full-time %	FRANCE part-time %	full-time %
Promotion	33	56	13	32
Initiative used	53	88	43	82
Bonuses	47	81	33	50
Pay	60	81	30	35
The work you do	80	81	77	77
The hours you work	80	69	73	80
Job security	67	94	80	62
Total (n)	30	32	30	34

(Source: Employee questionnaire)

In France there is a stronger preference for full-time hours, compared to Britain where women want to work part-time. As we can see from the data collected here, 80% of the French full-timers, compared to 69% of the British full-timers, were content with their hours. The reverse is true for part-timers: in

France 73% compared to 80% of British part-timers were satisfied with their hours. This would suggest that French women tend to be more satisfied working full-time than British women.

On the whole part-timers in Britain appear to be content working part-time, although there is less satisfaction with the attendant conditions of part-time employment. Part-timers, in both countries, were less satisfied with their promotion prospects, bonuses and the opportunity to use their initiative. In France part-timers were more content with their job security than full-timers which puts into question the precariousness usually associated with this type of contract. In Britain the relationship was reversed with fewer part-timers being satisfied with their job security. This could be a reflection of the different ways part-time work is used in the two countries, as outlined in Chapter 7. British and French women have significantly different attitudes to work: compared to British women, French women are less likely to want to work part-time, they give greater emphasis to social and monetary rewards as motivations for working, and they are also likely to express a higher level of dissatisfaction with work. But, how are the differences in attitudes identified here related to differences in structural arrangements?

4. Structural factors affecting women's labour market preferences

The attitude differences identified suggest that the norms associated with women's participation in paid employment differ in each society. Norms are created and sustained through the practice of individuals. This practice needs to be understood in relation to opportunities and constraints of societal institutions on the behaviour of individuals. In this section we are going to examine the differences in educational attainment, the provision of childcare, and how these structural factors shape women's attitudes to paid employment.

4.1 Qualifications and promotion

Lane (1991) has suggested that the differences in the national system of vocational and educational training can influence women's labour market position and their attitude to paid employment. For example, in Germany the certification of qualifications provided women with "valuable passports" to employment which, Lane argues, made it more difficult, although not impossible, for employers to assign women to the secondary labour market. Chapter 4 of this book pointed to the significant differences in the qualification levels of women in the British and French banks studied. It was argued that these educational differences affected employers' use of functional flexibility. This argument is developed further in this chapter to show how the differences in these systems influence women's attitude to paid employment.

In Britain women spend less time in the educational system, they start work earlier and have fewer qualifications compared to women in France (see Table 8.6) (Sullerot 1973; Barrère-Maurisson et al. 1989; Dex and Walters 1989; Hantrais 1990:28; Dex et al. 1993:169). More than twice as many French women, between the ages of 19 to 22, are in higher education, compared to British women (Eurostat 1989: Table 24). According to the data presented by Dex, Walters and Alden (1993:122-3) part-timers in both countries are more likely to have left school earlier than full-timers. They also point out that in France there is a significant minority of part-timers who are highly educated. They suggested that these part-timers are working reduced hours so as to avoid higher tax bands. This does not appear to be the case in Britain, if anything current tax bands encourage low hours part-time work (O'Reilly 1994a).

These differences in educational attainment were reflected in the sample of women interviewed in the case study banks. Despite doing comparable jobs, 21% of all the British women had no qualifications whatsoever, compared to only 5% of the French women in a similar position (See Table 8.8; and also Table 4.3, Chapter 4). The majority of women working in the banks in Britain had O-Level qualifications. French women, doing similar jobs to the British sample, were more evenly spread between those who had Brevet (equivalent to O-Level standard), and those who had a Baccalaureate (equivalent to A-Level standard). Educational qualifications were related to career expectations, as we can see from Table 8.9. (The number in brackets is the real number of respondents.)

Table 8.6
Young persons 14 to 24 in education
(as a percentage of the active labour force in 1989)

	BRITAIN		FRANCE	
	women	men	women	men
Age	%	%	%	%
14-18	11.3	8.4	15.6	11.3
19-22	2.2	1.8	5.6	3.7
23-24	0.6	0.6	0.9	0.6

(Source: Eurostat Labour Force Survey 1989, tables 01 & 24)

Table 8.7
Age left school by hours of work

Age left school	BRITAIN		FRANCE	
	part-time	full-time	part-time	full-time
	%	%	%	%
low (before 16)	63.4	51.4	36.9	27.2
medium (before 18)	27.4	31.3	28.0	33.0
high (after 18)	8.7	17.2	35.0	39.9
Total	99.5	99.9	99.9	100.1
(n)	910	441	314	1580

(Source: Dex et al. (1993) adapted from Table 5.14)

Table 8.8
Level of qualifications amongst British and French employees

	BRITAIN			FRANCE		
	None	O Level	A level	None	Brevet	Bac
Total %	24	73	3	8	45	47
(n)	(15)	(45)	(2)	(5)	(29)	(30)

(Source: Employee questionnaire)

Women with higher qualifications were more likely to want promotion. More French women said they would like to be promoted, and they were more likely to have higher qualifications than their British counterparts. The difference in educational attainment affects women's orientation to paid employment: where women have higher qualifications they are more likely to work on a continuous full-time basis, women with few or no qualifications are more likely to have lower career aspirations and an unstable pattern of labour market participation. These case study results were supported by the data of Dex et al. (1993:113). Full-timers have greater expectations of being promoted that full-timers in both countries. Part-timers tend to have lower levels of educational achievement, and French women, in general, have higher levels.

Table 8.9
Level of qualifications and a desire for promotion

	BRITAIN			FRANCE		
	None %	O Level %	A level %	None %	Brevet %	Bac %
Yes, want promotion	40	69	100	60	68	80
(n)	(6)	(31)	(2)	(3)	(20)	(24)
No, do not want promotion	40	22	0	0	21	10
(n)	(6)	(10)	(0)	(0)	(6)	(3)
don't know	20	9	0	40	11	10
(n)	(3)	(4)	(0)	(2)	(3)	(3)
Total%	100	100	100	100	100	100
(n)	(15)	(45)	(2)	(5)	(29)	(30)

(Source: Employee questionnaire)

4.2 Childcare provision compared

A second major factor to take into account is the provision of childcare. In comparison to the rest of Europe, Britain has a poor record on public sector childcare provision (Moss 1990; Bradshaw et al. 1993). In France the municipal "creche", "gardèrie" and "école maternelle" provide important support for working women. The strong tradition of the state taking on responsibility for education in France,[7] dating back to the Third Republic, has had the unintended impact of making it easier for women to work full-time (Durand-Prinborgne 1991). Although it is difficult to make accurate cross-national comparisons of childcare provision, because of the different forms of pre-school childcare and the different age of compulsory schooling,[8] the available data indicates that there is more extensive provision in France than in Britain. For example, in the period 1986-7, in France 95.4% of all three and four year olds were in full-time care/education.[9] In Britain, during the same period, only 46.7% of all children between the age of three and four were at primary/nursery school, and nearly half of these were on a part-time basis.[10] As children start school on a full-time basis the differences diminish, except for the fact that holiday camps and supervised studies after school are more widespread in France (Moss 1990; Hantrais 1990:133). For French women it is easier to return to full-time employment sooner after the birth of a child than it is for women in Britain: there are more facilities in France and they are offered on a full-time basis.

The availability of childcare and the terms on which it is provided affect whether women can take on a full or part-time job (Moss 1990:17-21 & 34-37; Horrell & Rubery 1991; Alwin et al. 1992). The type of provision also tells us about national differences in the attitudes to women's role in the family and the work place (Alwin et al. 1992; Pfau-Effinger 1993; Tilly & Scott 1987).[11] It is not just that the institutions and forms of provision are different, but that these institutions reflect the differences in the national culture and values.

Given the differences in structural provisions apparent at the national level, the aim of this research was to understand, how the individual women interviewed used these resources, and how this affected their experience of domestic work and paid employment. The women interviewed were asked how they currently looked after their pre-school children, or if their children were now older, how they had looked after them in the past, before they attended full-time school. The following data, presented in Table 8.10, take account that often several forms of childcare will be used. Respondents were encouraged to indicate all the forms of childcare that they used. Responses were recorded for each type of childcare and should not, therefore, be read as a column percentage.

Table 8.10
Part-time and full-timers' use of pre-school childcare in Britain and France

types of childcare arrangement	BRITAIN part-time %	full-time %	FRANCE part-time %	full-time %
myself	72%	0	15%	14%
my partner	31%	0	3%	14%
a relative	31%	100%	30%	24%
an unpaid friend	0	0	4%	5%
a paid friend	7%	0	0	10%
a paid child minder	10%	0	63%	43%
a play group/creche	3%	0	26%	48%
a work place nursery	0	0	0	0
Total (n) women with children	29	3	27	21

(Source: Employee questionnaire)

By looking at the data we can distinguish between formal and informal arrangements. Formal arrangements include state provided creches, play groups and paid child minders, and informal arrangements consist of family, friends and partner. This data confirms that in Britain childcare is dependent on informal provision, compared to France where greater use is made of formal care through the use of child minders, playgroups and creches. For example, in Britain 72% of part-timers with children said they were responsible for this early childcare compared to only 15% of French part-timers with children.

In both countries the family, with the exception of the partner, played a similar role in providing pre-school childcare. In this sample the British women with children were more likely to say that their partner helped looking after young children compared to the French women. Although we must be cautious of over interpreting this data to generalisations at the national level because of the small sample size, Hantrais (1985) confirms that British women are more likely than French women to arrange their working hours around their husband's job: British men have to relieve their wives of childcare if the women work. For both full- and part-time employees in Britain, relatives, usually their mothers, were essential if they were going to go out to work full-time. Connell (1987) argues that the gender regime of the family and cathexis contribute to the overall gender order, and this can vary both historically and between different cultures. Thus, the perception of 'suitable' forms of childcare can affect women's ability to take up paid employment. Comments by two full-time cashiers in Britain illustrate this,

> My husband was a bit funny about me coming back full-time, but when I arranged with my mum to look after the baby, he said it would be OK because she's family.(Full-time cashier, Britain)

> My mum looks after my baby while I'm at work. It's great she only lives around the corner, so I can drop him round on my way out in the morning, and my mum feeds him, and then I can collect him in the evening. It's hard though, because by the time he comes home he has to go to bed, so we don't really see much of him. If it wasn't for my mum I don't know what I'd do. (Full-time cashier, Britain)

British women in this sample relied more on their relatives for pre-school childcare than French women. The vacumn of comprehensive state regulated childcare in Britain has meant that British mothers have to rely more on their relatives for pre-school care compared to French women. Even for older children the French women could rely on using formal childcare compared to the British women. In France more part-timers used child minders, compared to full-timers who used play groups. This may be because it is more difficult for part-timers in France to find a place at play groups/creches which provide full-time care.

But the British part-timers interviewed were not unhappy with their childcare facilities. The French women were more likely to say that it was difficult (O'Reilly 1992:214). Amongst the part-timers in France 44% of those with children said they had difficulty, compared to only 28% in Britain. As British part-timers work shorter hours and rely on informal childcare they may find it easier to adapt their hours to childcare needs. The difficulty for French women could also reflect the criticisms made by Bouillaguet-Bernard and Gauvin (1988) concerning the inadequacy of childcare in France. Both part-timers and full-timers interviewed said that it was incredibly difficult to get a place at their local creche. *"You have to put your name down a year in advance, and then you might not get a place!"* (Full-time cashier, France). One woman even mentioned that knowing the local mayor personally helped her get a place for her son in the local creche. Another French part-timer explained how difficult it was for part-timers to find childcare when it was organised on a full-time basis.

> It's even harder if you work part-time because the minder wants to look after a baby full-time. It means more money for her, and when you only want part-time childcare it means you are taking up the place of a full-time baby. (Part-time tray agreer, France)

Although formal childcare is far superior, at an aggregate level, in France than in Britain, it does not meet all of the demands made of it. The frustration some French women experienced in obtaining childcare provision is often overlooked in cross-national comparisons of childcare.

In order to explore the relationship between childcare provision and attitudes to the hours worked, all respondents were asked if they would like the bank to provide creche/childcare facilities at work, and if it did would this encourage them to work on a full-time basis. There was a high demand for such facilities from all women with children, and especially those in Britain (O'Reilly 1992:215-6). However, only a minority of part-timers said that such childcare facilities would encourage them to work full-time. In Britain only 14% and in France 15% of the part-timers with children said they would work full-time if full-time childcare was available. This could be interpreted to mean that these women are constrained to work part-time because of the limited provision of childcare. We might have expected this to be higher in Britain given the differences in the provision of childcare. For the rest they are divided between those who said that such provision would not encourage them to work full-time and those who were unsure. If we take those who said they would not work full-time, we can suggest that for them part-time work is a choice rather than a position forced on them by the lack of adequate childcare provision. Evidently there is a demand for part-time work in France which has not been fully recognised. However, this demand for part-time work differs because of the differences in women's integration in economic production and social reproduction (Tilly and Scott 1987; Pfau-Effinger 1993).

5. The gendered construction of part-time work

The fact that part-time work is predominantly performed by women raises questions concerning the gendered construction of employment. The women interviewed were asked why they thought it was mainly women who did part-time work and who worked in the lower grades. They were encouraged to express themselves freely, so as to understand how they rationalised their situation. The aim of this data is to give a more in-depth insight into how these women experienced paid employment.

Part-time work was seen as a means for women to combine paid employment without disrupting their role in the home,

> Women need part-time work if you've got a family. It doesn't matter for the man, women have a family to look after, men have someone to look after them. (Part-time Cashier Britain)
> Men don't need part-time work, men are either managers in the branches or are up there in the bank (Part-time Tray agreer Clearing, Britain)
> You're not going to go anywhere on this job, and I don't really want to, I've got a family and a house to run (Part-time Tray agreer Clearing, Britain)

In France part-time work was more often associated with women who had exceptional difficulties, i.e. several children, or for people who were ill and therefore were unable to work full-time.

> Part-time work is often the choice of young mothers with several children (Full-time cashier, France)
> Part-time work is suitable for women with children or people who are ill (Full-time Clearing, France)

Part-time was more suitable for women, especially in Britain, because they were eventually going to have babies,

Men get promoted quicker, although they are trying to change it - they (the managers in the bank) assume women are going to have a baby and come back part-time (Full-time First Cashier Britain)

Men do not need to work part-time because they are expected to have careers. However, some of the women interviewed clearly had a sense that male interests operated against them.

This work here is mainly done by women because more men are executives, because of misogyny, and because women don't have the same opportunities. You never see a woman as a manager, I suppose they decide to have a private life and kids.(Full-time cashier, France)
It is misogyny and the tendency to have more confidence in men giving commercial advice. (Full-time cashier, France)
Men don't work part-time because of the money (Part-time cashier France)
Part-time work, sitting on a machine, isn't a job for a man. Men want more of a position. The boys here think it's too low for them. (Part-time Encoder, Clearing Britain)
You never see any women up in the 'heavens' as we call it (Full-time Supervisor, Clearing Britain)

Even amongst the younger staff there was a sense, especially in Britain, that the women were left behind as the men were offered a career. This was because the management pushed the boys on more quickly, but also because women were less motivated in having a career.

The fellas get their grade three and go to other floors or outside promotion, the girls are left behind, women don't seem to take their career seriously, for them its just a job (Full-time Supervisor, Clearing Britain)
It's only women who work part-time, it's not as developed for men, I don't know why...there are more secretarial schools for women, but, in the army men do the same jobs. (Part-timer, Clearing France)
It's mainly women because the salary is so low, and career development is limited, men don't bother about the kids, we're blocked and there is less money (Part-time cashier France)

One of the clearest expositions and rationalisations for the divisions between men and women was given by Claudine and Valeria. When I asked Valeria why she thought it was mainly women who worked in the Tray Agreement department this is what she said:

> Well,.... I don't really know. (Turning to her work colleague) Claudine, why do you think there are so many women in the bank?
> Claudine replied: It's a woman's job: there's more sitting involved and it's less tiring. Men don't like sitting down all day in an office.
> Yes,... I guess that's true, replied Valeria.
> Claudine continued: Women are more docile and are prepared to accept the hierarchy - and the hierarchy here is heavy - it's like the civil service. Men are more commercial - you find men employed in the branches, on the commerical side, getting new business and that. They have direct contact with the clients. Before it used to be only the men, but that's changing, I think customers prefer to see a man though.

This was quite a remarkable exposition of the gendered division of labour which could draw parallels with images of "man the hunter" and "woman the homemaker" (Collinson & Knights 1986). Women's position at work is more closely associated with the role of nurturing and support, whereas men are seen as more active and commercial (Kerfoot & Knights 1991).

The women interviewed in each country had a clear perception of how the differences between men's and women's employment operated. Whilst there were those who were prepared to accept this there were other comments, usually made by the younger staff, of resentment towards the fact that men would be promoted over them. Even in France where women have a more continuous pattern of employment it was evident that women saw themselves being held back in comparison to the men. Overall, the suitability of part-time work was clearly associated with women, especially during the period of child rearing. The only noticeable difference was that in France part-time work was suitable for women with exceptional burdens like a large family, whereas in Britain it was universally germane.

6. Conclusions

This chapter set out to examine whether employees attitudes affected the the type of jobs employers' offered. From the employee questionnaire and other sources of secondary data we have seen how there are significant differences in the attitudes of British and French women. British women were more likely to expect to work part-time at some stage, whereas French women expected to work full-time. Part-timers in Britain were more likely to see their wages contributing to household luxuries rather than essentials. The French women, and British full-timers interviewed were more likely to see the social aspects and the money they earned as equally significant reasons for working. French part-timers had more in common with French full-timers than with part-timers in Britain. Thus, in this chapter we have identified clear distinctions between the attitudes of different groups of women in each country.

This chapter has also sought to show how these attitudes are linked to structural factors like the system of educational attainment and the provision of childcare. In Britain over half the available childcare is provided on a part-time basis. Women are more likely to leave school at 16 in Britain than they are in France. Women with higher qualifications were more likely to want to be promoted. These factors contribute to forming an 'on-going' system of social relations in Britain where limited childcare and low educational attainment encourage women to look for part-time work; in France the situation is the reverse. By linking these factors this chapter has sought to show the social relations in the two countries have developed differently. This means that improving the provision of childcare in Britain, essential as this is, will not necessarily lead to producing similar patterns of women's employment comparable to those in France. Structural provisions of childcare and education reflect the values which have emerged over time within a specific society. These values are practiced and re-created on a daily basis in the practices of the people who live in a given society. As Granovetter pointed out, the characteristics of a specific society are embedded in on-going social relations.

Secondly it can not be assumed that despite the predominant social norms all women will follow them. Although full-time work is more common in France, there is a demand for women to work part-time. In Britain women with higher qualifications, higher career expectations and access to childcare facilities are more likely to want to work full-time. This recognition helps us to realise that one can not talk about women with the assumption that they are a homogeneous group with similar aims and aspirations, in the way assumed by Maruani and Nicole (1989). For some women part-time work allowed them to spend time with their children, whereas for other women it was because of the limited provision in childcare that they had to work part-time.

This chapter has identified differences in attitudes at the individual level and related them to structural characteristics, so as to draw a picture of how the female labour supply has been constructed in each country. In identifying these differences and the reasons for them we can see that despite considerable similarity, as evidenced in the women's rationalisation and perception of their position at work, there are also notable differences which mean that employers in each country are not dealing with the same type of female labour force, and whether consciously, or not, these employers engage women with different employment expectations.

Finally turning back to the questions and problems raised at the beginning of this chapter, clearly the nature of choice or constraint, strategy or structure, can only be understood in the context of social institutions of the particular society. In France where women in the banks chose to work part-time, they were often blocked by the management who saw no advantage for the organisation in this form of employment. The problem with the idea of choice is that it needs to be located in a social context. It is not employers' policy alone which shapes the characteristics of the labour force deployed: we need to understand differences in participation patterns in relation to other societal factors like education, childcare provision, and employment regulation.

Notes

1. Dex et al. (1993:5-6 and 165-6) argue for a rational choice model in their comparison of British and French mothers, in which they can identify the incentives and opportunity costs posed to women with children wanting to work.

2. Connell cites the example of Victorian women who "rejecting marriage were not free to adopt any other sexual life they pleased. Often the only practicable alternative was chastity."

(Connell 1987:95). In a contemporary context, Hantrais argues "Women who undergo higher education do not, however, seem able to avoid the impact of the social pressures shaping professional opportunities and face many of the constraints as women who have not reached such a high level of educational attainment. The obstacles to promotion may also be greater in that women in this situation are often encroaching onto traditionally male territory and therefore need to be equiped to compete on the same terms as men." (Hantrais 1990:173-4).

3. From each country 30 part-timers where interviewed, as well as 32 full-timers in Britain and 34 full-timers in France doing comparable jobs.

4. Association Nationale Pour l'Emploi, is broadly equivalent to Job Centres in Britain.

5. There were opportunities within the interview for the women to talk more freely about themselves. As all of these interviews were conducted during working time, at the place of work, the depth of information depended enormously on the degree of access permitted by the bank, and the pressure from supervisors for the women to return to work quickly.

6. The differences in attitude attributable to life cycle factors were less significant than the differences between countries, except for attitudes to promotion: full-timers with children were less satisfied than the younger women concerning their possibility for promotion.

7. This tradition was based on the principle of equality and state education was seen as a means of creating citizens loyal to the Republic, as well as removing disadvantage. See also the ideas on education expounded by J-J Rousseau in "Emile".

8. In Britain children start school at 5 compared to 6 in France (HMSO Social Trends 21, 1991, 49).

9. INSEE, Annuaire Statistique de la France 1989, Table F.01-1, p299

10. HMSO Social Trends 21, 1991, Table 3.2, p48.

11. Pfau-Effinger (1993) has argued, by comparing Finland and W.Germany, that the process of modernisation and industrial-

isation effects women's integration into paid employment. This has repurcussions on the acceptance of part-time work in each country: in W.Germany the concept of the family wage has facilitated a more extensive use of part-time work than in Finland. For a historical comparison of women's employment in Britain and France see Tilly and Scott (1987). They argue that the demand for women's labour is related to the interaction between the system of production and reproduction. The type of jobs employers offer is affected by the structure of the economy, the mode of production, the scale of organisation and the technology employed. Historically British women were brought into paid employment via the factory system, compared to France, where small scale domestic production predominated. Hantrais (1990:109) presents data to show that between 1901-10 in Britain 10% of married women were in paid employment; in France over the same period, the figure fell from 50% in 1901 to 44% of all married women by 1931. The process of industrialisation varied and has left a historical legacy on contemporary practices.

9 Industrial relations and labour regulation

1. Introduction

Previous chapters in this book identified distinct differences in employers use of labour flexibility. The aim of this chapter is to examine the influence of industrial relations and labour regulation on employers' policy. The core argument developed in this chapter is that where the labour relations are more regulated, as in France, employers use of flexibility within the firm develops in a formalised manner, or else, employers look for ways to evade regulation by subcontracting to small firms. Where there are fewer constraints on employment practices, as in Britain, flexibility develops in a very informal, incremental and capricious way.

In the literature on labour market segmentation Berger and Piore (1980) have shown how employment regulation varies between different countries, and they argue that this creates preferential treatment for different groups of workers. They are sceptical of conspiratorial explanations for these differences. Instead they claim that labour market divisions are "found" rather than "made" (Berger & Piore 1980:49). They view contemporary forms of dualism and discontinuity as a product of country specific forms of conflict resolution. Rubery (1978) has also drawn attention to the issue of conflict. She asserts that a more active role for workers, and their representatives, needs to be more fully integrated in these debates. Workers actively establish forms of labour market segmentation in order to maintain their bargaining position. As a result she suggests that "...*it is the limitations on capitalists rather than their ability to control that becomes the interesting question.*" (Rubery

1978:23). These studies suggest that the strategies adopted by trade unions, the type of employment regulation introduced by governments, and the policies pursued by employers associations can all work to constrain employers ability to use different forms of labour flexibility.

By adopting a broader perspective which takes account of these actors we can direct attention outside the immediate confines of the firm, and avoid presenting employers as atomistic decision makers. This approach also has the advantage of showing how relations between employers, trade unions and the state are part of an on-going process, although necessarily rooted in the specific historical and institutional development of a given society. The first part of this chapter outlines the general characteristics of the industrial relations system and the role of the state in each country. The second part goes on to examine how these relations have changed over time, with specific reference to the banking sector. The third section analyses the implications of state regulation and how this has impinged on employers' use of flexibility. The final section focuses on the nature and efficacy of trade unions' strategies towards the employers' flexibility initiatives. From this comparative analysis it will become clear that employers' ability to develop labour flexibility is closely tied to the nature of the industrial relations and labour regulation in each country.

2. The structure of industrial relations in Britain and France

A substantial literature on the differences in Western capitalist societies has shown how industrial relations and business systems vary between countries (Lane 1989; Sisson 1987; Hayward 1986; Cox 1986; Hall 1986; Boyer 1986; Gallie 1978; Whitley 1991). Britain and France are examples of two countries which have developed divergent paths in the management of their industrial policy. Whereas the French have adopted a system of indicative state planning, British economic development has been characterised by "economic liberalism" and "laissez-faire capitalism" (Lane 1989:255).

2.1 The role of the State

The tradition of state involvement in the economy in France has evolved historically. The late and gradual development of industrialisation in France encouraged the state to initiate measures to stimulate economic development, under the governments of Napoleon III, the Popular Front and the post-war government (Hall 1986). After 1945 the employers associations, which had been involved with the Vichy regime, were too weak to oppose government planning mechanisms. More recently state intervention in the economy has been reinforced by the existence of a highly qualified elite, symbolised by the "énarques",[1] with direct experience of industry and the civil service as seen in the tradition of "pantouflage"[2] (Hayward 1986). According to Hall, two-thirds of French business men surveyed by Le Nouvelle Economiste in 1985 supported this system (Hall 1986:279). Regardless of political affiliation, the elite of top civil servants in France today are more likely to think they have a right to be directly involved in industrial policy, than is the case amongst the ranks of their British counterparts (Hall 1986).

The character of elite industrial culture is quite different in Britain. Industrialisation came early and rapidly. Unlike France, where cartels and protectionist laws attempted to safeguard indigenous manufacturers, in Britain domestic industrialists and financiers looked abroad to the burgeoning empire for market opportunities. These economic developments reinforced support for laissez-faire government. Hall argues that British governments

> embraced the self-regulating market economy, an international regime of laissez-faire, and Keynesian demand management successively, so as to avoid more direct intervention into the affairs of industry. (Hall 1986:35).

One reason for the general reluctance amongst dilettante, British civil servants to "meddle" with the market has developed out of the sharp segregation in the educational system: civil servants and senior managers often came from an academic background, whereas engineers were trained up from the shopfloor through apprenticeships. Unlike France, after World War II business organisations in Britain remained strong and impeded the development of the National Economic Development Act 1947 (Hall 1986: 267). Attempts at state intervention in Britain have, in general, been short-lived; British industrial and political development has been typified by a resistance to state intervention, supported by a culture of individualism and pragmatism. These different historical legacies were vividly symbolised in the 1980s by the Thatcher government in Britain and the Mitterrand Presidency in France.

2.2 Pattern of trade unionism

The origins of the trade union movement and their interaction with the state and employers has also created distinctive systems of collective bargaining in the two countries. Hall (1986:267) argues that the repression of the unions by the French state in 1848, 1870 and later contributed to the long-term weakness and fragmentation of French unions. The comparative tolerance of the British state to the union movement, in the early period of industrialisation, allowed its development to take place on firmer grounds. Lane (1989) argues that up until the Thatcher government the union movement

> ... has been integrated into British society by relatively liberal and flexible political and economic elites. For most of this time, the state has left the industrial opponents to sort out their difference in their own way. (Lane 1989:197)

The early experience of industrialisation was important for shaping the contemporary characteristics of the union movement in each country.

Industrial relations in Britain have been traditionally characterised by craft and industrial unions tied to specific sectors or types of employment, and loosely held together by a rather weak national confederation, the Trade Union Congress (TUC). In recent years there has been an increasing trend for smaller unions and those with a declining membership to merge into larger federations, for example with the TGWU, MSF or the GMB. In France the union movement has been characterised by political fragmentation. There are five major confederations, and several smaller ones in France competing for the allegiance of a small number of paid up trade unionists. The unions in Britain have been enjoyed a higher rate of membership compared to the unions in France: in 1988 approximately 10% of the working population in France were members of a union, compared to approximately 47% in Britain (Bibes & Mouriaux 1990).[3] Union membership has experienced a dramatic decline in both countries, and particularly in France.

The main French trade unions are the Confédération Générale du Travail (CGT), Force Ouvrière (FO), Confédération

Française Démocratique du Travail (CFDT) and the Confédération Française des Travailleurs Chrétien (CFTC). The Confédération Générale des Cadres (CGC) is smaller and orientated to higher grade employees and managers. In the banking sector there is also the Fédération Générale Agro-alimentaire (FGA) for the Crédit Agricole.

The CGT, is the largest union, and has close links with the Communist Party. Its membership is largely drawn from the traditional working class aristocracy. Politically it sees the immediate struggle for demands at the work place as indispensable, but insufficient as a means to overthrow capitalism. Their aim is to create a society based on common ownership and democratic planning.[4] As a result it sees its role as one of raising consciousness and mobilising "the masses" rather than pursuing narrow economic gains and being involved in compromising collective negotiations.

FO is characterised by its' fierce anti-communism, having formed as a result of a split with the CGT in 1948. Its leaders believe that trade unions should have a more limited role in representing the workers, rather than seeing themselves as a political vehicle; strikes should only be used as a last resort and only after extensive negotiations.

> Its emphasis on negotiation and partial reform, as against what it regarded as the millenarian perspectives of its rivals, led to sharp ideological clashes that ensured that co-operation between the unions was very rare and transient. (Gallie 1983:112).

FO draw most of their support from white collar workers, professionals and those in the public sector.

The CFDT was established after a break with the Catholic (CFTC) in 1964 when it set itself up as a more radical and secular trade union. Its membership is based amongst the urban proletariat and those from a rural background, together with some of the élite of the working class (Geledan 1978). During the 1970s the CFDT argued for workers' self management ("autogestion"). Today it tends to support the Socialist Party and has sought to encourage the pursuit of short term goals through increased collective negotiations. They advocate a radical but more pragmatic approach to achieve socialism (Jacquier 1986:62). Competitive hostility between these three unions has been a long-term characteristic.

The CGC is seen as the union for higher grade managers, 'cadres' and above. They believe that élitism is necessary and natural, equality is unjust, and there is a need for a mixed economy. They are guided by the ideas of responsibility and professionalism, and as a result they have been willing to sign negotiated agreements much to the fury of the other unions who claim they are unrepresentative. They often associate themselves with the CFTC and FO, or from time to time with the CFDT, but rarely with the CGT. The organisation and ideology of trade union traditions vary significantly in each country.

2.3 Trade unions in the banking sector

In France, each national confederation is made up of federations, with considerable autonomy, from all branches of industry and commerce. Defining a branch federation is not as clear cut as it may first appear. For example in the banking sector the Caisse d'Epargne negotiate separately from the banks which are covered by the employers 'Association Française des Banques' (AFB); and the Crédit Agricole negotiate within the Fédération Générale Agro-alimentaire. Each of the major confederations have representatives working in the banking sector.

In Britain, the system of staff representation in the banking sector has traditionally been divided between the national union and company level staff associations. The Banking, Insurance and Finance Union (BIFU) as a trans-enterprise union has aimed to negotiate at the national level. Employers' hostility has encouraged it to adopt a more militant attitude, which is reflected in its' membership of the TUC and its willingness to use sanctions in negotiations, including strike action. The other TUC affiliated unions which have some representation in banking are MSF (formerly ASTMS) and APEX, but these are less influential.

BIFU's main rivals are the staff associations. They were set up by the banks to undermine the national union. As a result they were considered as little more than management adjuncts until they became more independent in the 1960s. The staff associations represent approximately 41.7% of all bank employees. BIFU, whose membership is based in the lower clerical grades, claims to represent approximately 29% of all bank staff in Britain (Morris 1986:101). There is constant and bitter rivalry between these organisations. The staff associations believe in enterprise level negotiations and have preferred unilateral arbitration to the threat of sanctions. They have emphasised the distinctiveness of banking as a career so that national level negotiations were considered irrelevant. They also argued that the traditional militant style of trade unionism, found in the manufacturing sector, was inappropriate to banking. These two bodies in Britain have for the most part been hostile to each other leaving management room to benefit from this weakness and division.

2.4 Collective bargaining and labour law

Collective bargaining in Britain developed in a fragmented and informal manner. This was largely due to the importance of craft unions, especially in manufacturing, which were vigourously implanted at the firm level early in the process of industrialisation. Employers failure to defeat these unions resulted in a system of negotiations around procedural rules at the level of the firm. The system of collective bargaining developed differently in Britain, compared to struggles in continental Europe (Sisson 1987:35). In France there were fierce struggles over the most legitimate system of collective bargaining, reflecting the intense struggle between trade unions and employers. Sisson argues

> ... both recognition and the structure of collective bargaining are rooted in very specific compromises - in most cases struck relatively early in the process of industrialisation - involving large numbers of employers more or less regardless of their individual views. (Sisson 1987:11)

British trade unions gained legal status by 1824 and by the end of the century they were recognised and tolerated by British employers. This did not occur in Continental Europe until mid-way through the twentieth century. Employers and government recognition of trade union was usually the result of attempts to resolve political or industrial conflict. Willingness on the part of employers to negotiate did not come from a desire to co-operate with the unions, but rather, Sisson (1987) argues, from employers' attempts to institutionalise compromises arising from industrial conflict. Collective bargaining established the boundaries between issues that were negotiable and those that would remain under the employers' prerogative.

The historical legacy of the struggle between the trade

unions and employers in each country can be observed today in the distinctive differences between the negotiating structures in each country. In Britain bargaining has tended to take place on an informal basis in the workplace. Multi-employer and single company bargaining have operated on the basis of "gentlemen's agreements" in Britain; in France collective agreements are contractually binding (Doyle 1986:119). In France negotiations take place on essentially three levels: inter-professional negotiation, branch negotiations and enterprise negotiations. Inter-professional discussions at the department or regional level have been a means for employers to avoid giving the unions a national platform (Sisson 1987). The inter-professional agreements are essentially general outlines.[5] Although superficially these negotiations appear restrictive, the general nature of these agreements, and the minimal way in which employers implement them, undermines their potential strength (Sisson 1987:14; Gallie 1985; Wilson 1985; Berger 1985).

Finally, it is important to take account of the different legal traditions in each country and how this affects the way employers behave. In Britain, where labour law closely dovetails with the principles of common law, employers have greater freedom to contract. In France the legal system is based on roman/civil law, or what Sisson (1987) refers to as "statute law". This means that in France employers are only permitted to enact employment contracts as stated in the law, whereas in Britain employers have the freedom to contract, i.e. they can do what they like so long as it is not prohibited by law (Deakin 1992).

The effect of these differences in collective bargaining and labour law is that in Britain, although employers have greater freedom to make unilateral decisions, they are more susceptible to challenges from the trade unions than is the case for French employers. This is because the British system to settle industrial disputes is based on voluntarism, which leaves employers vulnerable to industrial action. In France collective bargaining is limited by the ubiquitous and detailed coverage of labour law. Where negotiations do take place in France these are largely, in Sisson's terms "administrative" or "supplementary". Branch negotiations are restricted to the period immediately following the multi-employer agreement, so that it has been more difficult for French trade unions to get employers to the negotiating table at other times.

By identifying the national paradigms of industrial relations we can gain an insight into how the issue of flexibility has been treated in both countries. In Britain, where labour law resembles common law and where collective bargaining has been more entrenched, employers have been more likely to introduce or negotiate change in an informal and ad hoc manner. In France, in contrast, employers are more likely to make a unilateral decision and introduce change more formally by using specific contracts or by subcontracting operations to smaller companies not covered by the legal regulation. This is because of the predominance of civil law and state intervention in France, coupled with the weakness of the trade unions and the system of collective bargaining.

This section has attempted to compare and contrast the core features of the industrial relations system in each country. By doing this it has sought to show how the historical legacy of industrialisation has shaped the industrial relations system in each country. Clearly this has not been a static development. In order to understand how this dynamic has developed the following section looks specifically at the history of collective bargaining in the banking sector, before going on to examine how flexibility issues have been dealt with more recently in each country.

3. The historical development of negotiating systems in the retail banking

3.1 Britain

In Britain the development of industrial relations in banking can be briefly summarised into three periods. In the first period, from 1917 to 1960, the banks staunchly refused to recognise the Bank Officers Guild (BOG),[6] and set up rival staff associations to thwart its development. In 1950 formal negotiations were set up between the banks and the staff associations, so as to repudiate demands for recognition from the more militant National Union of Bank Employees (NUBE). The staff associations were effectively management adjuncts, but in order to give them some credibility the banks agreed to unilaterally binding arbitration. This meant that either party could refer negotiations to an outside arbitrator whose decision was mutually binding. Whilst this imposed restrictions on the banks, it guaranteed against strike action and legitimated the associations as independent representatives, without involving the more "militant" NUBE.

The use or threat of unilateral arbitration was not seriously used until the 1960s.

In the second period, 1960-78 the banks were forced into joint negotiating procedures with the national union and the staff associations. This came about for two reasons: the banks needed to establish labour market control and managerial control. Firstly the banks were favourable to national discussions as a way to reduce inter-bank competition for labour and wage "leap-frogging" in a period of a tight labour market. Secondly strike action, announced for the end of 1967 (the Action '67), posed a sufficient threat to merit the intervention of the Minister of Labour, who tried to encourage the banks to recognise the NUBE (Morris 1986). However the banks were only prepared to accept discussions on limited issues of pay and conditions, and the government was not prepared to intervene to push the banks further. Pensions, automation and conditions of work were all designated as the "domestic concerns" of management alone.

There was an important distinction between company and national level bargaining. In banking, issues negotiated on one level could not subsequently be resolved on another level. These developments support Sisson's (1987) argument that employers do not negotiate willingly with trade unions: collective bargaining is a way of establishing the boundaries between "legitimate" negotiating issues and those which remain under managerial prerogative. The negotiating structure in the banking system in Britain has been exceptionally centralised, compared to the more decentralised system of industrial relations in manufacturing, where shop stewards have played an important role in negotiations. Unlike workers in manufacturing, bank workers have never exercised job property rights or control over job demarcation. Sisson (1987) also argues that negotiating structures are a reflection of historical compromises and attempts to undermine worker militancy. The main struggle for the national union in Britain has been over recognition. The limited areas open for negotiation, and union rivalry, have left the banks with considerable flexibility and control to organise jobs at the local level.

In the third phase, since 1978, the rivalry between the NUBE and the associations came to a head and joint national negotiations broke down. In order to obtain recognition in 1968 the NUBE had put aside its aim for sole representation. They had hoped that the massive increase in membership which followed the "Action 67" would continue, and they could claim to have sole representation on the basis of membership alone. However the associations had maintained a secure base by becoming increasingly more critical of management, although they continued to be reluctant to take sanctions into bargaining. In 1979 the NUBE changed its' name to the Banking, Insurance and Finance Union (BIFU), as a reflection of its cross sector membership, and launched successful strike action in the banks' computer centres. Joint negotiations could no longer contain this union rivalry. Between 1978 and 1980 the situation was in limbo. It became impossible for the banks to return to a single union relationship and the solution arrived at, after an experiment at the Midland Bank, was to have separate but identical negotiating procedures with a conciliation stage bringing all parties together. No other form of joint co-operation could be agreed.

The negotiating environment has become increasingly more hostile to the unions. National negotiations have become less relevant with the increasing organisational diversity and application of new technology (Morris 1986). The banks have challenged the unions monopoly on information by extending their internal communications and consultation. Employers in the banks in Britain have sought to create a more predictable industrial relations environment for the introduction of new working practices, and they have profited from union rivalry, which they in effect instigated. At a national level the unions have had a limited, but successful, impact on the issues of pay and conditions because of employers reluctance to go into arbitration. With the break down of national negotiations and the end of arbitration the unions have tried to exercise a more consultative role on the introduction of new technology and work practices, but in effect the divided unions are very weak. BIFU's attempt to widen the areas of negotiation were unable to undermine the tradition of strong managerial control. The voluntarism of collective bargaining, the weakness caused by union rivalry, the reluctance for the state to get involved and the comparative flexibility to contract provided by labour law, have left the banks in Britain with considerable freedom to experiment with flexibility on an ad hoc basis.

3.2 France[7]

The situation in France presents a somewhat different picture.

The dominant role played by the state, the autocratic nature of the banks and the politically divided unions, have given form to a contrasting system of collective bargaining. The first phase of negotiations in the banking sector in France was ushered in under the auspices of the Popular Front government, with the signing of the first collective agreement, "Convention Collective", in 1936. The initial gains made by the short lived Popular Front government inaugurated a reduction in working time to 40 hours a week; this was applied by decree in 1937 to the banking sector. However delays caused by the war were used to justify an increase in working hours, to 45 hours a week. Trade union demands were effectively stifled by the corporatist style of collective negotiations set up by the Vichy government. After the war there were attempts to strengthen the works committees, "comités d'entreprises". However employers found they could undermine the strength of these committees by implementing them on a minimal basis and curtailing their sphere of influence.

State intervention was reinforced in the post-war government. After the war the banks were nationalised and therefore under the control of the Ministry of Finance and the Ministry of Labour. The unions were constrained by the government wage plan for nationalised industries, and they were involved in a form of corporatism in which they were the weakest partner. Wage demands supported by unified strike action in the early 1950s were eventually settled by the Commission National de Conciliation, which had been brought in to resolve the conflict in 1954. They imposed a unilateral decision on all the parties involved. Although there had been important gains for pensions, employment protection, and holidays, Adam et al. (1972:12) argue that these do no more than recognise the modesty of contractual relations in France. The state has historically played a far more active role in industrial relations in the banks in France than is the case in Britain, and nationalisation of the banks by De Gaulle after the war reinforced this position.

The second phase of industrial relations marked a move towards limited collective bargaining from the late 1950s onward. Provisions for negotiation had been systematically violated by the government because their economic policy was opposed to wage rises: the government wanted to reduce domestic credit and internal consumption, in order to meet the balance of payment deficits. In 1957 a three week bank strike created such conflict between the government and employers on one side, and the unions on the other, that the National Assembly pressurised the government to allow free discussions between the unions and the banks by applying the law of 11th February 1950, and the convention collective of 20th August 1952. With some delay the 1957 convention, which allowed negotiations on wages, was agreed. The weakness of collective bargaining in France usually meant that achievements could only be made after effective disruptive action. During the 1960s the unions were involved in fairly regular negotiations on grading, wages and pensions. In 1966 they tried unsuccessfully to open discussions on the issues of hours, mechanisation, employment security, and the repercussions of the re-organisation that was taking place as a result of concentrations and mergers. But employers, as in Britain, were resistant to negotiations on areas they considered to be governed by managerial prerogative.

The reforms which followed the events of May 1968 attempted to strengthen the position of trade unions. Although the role of the comités d'entreprises was reviewed, and trade unions were given the right to organise within the company this was of limited advantage because the employers ignored them (Gallie 1985:206). In the 1960s the unions improved their position in negotiations on grading and wages, but usually only after the employers had conceded to militant action. By the seventies as more and more banks were privatised and services subcontracted these gains diminished. Work formerly performed by employees covered by the Convention Collective des Banques was sent out to cheaper labour not covered by this agreement (see Chapter 6). Union divisions made a collective and coherent response to these changes impossible, and gave the banks the excuse not to negotiate. During the seventies privatisation encouraged further re-organisation and subcontracting in the banks. There was a tendency for the employers federation, the APB, to make unilateral decisions, even after tripartite discussions at the Commission National Partaire (CNP). Trade union demands were ignored. Wage control imposed by the Barre government in 1974 further restricted negotiations despite the show of militant demonstrations. The move towards increased collective bargaining was set back towards the end of this period by economic crisis, lack of employer co-operation, government intervention, and signs of inter-union animosity from 1977 onwards (Wilson 1985:257-8).

The third phase was marked by the election of Mitterrand in 1981, a result which caught the unions by surprise (Segrestin 1985; Wilson 1985; Bridgford 1990). This marked a distinct change in the social climate of France. The Socialist government re-nationalised the banks on the 11th February 1982 (Fabra 1985). But the unions were unsure of the rules of the game: in previous periods of nationalisation they had been subject to the dictates of the Ministry, but under the new Socialist regime the unions were expected to play a more participatory role as signaled by the Auroux laws. The Auroux laws, altered nearly one third of the existing Code du Travail, and marked an attempt to steer a new direction in the pattern of industrial relations in France (Gallie 1985). These laws aimed to stimulate collective bargaining (the laws treating employment regulation are discussed later). Although the CFDT had been extremely supportive of this policy, the CGT viewed these developments with suspicion, and charged the government with attempts to integrate them and weaken their independence. The aim of the government was to bring the unions and employers associations together, although it could not make them negotiate. Legislation[8] introduced in 1982 increased the pressure for employers and unions to meet i) at the industry level every five years, to negotiate on salaries and grading, and ii) at the firm level to negotiate real wages and working time on an annual basis.[9] The government also tried to avoid employers signing agreements with an unrepresentative union: for a company to amend a branch agreement the signatory union had to have "at least 50% of the electors at the last Company Committee election" (Gallie 1985:208). Other aspects of the reforms aimed to improve workers right of expression and worker representation within the firm (Chouraqui & Tchobanian 1991). It is widely regarded that the aims of the laws have fallen short of the initiators initial aspirations, and employers have implemented only the basic minimum required (EIRR 1993: June pp.30-32).[10]

From this review of the development of negotiations in the banking sector we can see how in France the unions have had difficulty in establishing a tradition of free collective bargaining because of the important role played by the government and employers unwillingness to negotiate. The unions have made gains in periods of general discontent. Where negotiations have failed, as for example on the issue of reduced working time in France (Autrand 1987), the government initiative to legislate has undermined attempts to encourage collective negotiations. In Britain the main problem for trade unions has been obtaining formal recognition. In Britain the system has become more fragmented and the traditional paternalist prerogative of management has frustrated attempts by BIFU to broaden the agenda. Where the government has been reluctant to legislate, labour market conditions have been the barometer of union bargaining power in the banking sector in Britain. We now turn to examine how these differences have affected employers opportunities to develop labour flexibility.

4. Employment protection & employers' flexibility policies

The provision of employment protection for permanent employees, part-time and temporary workers differs significantly in the two countries. In preceding chapters we have seen how functional flexibility and temporary employment were more developed in France than in Britain (Chapters 4 and 5). In Britain part-time work was more popular than in France (Chapters 7 and 8). Berger and Piore (1980) suggest that employment protection serves to create a dualist labour market. In this section we examine the differences in the provision of employment protection and examine how relations between employers and the state have developed in each country. This focuses on how employers have reacted to the constraints imposed on them.

4.1 Employment protection and labour legislation

Berger (1980:92) argues that the distinctions found in industrial legislation have been "*determined as much by societal and political forces as by economic factors.*" One of the key features in French legislation is the distinction made between small and large companies: small firms have historically eluded the restrictions imposed on larger companies. For example, in terms of work place representation the 1936 Matignon agreement which introduced employee delegates was only applicable to companies with 10+ employees.[11] Later legislation related to works committees and union delegates only applied to companies with 50+ employees (Dayan 1987; Berger 1980; Sisson 1987). The limited implementation of employment protection in smaller firms is related to the historic and political privilege given to small companies in the process of industrialisation in France.

In Britain continuity of employment over a two year period ensures entitlement to employment protection. A break in continuous employment with the same employer can easily result in disqualification from statutory protection. Deakin (1992) points out that in Britain full-time permanent employees with long service have been known to loose their rights to employment protection, as in the case of the Hull fishermen.[12] In France the Code du travail has provided French employees with greater statutory protection than is the case in Britain.

A key area which provides an insight into the differences in each country is highlighted by the law on redundancies. In France the post-war government introduced restrictive measures to deter employers from making massive redundancies. In 1974, due to the perceived threat of social unrest that could result from high unemployment, the conservative government of Giscard d'Estaing introduced legislation to provide generous redundancy payments of 90% of the redundant employees previous year's salary, to be paid for a period of one year (Bernard 1987:13). When a company wanted to make redundancies, for economic reasons, these had to be verified through a long drawn out procedure, with the ultimate decision been left to the inspecteurs de travail.[13] Berger argues that,

> ... the CNPF not only agreed to the new social charges and constraints, but it also insistently lectured its constituents about the dangers of lay-offs for la paix sociale. (Berger & Piore 1980:227-8)

Employment protection was seen by the patronat as a means of fending off the threat of social unrest. The aim of this legislation was to restrict employers making large scale redundancies.

These comparatively restrictive laws in France have in recent years been amended. With the return of Chirac to power in 1986 many of the restrictions on redundancies were lifted. The powers of veto by the inspectors have been effectively reduced, so that they have became rubber stamps for employers decisions. In 90% of the cases submitted to the inspector, redundancies were accepted.[14] Under this new law they were paid 70% of their previous years salary, for a period of five months, while they underwent retraining. However this legislation only applied to employees with two years service, and companies with more than 10 employees. Small businesses in France have not been forced to comply with the legislation used to regulate larger companies.

The system of administrative arbitration has enabled employers to gradually make small scale redundancies more easily because it reduced the risk of industrial action. Bernard (1987) suggests that, even before these changes, French employers had been able to interpret these restrictions in a very flexible manner: between 1975-85 the number of people being made redundant doubled.[15] However, the majority of these redundancies occurred on a small scale in companies with less than 10 employees. For larger companies, especially those like the banks which are owned by the state, it has been more difficult to evade these restrictions. The French banks have been able to develop flexibility by subcontracting services to smaller companies not covered by these redundancy laws. Employees in these smaller companies do not qualify for the privileges guaranteed by the collective agreement applied to bank staff, and the restrictions on working time specified in the 1937 decree do not apply to these companies. The nature of employment law in France has established a specific set of rules for the banks. Compared to the British banks, French employers have developed flexibility in a different societal context.

In Britain, Hepple and Fredman (1986:141) point out that the definition of redundancy is not as strict as in France.[16] Statutory provision for the implementation of redundancies requires employers to inform and consult recognised trade unions, which represent the targeted employees, about their proposals (Anderman 1986:439). However one of the major difficulties for trade unions in Britain has been in obtaining formal recognition, as seen in the case of the NUBE discussed earlier. Employers do not have to obtain authorisation from the Department of Employment as in France, but they are required to notify them if they plan to dismiss 10 or more employees.[17] Employers have not found these restrictions onerous. This is because of the generous interpretation given in the industrial tribunals of employers right to manage, and because very few trade unions have litigated against employers who have not negotiated correctly (Anderman 1986). Voluntary redundancies have been encouraged by union negotiations for lump sum severance pay. Anderman (1986) argues that redundancy legislation has not been designed purely to constrain managerial discretion. Instead,

> the legislation has also been to reform managerial practice in order to enable management to achieve its economic objectives more effectively in the sphere of redundancy and discipline. (Anderman 1986:416).

In Britain employment protection has not provided a universal basic floor of protection from which collective bargaining can be built because many groups have been excluded from the statutory protection. Employment protection in Britain is more closely related to the presence of a powerful union which can engage in effective collective bargaining.

One conclusion which could be drawn from the differences between the two countries is that where the unions are weak and politically divided, as in France, employers have sought to legitimise their actions with the aid of state intervention. In Britain, even though the unions in the banking sector have been weak, the practice of collective bargaining and unilateral arbitration have been the main sources of management legitimacy. Employers in France have been able to manipulate existing provisions with greater ease than may be suggested by a superficial comparison of legal protection in the two countries.[18] Where employment protection is more restrictive for larger companies, as in France, this leads to employers developing flexibility in a more formalised way than is the case in Britain, or else it encourages them to subcontract to smaller companies not covered by the same regulations.

4.2 Employment protection for temporary and part-time workers

The characteristics of formalised practices in France and casualised initiatives in Britain can also be seen with regard to the use of part-time and temporary workers. In France there have been three major changes to the legislation on temporary employment since 1981. In the early years of the Mitterrand government sharp guide-lines were established defining a code of "legitimate" reasons employers could use to employ temporary workers. In 1986, when Chirac became prime minister many of these restrictions were removed. However in 1990 these restrictions, albeit in a milder form have once again been introduced (Liasons Sociales 1986, 1987b, 1988b, 1990b, 1990b, Liasons Sociales Mensuel 1990). In Britain there is no legal recognition of the use of temporary staff as distinct from permanent staff. In fact the nature of employment protection raises questions as to how secure permanent employees are in Britain. Thresholds to entitlement for employment protection are based on the number of hours worked per week and the length of service.

The number of hours worked per week makes a significant

difference to employment rights in Britain, which can act as an incentive for employers to use part-timers. For example, until March 1994 any part-timer working between 8-16 hours a week had to be employed for 5 years continuous service before they are entitled to appeal against unfair dismissal, or receive maternity leave. This incentive to use part-timers is supplemented by the system of National Insurance payments, so that people earning less than £57 a week (1994-5) are exempt from payment and do not receive employers contributions; this ultimately affects the type of pensions and insurance cover they are entitled to. This can encourage employers to offer less hours so as to reduce their contributions; Chapter 7 pointed out that British part-timers are more likely to work shorter hours than part-timers in France where similar tax thresholds do not exist.

Unlike Britain where employers have the freedom to contract, in France employers can only employ staff according to the Code du Travail. Part-time work was officially recognised in legislation and collective agreements during the 1970s when it was designated a suitable form of employment for people returning to work after a long illness; it was seen as a gradual means of re-integrating them into the pattern of full-time work. The question of part-time work became popular again in the early 1980s with discussions on a reduction in working time (Autrand 1987). The Auroux laws provided part-timers with exactly the same rights as full-timers, i.e. not on a pro-rata basis as is often the case in Britain.[19] In 1981, part-time work was defined as half time working, although in 1982 the legislation was adapted to allow for 80% of full-time hours as the maximum hours a part-timer could work, therefore a series of schemes between 80%, 70%, 60% or 50% of full-time hours was acknowledged as being part-time (CIC 1984).

At the same time the Auroux laws were trying to encourage collective bargaining, particularly on the issue of working time. One result of these developments was to formalise the use of part-time work in France. Chapter 7 outlined how in practice the use of part-time work in the banking sector in France corresponds to fixed formulas between 50% and 80% of full-time working hours; in Britain employers had considerably greater freedom to draw up new contracts to meet changing needs as was seen in the change from alternate week contracts to two or three day a week contracts. Although the Chirac government introduced some minor changes to employers contributions, to encourage them to use part-timers this did not fundamentally change the legal protection for part-timers in France.

These national differences can also be identified in the use of temporary work. Chapter 5 demonstrated how in France temporary work was more regulated and formalised than the casualised system in Britain. This was exemplified by the use of the on-call pool of former employees in Britain. In France it is extremely difficult for the banks to use staff in a comparable way. Protective legislation has the effect of formalising employment relations, with the result that it is easier for British employers to adapt employment contracts to their needs in a way that is not open to French employers. This clearly shows how the differences in employment protection can impinge on the type of labour flexibility used by employers in the two countries.

4.3 Regulations on working time

The differences in state regulation extend beyond the restrictions on employment protection to the area of general working hours. Opening hours have traditionally been a contentious issue in the history of industrial relations in each country. In France, where most of the banks are under public ownership, employers have been more constrained in extending opening hours because of the 1937 decree on working time. This entitles bank employees to two consecutive days holiday one of which must be a Sunday; therefore the branch must be closed on Mondays or Saturdays. Secondly it outlaws the use of shift work in the branches which only allows banks to be open 5 days a week. After the war, between 1951-6, the banks were temporarily successful in extending opening hours because the minister was prepared to sign "un arrêté" which derogated the 1937 decree. The government wanted to improve productivity which they saw as being linked to longer opening hours and their own policy on credit.

However, a reduction in working time had been demanded since the end of the war, but nothing was achieved until April 1956 when the Employment Minister announced an experiment with a return to a five day week for civil servants. For the banks the Finance and Employment Ministers considered that a reversion to the decree of 1937 would no longer hurt the national interest, although they still worked 45 hours a week.[20] In 1956 the deficit in the balance of payments encouraged the government to suppress credit and domestic consumption with the aim of reducing inflation. Ending Saturday opening was also a way of placating some of the demands for reduced hours made throughout the 1950s; it also marked a stage of "normalisation" after the war. More recently with increased competition in the personal sector, the banks in France have been demanding the abolition of the 1937 decree, so that they can open six days a week (CNC 1989).

There has also been a move to extend opening hours in Britain. In Britain, Saturday opening and extended hours developed in the 1950s when there was competition to attract personal deposits. The banks eventually put an end to Saturday opening in an attempt to reduce the high turnover of young female employees and because of its limited profitability (Morris 1986). But once again the practice has re-arisen to extend opening hours in selected branches. The British banks were able to offer their existing staff, who wanted to work on Saturdays, a separate contract. The banks made Saturday working popular because of the higher rates of pay offered, although BIFU was opposed to this policy.

Opening hours are not just a matter of peripheral interest, in both countries they have been linked to economic policy. The increased competition for personal finances has occurred with a move to increase opening hours in both countries. However French employers are more severely constrained by the provisions of the 1937 decree on opening hours in the banking sector. Even so there have been periods when the government has been prepared to derogate this decree on a temporary basis. In Britain employers have been subject to very few restrictions, and Saturday opening is a good example of the way British employers have been able to contract flexibility according to their immediate needs.

Here lies a significant cross-national difference in the system of industrial relations and legal regulation, which is the major focus of this chapter. In France the state has played a more interventionist role, employment protection is codified, although smaller companies have evaded its strict application. As a result employers use of flexibility is more constrained and formalised than is the case in Britain. The weakness of collective bargaining in France encourages employers to legitimise their action in terms of collusion with state regulations. In Britain state intervention has been minimal. The strength of employment protection, defined in terms of continuity of service and hours, is closely tied to the effectiveness of unions in collective bargaining. In the banks, where the unions are weak and divided, employers have had the freedom to contract labour flexibility in a mercurial fashion to meet their changing needs.

5. The unions response to employers flexibility and employment regulation

The final section of this chapter focuses on the nature and efficacy of trade unions activity to counter employer labour flexibility initiatives. This will show how union rivalry in the banking sector in both countries has given employers considerable scope to unilaterally develop labour flexibility. This also examines the extent to which trade unions have reinforced labour market divisions in order to maintain their bargaining position (Rubery 1978). In Britain union campaigns to improve the conditions of part-timers, on a pro-rata basis, have reinforced part-timers as a distinct category from full-timers. In France the employment protection provided by the state and the ideological stance of trade unions, together with their limited capacity to negotiate, has given the unions a minimal role in segmenting the workforce.

5.1 Part-time and temporary work

The campaigns launched by the unions in Britain and France on the issue of part-time work differ significantly. This is because of the distinct forms of employment protection provided in each country; and secondly, because the use of part-time work has been more extensive in Britain than in France.

In France, where part-time work is a comparatively recent development, French trade unions have been virulently hostile to its development. Despite the provision of statutory protection and equal terms and conditions for part-timers in France, the unions view it as a form of precarious employment, which undermines the status of full-timers. As a result of this hostility, and the comparably lower rate of part-time employment in France, the unions had not specifically orientated their organisation to focus on part-time work. Part-timers in France were not treated as a special case, union demands for wages, training and reduced working time applied to all workers equally.[21]

In Britain the statutory protection for part-timer workers is dramatically inferior to that of full-timers. This disadvantage is accentuated by the fact that employment protection in Britain is closely tied to the bargaining power of trade unions, and part-time workers are commonly found in sectors where trade unions are weak. In the banking sector the unions have campaigned to improve the terms and conditions for part-timers on a pro-rata basis i.e. according to the number of hours they work. Towards the end of the 1980s the unions made some important gains for part-timers. These have included pension rights and access to cheap loans and mortgages. Employers in Britain, and especially in the banks, have been prepared to concede to these improved benefits for several reasons. Firstly the European Court Ruling on the case of Bilka Kaufhaus v. Weber von Hartz [1986 IRLR (317)] stated that indirect sexual discrimination could exist where any group of workers, who were predominantly women, were being systematically discriminated against. Part-time work is overwhelmingly performed by women and therefore any inferior terms and conditions could be interpreted as indirect sex discrimination. In order to save the expense, and the bad publicity of being taken to the Courts, the British banks had decided to take the "initiative" in improving the terms and conditions of part-time employment. The banks in Britain did not want to face future litigation charges. Secondly the banks saw part-timers as a way of solving future labour shortages, and were prepared to improve their conditions so as to attract them back to work. By improving the conditions for part-timers the bank could promote its image as a "good employer". In the 1990s part-timers have been seen as a way to reduce labour costs.

In Britain union campaigns to improve the position of part-timers have sought to obtain hourly pro-rata conditions equivalent to those of full-timers. Although in the banks part-timers are increasingly entitled to pensions, cheap loans and mortgages, such campaigns continue to leave part-timers in a disadvantaged position vis à vis full-timers. Part-timers in the British banks have become relatively more expensive to employ, but they are still cheaper than part-timers in France who are entitled to exactly the same benefits as full-timers.

The unions in both countries have been opposed to an extensive use of temporary work. This has not been a major issue because temporary work has not been used to substitute permanent employees, and its use is comparatively low: in 1989 4.5% of people employed in financial institutions were on temporary contracts in France compared to 2.4% in Britain

(Table 5.3). Recruitment of temporary workers in the banks in Britain has been a problem for the unions, not only because of the intermittent nature of these contracts, but because of the restrictions imposed on inter-union rivalry, such as the Bridlington agreement. This is illustrated by the comments of one trade unionist,

> We have become aware over the last few years that more and more short term contract staff and temporary staff are being used especially in credit card processing and on the secretarial side. Our big problem has been initially whether or not we can recruit them because there are all sorts of problems involved in that. For example, according to the Bridlington agreement we could be encroaching on other unions ground. It could be that if they work for a particular organisation, like 'Manpower', there is a union already operating within it. Our policies haven't been fully sorted out on this yet. (BIFU Representative)

The diverse nature of temporary work and the strength of managerial prerogative has made it extremely difficult for the unions to negotiate effectively on this issue. In France employers have been able to use temporary work according to the provisions laid out in the Code du Travail; in Britain the banks have no restrictions on the type of temporary contracts they can use.

5.2 Extended opening hours

The unions in Britain have found it very difficult to broaden negotiations to the areas of extended working hours. The demand for reduced working time has been less important in Britain than in France.

> The only campaign the union has had to reduce working time is in terms of shift work. A few years ago there was a bloody great argument at BIFU's conference about extended opening. A motion was passed at BIFU's conference that we should negotiate if extended hours were mooted by the banks for at 28 hour week, 6 day working with adequate shift premia and extra time off.
> Funnily enough two weeks later the Bank said that they would open on Saturdays, but it is not part of peoples' 9 to

5, five day a week contracts, it's a separate contract, and now you see most of the banks open on Saturdays, a lot of them are getting involved with extended opening hours and nowhere have we negotiated that union policy put forward by the conference.

We have come close to it in some of the smaller banks, in sort of one-off operations like in a shopping centre where they wanted to open a bank up, and we have got very close to it. But for everyday branch banking the banks have wanted to introduce extended hours and we have got nowhere near.

Rather than reduce working hours you can say that they banks are extending them and BIFU's policy remains in most circumstances to get people onto shifts. (BIFU representative.)

Rather than negotiate extended opening, the banks in Britain have been able to contract existing staff to work longer hours on a voluntary basis, with separate contracts.

Whereas in Britain the unions have argued for shift work to meet employers demands for longer working hours, in France the unions have been staunchly opposed to this practice, which infringes on the protection provided by the 1937 decree. In France the issue of working time has been more predominant in union, employer and government concerns. The unions have been opposed to any move which will undermine the gains of the 1937 decree on working time. However, attempts to negotiate this issue have highlighted the tension between the unions, and within union hierarchies, as well as within the employers' association, the AFB. A good example of this can be seen in negotiations on working time at the Crédit Lyonnais.

In 1987 the Crédit Lyonnais tried to override the 1937 decree by signing an agreement with the local branch of the CFDT de Valence and Béziers and with the SNB-CGC. This agreement conceded to union demands for a reduction in working time. This was a reduction of two hours a week and in return branches, in that area, were to open from 9am to 9pm. This agreement was ratified by the National Confederation of the CFDT and also had the support of the minister, Phillippe Séguin. However it was seen as a radical and undesirable development which "a mis le feu aux poudres dans la profession". All the other unions were extremely hostile and the banking federations of the CFDT and the SNB-CGC were also opposed to the local agreement. The local branch of the CFDT justified their action on the grounds that it would save jobs, given the redundancies which had been made at the Société Générale and the BNP.

Even the employers fédération, the AFB, were taken aback at the rapidity of this agreement on a subject which they were in the process of discussing at the branch level,

> ... one has the impression of having been short circuited by a single company even before any negotiation at the level of the branch could begin to be pieced together.

The AFB accused the Crédit Lyonnais of frightening the trade unions who were becoming increasingly intransigent in negotiations. M. Pelletier at the AFB is quoted as saying:

> There is nothing imperative about a branch agreement but it would be preferable that there was one. In relevant cases, the agreements we have already established will be applied progressively according to the letter. What's more the agreements made by the Lyonnais take upon themselves the allure of being a branch agreement.

The implications of the Crédit Lyonnais case were that it would set a precedent. This case is very important and reveals the weakness of negotiations in France and the nature of divisions within and between the unions. In this case the employers at the Crédit Lyonnais did not benefit from union division because of the hostility from the employers association the AFB.

Autrand (1987) clearly highlights the difference between the unions on the issue of a reduction in working time. Although the CFDT, like the CGT, believe that mass mobilisation to support the demand is vital, the CFDT considered that inter-professional negotiations needed to be backed up by a cascade of negotiations at the branch level on the issue of reducing working time. It was only at the level of branch and company level negotiations that the trade unions could propose concrete measures to create employment.

> The CFDT puts no importance on inter-professional negotiations unless they are meant to be an opening prelude to a cascade of negotiations at other levels. (Autrand 1987:93).

In contrast the CGT had little faith in centralised accords and preferred to mobilise before negotiations. When there was limited support from the membership, the CGT were unwilling to compromise at the central negotiations, and looked to the government to regulate the situation on working time. FO, on the other hand, wanted to protect *"la poltique contractuelle"* which they saw as been stronger at the national level than at the company level. (Autrand 1987:94).

In France where there have been local initiatives these too have been controlled from 'on high' by the intransigent union federations, the employers associations and government intervention. In Britain whilst the unions have been more willing to discuss the development of extended hours and shift work, they have not been invited to participate in such negotiations.

6. Sources of union weakness

Despite specific differences in the way the unions in each country are organised there are three main reasons why they have been unable to successfully block employers labour flexibility initiatives. These reasons revolve around the nature of union divisions, the fierce anti-unionism of the banks in both countries, and the difficulty in mobilising bank employees to take industrial action.

6.1 Union division

In Britain the rivalry between the staff associations and the national union, BIFU, has prevented the organisation of effective collective action. This division has been instigated by employer anti-unionism and the history of the growth of trade unions in the banking sector. Today the separate bargaining structure is a clear example of this lack of co-operation.

In France, the unions have historically been divided on political grounds and this tradition is pertinent in the banks today in the difficulty of organising collective action and bargaining. Despite attempts by the Socialist government to improve the position of unions, these divisions have perpetuated a situation where government intervention overrides collective bargaining.

6.2 Employers' anti-unionism

Employers' hostility to unions was identified earlier in the analysis of the growth of trade unions in each country and in the banking sector. In both countries where employers have gone into bargaining this has often been seen as a way to resolve social unrest. As Sisson (1987) argues, collective bargaining is often a means for employers to draw the boundaries between legitimate issues of negotiation and those which remain under the employers' prerogative. Despite attempts by the unions to widen these terms they have often been reduced to negotiating on wage issues. The use of technology, restructuring and flexibility have been excluded from collective bargaining.

6.3 Limited support for collective action

A further problem for the unions has been the difficulty in persuading bank staff to take industrial action. Bank workers' reluctance to take strike action, together with their desire to remain "respectable", have meant that minimal forms of action have been used, for example, stopping work for half an hour at the end of the day or coming in half an hour late. As Lockwood (1989) and Morris (1986) have shown the ethos of bank employees has been hostile to the traditions of trade unionism which have been more popular in the manufacturing sector. The tendency today in the banking sector in both countries has been towards localised and company specific action.

In Britain the staff associations have traditionally been unwilling to take strike action compared to the more militant national union. Where there have been important strikes in the banking sector these usually occurred at moments of wider social discontent, for example in the 1950s and in 1967 and 1968. In Britain at the end of the 1970s BIFU successfully utilised a "vanguard" strategy in the computer and data processing centres, notably at the Co-op Bank and the TSB. Computer technicians, in demands for collective improvement for all staff, threatened to "pull the plug out" of the centralised computer. This had serious consequences of drastically reducing the money which could be traded on the financial markets. The banks curtailed these "vanguard" strategies by separating computer and engineering staff into other bargaining units. The second phase of computer technology has allowed a decentralisation of processing operations and the banks have set up by-pass operations to avoid the possibility of a specific section of workers disrupting the entire network. The banks are increasingly introducing micro-computers into each branch which will end the possibility of such forms of action in the future.

Wider calls for action have only been partially supported reflecting the unions weakness and division. Every year BIFU has balloted its members for strike action over pay. In 1983 the first strike for 16 years took place over Christmas opening in Britain,

> but the action was only partially supported and appeared to make little impact on the banks, thereby revealing BIFU's weakness in the existing division of representation. (Morris, 1986:63).

More recently, in Britain, the staff associations have increasingly been prepared to accept strike clauses in their constitution. Although the general secretary of one staff association said in an interview: "You wouldn't get the support to go out on strike". The BGSU in 1983 recommended limited industrial action over the re-introduction of Saturday working and over pay negotiations in 1985. The banks however got away with Saturday opening because of the willingness of sufficient number of staff to work on Saturdays. The banks have had the greatest success where they can get staff to comply voluntarily with employers demands for flexibility, as was seen in the case of Saturday opening. In Britain BIFU has also had more success at the level of local action where it is not in competition with a staff association and where there have been redundancies, for example at the Midland and NatWest. It has exercised some influence in negotiations on work organisation and in the redundancy of messengers displaced by the automated CHAPS II system.

In France during the 1950s half hour stoppages at the end of the day and a rally outside the Ministry of Finance were the extent of collective action. Later 24 hour stoppages became more common. The greatest success was in the administrative centres rather than in the branches. These demonstrations took place mainly in Paris, as well as in the provinces. However attempts at inter-union co-operation usually ended in bitter back biting. The dominant role played by the government and the intransigence of the banks in France left the unions with little room for manoeuvre although important concessions were gained after the 1957 and 1968 strikes. Bargaining in France has been conducted at "arms length". Whilst the employers appear to act unilaterally, the militant demands for action by the trade unions allows them to take the credit for concessions without signing agreements which would compromise their radical stance. In France direct action "... is about making a strong opposition to the bosses and emphasising action compared to negotiation." (Adam et al. 1972:30).

There has been an increasing tendency for action to take place at the company level in France. A three week strike at the BNP in December 1989 is an example of this. The strike came shortly after the publication of an AFB report which showed that the BNP paid the lowest wages of all the banks. Staff were more likely to take company level action for tangible demands than to take action for the sector as a whole. At the Crédit du Nord the initial demonstrations against announced redundancies waned when the company declared that these would be deployed on a voluntary basis. Strike action is becoming increasingly fragmented.

Bank workers have traditionally been reluctant to take militant action. Although there have been periods of important strikes, these are rare and intermittent. The tendency today, in both countries, is towards a fragmentation of local action where employees feel they can exercise greatest influence to achieve their particular demands. The diversity of action experienced is often related to the divergence of company specific policy, for example over redundancy announcements in Britain and over wages, for example at the BNP in France.

Overall, the unions have not been able to consistently counter employers moves to develop labour flexibility. In both countries the unions have been hampered by different forms of inter-union rivalry, employer hostility, and limited rank-and-file support for industrial action. In the banking sector, unlike manufacturing or printing, the unions have not been able to exercise job property rights and exclusive practices. As a result the unions in the banking sector have played only a minimal role in segmenting the workforce. The banks have had considerable scope to unilaterally develop labour flexibility because of the nature of union weakness in both countries.

7. Conclusions

This chapter set out to show how employers use of labour

flexibility was shaped by the system of industrial relations and labour regulation operating in each country. The central argument of this chapter has been that in France employers have developed flexibility in a formalised manner, whereas in Britain employers have had greater scope to offer a diverse range of flexible contracts to meet immediate needs.

In both countries the unions in the banking sector have not played a major role in influencing employers' use of labour flexibility. In France the unions have been fiercely opposed to the development of part-time and temporary work. They have for the most part taken a political stance of total opposition to employers' use of labour flexibility. However, the inadequacy of collective negotiations in France has meant that the state ultimately imposes a legislative solution, as in the case of the reduction in working time. In Britain the unions have been arguing for the protection of disadvantaged workers, like part-timers, albeit on a pro-rata basis. They have been using core groups of workers in computing services to develop a vanguard strategy to make improvements for all workers, until they were obstructed by management policy. The banks have been opposed to formally widening the terms of negotiation, and the unions have largely been left out in the cold.

The system of employment regulation varies significantly in the two countries, and this has had a significant influence in shaping the context of employer decision making. In France employment relations have been subject to greater regulation because of the role of civil law; there has been a longer tradition of state intervention in industrial affairs; the practice of collective bargaining is extremely weak and the trade unions are politically fragmented. Employers have behaved in an autocratic manner implementing the statutory requirements in their mildest form. The protection provided by the Labour Code forces employers to develop labour flexibility in a formal way, or else, it has encouraged French employers to develop flexibility amongst those who do not benefit from full protection, as in the case of subcontracting. In Britain labour law has given employers considerable scope to contract around existing provisions. The major problem for unions in Britain has revolved around the process of recognition. The state has largely taken a laissez-faire attitude to industrial policy, and the Conservative government has been overtly hostile to the unions. Employment protection, in Britain, has been closely tied to the strength of unions in localised collective bargaining, but in the banking sector union weakness has allowed the banks to act with a free reign. As a result employers in the banks in Britain have had considerable capacity to introduce flexibility initiatives to meet changing requirements. The main contribution this chapter has made to the flexibility debates has been to take these discussions beyond the realm of individual employers actions by situating them within a wider societal context. It has sought to identify the resources and vulnerabilities of the major actors in their ability to achieve their desired goals (Hodson and Kaufman 1984). Employers' capacity to develop different forms of labour flexibility depends on the nature of the on-going system of industrial and forms of labour regulation that exist in a particular country.

Notes

1. Top civil servants who have studied at the Ecole Nationale d'Administration.

2. This refers to the interchange between top civil servants, business men and politicans who move between administrative, commercial and political jobs. The word derives from 'pantoufle' meaning slippers, suggesting the ease with which these people move around, as if they were at home.

3. Accurate figures for union membership are notoriously difficult to obtain, especially for France. There are a range of explanations for this which are linked to the industrial relations systems in each country. For example, in France the closed shop isillegal and there has been very little experience of a check-off system. There have been moves recently to strengthen the unions and imporve their finances with the "Accord sur l'exercise du droit syndical GIA-AXA 2/7/1990. This gives every employee a token of 4 hours worth of pay which they can give to the trade union of their choice in the company elections.

4. "...la C.G.T. s'assigne pour but la suppression de l'exploitation capitaliste, notamment par la socialisation des moyens de production et d'echange." Article 1 of the CGT statuts adopted at the 37th Congress of Vitry.

5. Accords which are 'perfect', like maternity leave, do not need to be clarified at the branch level. Other accords like

monthly payment of wages, professional training and reduced working time have to be clarified at the branch level.

6. The BOG was set up in 1917, by 1921 it had a membership of 35% of all bank employees (Morris 1986:27). Affter the was the BOG became known as the National Union of Bank Employees (NUBE) to reflect its wider cross grade membership.

7. There is no history of industrial relations in the French banking system equivalent to the British work by Morris (1986). This data has been drawn from archive research of tracts published by FO and the CGT, held at the banking federation in Paris. These tracts dated back to 1936. Supplementary information was obtained from interviews with the major trade unions.

8. La loi relative à la negociation collective et au reglementation des conflits collectifs du travail, 13/11/1982 (Gallie 1985:208).

9. Galllie (1985) points out that prior to this bargaining had been restricted to minimum wage rates.

10. By 1990 the goverment introduced further reforms so as to appear less heavy handed. This involved drawing on the use of consutant arbitrators. If discussions break down, an outside consultant is called in. This is someone who is chosen by common agreement from a certified list held by the Prefet de Region. This expert can only choose to accept one of the written propositions by each of the parties after hearing their case. The decision taken is mutually binding.

11. This agreement was legally enforced by the law of the 16th April 1946.

12. Their period of employment was related to going on sea voyages, and as the North Sea fishing industry declined the time between voyages became greater, to the extent that their continuity of service disqualified them from employment protection.

13. This law of the 3rd January 1975 stated that companies making more than 10 people redundant within a period of 30 days had to receive administrative authorisation. This modified the law of 24th May 1945, by reducing this authorisation only to redundancies made on economic grounds (Bernard 1987:13).

Where less than 10 people were being made redundant for economic reasons the inspector need only verify the demand; where there were more than 10 the inspector verified the causes, sought consultation, suggested measures for redeployment, and analysed the costs of payment required and the needs for retraining and redeployment (reclassement).

14. This is based on the research conducted by Elbaum and Tonnerre "La procedure de licenciement economique, influence sur les decisions de gestion du personnel et de l'avenir de l'entreprise" in Dossiers statitiques du travail et de l'emploi, No. 19 feb 1986:5-27 cited in Bernard (1987:14).

15. In 1975 a total of 260,186 people were made redundant compared with 440,000 in 1985 (Bernard 1987:14).

16. This is partly because employees in Britian have to be employed for at least two years before they are covered by this provision. This threshold of service continuity does not apply to permanent workers in France.

17. Employment Protection Act ss.99-107. A cluster of employment rights also inclue "the right to a minimum payment of compensation for redundancy, a right to a minimum period of notice of dismissal or pay in lieu of notice; a right to reasonable time off from work with pay during the notice period to look for another job or make arragnement for training for future employment; a right to a guaranteed weekly payment in case of layoff or short time; and protection for employees where the employer has become insolvent" (Anderman 1986:413).

18. For example the clause permitting automatic clearance for redundancies of less than 10 people per month means that forward looking employers will take a more gradualist approach in reducing the size of their workforce, so that these redundancies will be authorised automatically. The law is designed to deter large scale redundancies.

19. L'Ordonnance on part-time work No. 82-271 26 mars 1982, "assure aux salaries qui la pratiquent des guaranties collectives et individuelles comparable a celles des salaries a temps complet, a fin de mieux les inserer dans la collectivite du travail." Part-time work cannot be more than 4/5ths of full-time hours.

20. "J'ai connu le temps ou l'employe de banque, un chapeau melon et col-celloid, s'en allait au bureau abattre comme il pouvait les 54 ou meme 60 heures de travail par semaine." A trade unionist writing about the demands for reduced working time in L'Echo No16 jan 1955, p.2.

21. In the CGT the women's section, together with the youth and immigrants section had been merged into the central union structure since 1989. Although at the CFDT they had a special section to raise women's issues at all levels of the orgnaisation. A quota system had been in operation since 1981 to try and secure womens's involvement in the union. However, it was not always easy to attract many candidates depite the existence of financial assistance for childcare and domestic help give to activists.

10 Conclusions

1. Introduction

This book set out with a cross-national perspective to examine how accurately contemporary labour market theories accounted for the way employers use flexible forms of employment. These debates were examined within the context of an empirical study of the retail banking sector in Britain and France. From this research we have seen that the concepts of numerical and functional flexibility over-simplify current developments. These strategies have been mechanically tied to the categories of core and peripheral forms of labour. The diversity of employers' rationales for developing flexibility, the way in which people move between sectors, and the gender basis of different forms of flexibility are poorly accounted for in this literature. One of the key arguments developed in this book has emphasised the need to develop a perspective which can identify a variety of factors which shape the social and economic context within which employers act. The literature has had a tendency to identify employers as the key decision makers, but this pays very little attention to the constraints on employers behaviour, the role of trade unions, labour regulation and the work preferences of employees. Granovetter (1985) has argued that organisations need to be understood in terms of how they are embedded in the social fabric. This approach needs to be developed further to take on a more gendered aspect. Rubery (1988 and 1993) has argued that a more integrated approach needs to be adopted to understanding the relationship between forms of economic production and social reproduction. Some of the observable differences between countries can be explained by understanding how the structure of the family can affect the availability of its members to participate in the labour market. The work of Connell (1987) proposes a conceptual framework within which various gender regimes can examined simultaneously. The concept of a gender order composed of these regimes further allows us to understand the nature of economic production and social reproduction both over time and between societies. The research presented in this book has shown how a far richer picture of employers behaviour can be presented by taking account of these factors. This chapter sums up the criticisms made in earlier chapters, and it suggests how a more fruitful analysis of employers policies and labour flexibility could be conducted in the future.

2. Comparative research, labour market theory and the flexibility debates

The main theoretical interests of this research were set out in Part I. Chapter 1 outlined various theoretical and methodological approaches to cross-national employment research. It showed how that whilst some researchers have emphasised the importance of cultural differences, this aspect has been neglected by others. It also identified the problems of relying exclusively on quantitative or qualitative methods and argued that an integrated approach needed to be developed to account for both differences and similarities. A range of research tools need to be developed to synthesise analysis at the micro and macro levels.

Chapter 2 examined the literature on labour market theory and flexibility. Dual labour market theory, which developed as a critique of Human Capital theory, argued that employers policies actively created divisions between primary and secondary labour markets. Labour market status was related to company size and the use of technology (Doeringer and Piore 1971; Berger and Piore 1980), or systems of managerial control (Edwards 1979; Gordon et al. 1982). However, these explanations gave too much emphasis to economic structures, and insufficient attention to the power relations between different groups (Hodson and Kaufman 1982). The strict boundaries between primary and secondary labour markets eluded empirical findings, especially those derived from cross-national research. Attempts to explain the position of secondary sector workers focused on their behavioural characteristics. These workers led lives that

246

were different from the "average American", and they were unreliable workers. This failed to examine how women's "unstable" commitment to work was linked to the ideological acceptance of women's primary role in the home and men's in the market place. And, the lack of stable employment amongst Afro-Caribbean men was not linked to the effect of discriminatory recruitment practices by white "average American" employers. The model of the dual labour market was shown to be too simplistic and equivocal.

The flexibility debates have grown out of this earlier research on labour market divisions. It has been suggested that flexibility initiatives represent new employer strategies, which have developed as a response to increasing fluctuations and uncertainty in product markets, intensified competition and technological change. As a result of these changes employers are seeking to re-shape their workforce in terms of developing functional flexibility or numerical flexibility and subcontracting.

However, there were several problems with these concepts. As with early dual labour market theory, dichotomous models over-simplifies a heterogeneous group of employees and employment contracts. The distinction between using additional and existing employees was not fully brought out in these debates. The nature of job security was also inadequately analysed. The importance of training is poorly considered in relation to skill development and the expectation to increase the variety of tasks performed by one employee. There has also been a tendency to overstate the ability of employers to act strategically, without fully problematising the concept of strategy itself. Finally, the theory has been developed in a cultural vacuum with limited reference to cross-national differences.

2.1 Research design

The banking sector was selected for detailed examination of these debates. This sector provided an apposite arena in which to examine these issues. In recent years the banking sector, in both countries, has experienced an increase in competition and profit instability. The banks have sought to adapt to these changes by diversifying their services and extending their opening hours. These developments have occurred at the same time that technological innovation has allowed the banks to reconsider service delivery. This book has shown how British and French employers have developed different flexible labour strategies to meet these changes.

The research conducted for this book involved interviewing personnel managers in each of the major banks in both countries. More in-depth research was conducted with a major bank in Britain and France. This research involved interviewing managers and supervisors in the branches and clearing department. A sample of 126 full- and part-time female employees in comparable occupations were also interviewed, and observation research was conducted on several premises. This workplace research was supplemented by interviewing representatives from the leading trade unions active in this sector. Documentary evidence was provided by the unions and the companies studied. This research method permitted a cross-referencing of various sources of information, so as to build up a clear picture of the range of flexible labour options used by the banks, and the reasons for their use. Where possible cross-national differences identified at the case study level were related to known survey data for each country. This allowed specific findings to be generalised to the national level, where possible. The originality of the data collected was used to address specific questions arising from the flexibility literature. This method permitted a careful comparison of tasks and organisations that would not have been possible to achieve by relying solely on large-scale data sets and secondary analysis.

3. Strategies to achieve flexibility

3.1 The concept of employers strategy

The flexibility debates have given great weight to employers capacity to act strategically, although the concept of strategy is often treated as un-problematic. In Chapter 2 it was argued that strategy cannot be handled so casually. Employers have been identified as the key actors, although we have seen that their strategies are not always coherent. The flexibility literature fails to recognise how employers negotiate control and co-operation with other social actors, in order to legitimise and implement their "strategies".

There was some limited evidence to show that employers do think strategically. For example, where operations have been restructured, temporary workers and subcontractors have been employed to manage these changes. This was part of the banks strategy to restructure operations. In the case of the French bank which subcontracted its courier services this change was aimed at undermining union power, as well as re-directing financial investment to the smaller subcontracting company.

However for the most part employment in the banks has been managed on the basis of ad hoc, incremental change. As Purcell and Sisson (1983) have argued managerial strategies are often incremental and contradictory. Advocates of flexibility often overstate the coherence of managerial strategy. Employers usually do not have one coherent strategy, instead there are frequently several competing rationales. Child (1985) has argued that strategy has to be located in the "contextual factors". A more useful way to talk about managerial behaviour is to set it in a broader social and economic context. The emphasis on the strategic capabilities of managers fails to recognise the commercial, organisational, technological, regulatory and social constraints which have been established over time. It is usually impossible for employers to start with a "clean slate" when deciding how to structure their labour force.

3.2 Functional flexibility

Functional flexibility is about increasing the number of tasks performed by an employee. A basic assumption is that an increase in tasks leads to an increase in skill. The concept of functional flexibility can be operationalised in either of two ways. A broad definition allows for any increase in the number of tasks performed to be accepted as a use of functional flexibility. Alternatively, a tighter definition states that only where task enlargement has occurred with an increase in training can this be considered as a strategy to develop functional flexibility. The conclusion drawn depends upon the definition adopted. In the first case, we might expect to find a wide spread use of functional flexibility, whereas in the second case its use is likely to more limited. In Chapter 4 it was argued that this distinction is important in allowing us to identify where a deliberate strategy to develop functional flexibility has been accompanied with increased training, compared to where it has been an inadvertent and ad hoc policy to increase the tasks performed by certain groups of workers. The problem in the literature as it stands is that the wider definition is used implicitly, and a diverse range of employer rationales are bundled together in a slipshod manner.

Overall, it was seen that there has been a move to increase the variety of tasks performed by bank employees in general. There were, however, noticeable national differences in the development of functional flexibility, which were highlighted by the data collected from the employee questionnaire. Using a broad definition, functional flexibility was more developed in France than in Britain. There are several reasons for this cross-national difference. In France the banks had increased entry level qualifications, because they thought better qualified employees would be more adaptable to change. In Britain the banks tended to recruit younger staff with O-levels qualifications.[1] A policy of service integration, access to computer terminals for cashiers, the organisation of security in the branches, and the comparatively smaller size of the French branches and clearing departments also encouraged a more extensive use of functional flexibility in France than in Britain.

Employees who were defined as being functionally flexible were more likely to say that their skill level, their use of initiative and responsibility had all increased, compared to employees who were not functionally flexible. However, the increase in task variety was not closely tied to a wide spread increase in training. The French banks had increased entry qualifications, and according to Bernoux et al. (1990), French banks spend more on training than banks in the UK. However, less than 50% of employees defined as being functionally flexible, in both countries, said that their training had increased.

Functional flexibility more often implied a sideways extension of tasks. The move to increase the variety of tasks performed by one employee often came about as the result of an ad hoc policy of filling-in for staff who were displaced because of restructuring operations and services. This could be seen in the practice of borrowing staff between different sections, which occurred in both countries. Banking staff have traditionally been expected to be locationally flexible, especially if they want to be promoted. However this type of flexibility crosses the boundaries of the division between functional and numerical flexibility. Permanent full-time staff were often used to meet temporary staff shortages in other branches or departments, often because of illness or holidays. These staff were persuaded to be locationally flexible on the basis that this would improve their career prospects. This highlights the complexity of employers rationales in using different forms of flexibility.

3.3 Numerical flexibility

Numerical flexibility is a 'strategy' used to match the number of workers to fluctuations in the work load. However, this concept has been criticised for confusing the difference in the way employers use their existing staff to meet these fluctuations, (for example, locational flexibility, overtime and part-time work) and when they use additional employees (for example temporary workers, or subcontracting). Different forms of employment are all clustered together into a catch-all category of peripheral employment, which it is claimed provides 'numerical flexibility'. Whilst this neat simplicity may be attractive, analytically it provides us with a very blunt tool to understand how employers develop different forms of labour flexibility.

Overall, there has been a slight increase in the use of part-time and temporary work, and subcontracting in the banks. However, there are important differences between the two countries. It was more common in France to subcontract tasks like encoding, whereas in Britain these were performed by part-timers. Part-time work was more popular in Britain than in France. The banks in France used more fixed-term contracts compared to the British banks which used casual temporary workers. However the use of temporary workers was limited by security considerations, and the need for qualified personnel.

The use of these staff depended on the banks ability to predict the intensity and duration of work load fluctuations. Regular fluctuations in customer activity in the branches in Britain, for example, were managed using part-timers. In France this was not the case. Branches were smaller, with fewer clients, and full-time cashiers were expected to perform a wider range of tasks, or else customers had to wait in a queue.[2] The use of part-timers in France was more recent. Part-timers were only employed in branches where an increase in customer accounts was insufficient to justify a new full-time member of staff. Where the British banks often used part-timers to cover lunch breaks, in France the 1937 decree on working time prohibited the use of overlapping shifts. This also prevented the French banks from using part-timers in clearing, in a comparable way to the British banks. For example in the clearing departments in Britain, the banks often used part-time shifts in the mornings, the afternoons, and on 2 or 3 day a week contracts. In Britain the morning part-timers encoded cheques; in France the same task was performed either by full-timers in the branches or, this work was subcontracted. The French banks also used students on fixed-term contracts to meet seasonal fluctuations. In Britain part-timers were often asked to work longer hours, or former employees from the on-call list were employed. The French banks were not able to offer employment in a similar manner. Where fluctuations are more irregular and less predictable the banks were more likely to expect their own staff to be locationally flexible or, for low grade work they would employ temporary workers from the external labour market.

The flexibility literature has over-emphasised the importance of fluctuations as the main reason for using temporary workers, part-timers or subcontracted services. Chapter 5 argued that temporary workers were also used to restructure operations, recruit future employees and obtain specialised staff like computer systems analysts. In chapter 6 we saw that subcontracting was used for a diverse and complex set of reasons: subcontractors can provide technology specialists, reduce indirect control costs, employ cheaper labour, disperse risk, protect core workers and undermine union strength. It was possible to identify many competing and complementary rationales behind the decision to subcontract in the banks. In the light of this evidence, the argument that part-timers, temporary workers and subcontractors are used to meet 'fluctuations' only provides a shallow analysis of employer behaviour.

The concepts of core and peripheral employment are usually used in a way that implies that the boundaries between the two are impenetrable. Thus little attention has been given to understanding how employees move in, and out of, permanent employment. In this book we have seen how the banks have used subcontracting and temporary work (and in the French banks part-time work) to move jobs, or people, they consider less essential to their business out of core employment. For example as the banks restructure operations and subcontract services core employees are being re-deployed, or encouraged to leave, and temporary workers are used to manage these services until they are closed down. The banks, especially in France wanted to ease out low grade administrative employees and replace them with more highly qualified staff. Part-time work, as was seen at the Crédit Lyonnais, has been used as a gradual policy to reduce the size of their full-time work force, especially amongst older female employees in low grade administrative jobs. At the same time secondary employment has also provided gateways to move into more permanent employment. It has been common, during the 1980s in France for the banks to offer temporary contracts as a testing period, before offering permanent employment. This was supported by data provided by the BNP and also by the responses of the French employees at the Crédit Agricole, 12% of whom said they had first started work in the bank on a temporary contract. According to Brunhes (1987) this is a common trend in France. This practice was not used in the British banks. This cross-national difference is related to the distinctions between permanent and temporary workers in statutory employment protection in France, which were discussed in Chapter 9.

In Britain the banks were more likely to use part-time work to encourage former permanent, full-time female employees to come back to work. One of the reasons the banks were keen to encourage part-time work during the 1980s was because of the predicted drop in the number of school leavers entering the labour market, at a time when retail banking was booming. As the recession hit at the beginning of the 1990s part-timers provided a way of reducing costs. Part-time work in Britain has often been seen as a transition stage between full-time work, or not working. However it was not clear, from the data collected in this research, that most part-timers then went on to full-time employment; although the Career Break schemes sought to facilitate this for higher grade staff.

These results also raise serious doubts about the tendencies to equate part-time work, in general, with precarious employment. The use of part-time work in France has been accompanied by extensive legislative protection. First, part-timers are entitled to the benefits on the same basis as full-time, permanent employees. This makes it more difficult to categorise part-time work as a precarious form of employment in the secondary sector. Second, the way employers can use part-time work is strictly defined in the Labour Code. In Britain employers have had the freedom to contract part-timers as they like. In France part-time work has been subject to greater regulation. These practices also indicate that the boundaries between full and part-time employment are more permeable than the strictly dichotomous model suggests. The same employees were found to have moved between different categories of employment, in the same company, at different stages in their working lives.

Finally, although the question of job security has been

poorly developed in these debates, it is of central importance. Job security, as defined by employment protection varies between countries: in Britain it is based on working hours and continuity of service; in France the difference between permanent and temporary workers is specified more clearly in the Labour Code. The concept of job security is not a purely legal definition, but is closely tied to the economic climate, and the strength of employee representatives. When there is a boom and a labour shortage, even those on temporary contracts can find themselves in continuous employment with the capacity to earn high wages. In a recession, clearly these workers are more vulnerable, but so too are "permanent" employees, if the company is likely to cut back on staff or to close down. Part-timers in this survey experienced little sense of job insecurity, despite being theoretically allocated to the secondary sector. In Britain permanent employees' job security is closely tied to the strength of trade unions in collective bargaining in that sector. Even in France, where the unions are very weak, more restrictive redundancy laws have been aimed at deterring mass redundancies. Nevertheless, where redundancies have been introduced more gradually French employers, especially those in smaller firms, have been able to negotiate their way around the vetoing power of the local inspectors (Bernard 1987). The boundaries between core and peripheral employment are more susceptible to flux than a rigid dual model of flexibility would suggest. Throughout this book it has been argued that managerial behaviour needs to be more firmly situated in the social and economic context of a given society.

4. The societal context of employers' decision making

4.1 The economic and organisational context of employers' decision making

The economic and institutional characteristics of the retail banking sector in each country were set out in Chapter 3. The aim of this chapter was to draw out the similarities and differences which have occurred in this sector, and identify how the arena of employers' decision making has been shaped. In both countries the banks have been faced with increased competition and unstable profit margins; as a result they have diversified services and restructured operations in attempts to gain greater flexibility.

However, distinct historical legacies have bequeathed significant differences in the retail banking system in each country. In France the banks, despite nationalisation, have operated in an intensely competitive environment. In Britain the banking sector has been dominated by a few large companies. Until quite recently they have been able to operate like a private cartel, setting industry wage levels. However, this cartel has broken up since government deregulation of the financial sector in the mid-1980s. This was partly as a result of intensified competition coming from the Building Societies. The repercussions of competition in Britain were delayed because limited penetration of the personal finance sector left considerable scope to attract new accounts. In France the market for personal accounts has been saturated. The banks, in both countries, have competed on the grounds of service diversification and extended opening hours. But as we have seen the French banks have been more severely curtailed than the British banks in their ability to do this. The operating costs of the cheque clearing system are also considerably higher in France than in other European countries, and compared to Britain the wage costs of bank employees are also much higher. Although capital-assets ratios are lower in France, profitability is more stable and the government has been willing to support the banks during difficult periods. In Britain the banks have been increasingly vulnerable to erratic profitability in recent years. There are significant differences in the economic pressures encouraging the banks to look for labour flexibility in the two countries: in France there has been a long term concern to reduce staff numbers in the banking sector, although during the 1980s the socialist government was reluctant to allow this to take place in a savage manner; in Britain the concern with job reduction is more recent, and has been more radical in recent years.

In France the banking system is more decentralised than the British one, which has been concentrated around the City of London. This creates a different organisational structure in the two countries. For example, the administrative cheque clearing operations in Britain are centralised in London. In France these operations are treated at the regional level. This organisational difference effects the volumes of work coming into these centres, and the type of labour required to treat this work. In Britain these centres are considerably larger than in France, and there is a more extensive division of labour. This has encouraged the use of part-timers in Britain, who are used to meet weekly fluctuations in the work load. In general, the average size of the branches in France is smaller than in Britain, which has encouraged and facilitated a more extensive use of functional flexibility in France.

Automation during the 1960s was focused on centralised mainframe systems, in the 1980s and 1990s there has been a move to more decentralised computing systems. Electronic banking is still comparatively new in both countries, but depending on how quickly it is developed this will have serious consequences for employment in the banks in both countries (Child & Loveridge 1990). One major difference identified in Chapter 4 was the use of computers terminals for cashiers in France. The French banks have pursued a policy of service integration and these terminals have enabled cashiers to perform a wider range of tasks than their British colleagues. The British banks had not to develop technology as extensively, and they have introduced terminals selectively, which complements their policy of service segmentation in the branches. In France the national Minitel system also allowed cashiers in the branches to access financial information in a way that was not available to British cashiers. Technology solutions have been adopted by the banks in relation to the existing organisational structure and the way service policy is being developed.

Despite a general increase in competitive pressures forcing the banks to re-evaluate their organisational and service policy, the nature of competition in the two countries has differed. The differences in organisational structure and access to technology also suggest that these competitive pressures have encouraged them to handled employment questions differently. These concerns need to be located within a specific societal context to understand how employers negotiate and legitimise their actions. This is why it is important to take account of the differences in the system of industrial relations and labour regulation in each country.

4.2 The effect of industrial relations and labour regulation

The role played by the trade unions and employment regulation in segmenting the work force affects the arena in which employers can have recourse to different forms of flexibility. The main argument developed in this book has been that employers in each country are developing different types of flexibility: in France, employers' use of flexibility is more formalised; in Britain, employers have had more scope to use a diverse range of flexible contracts to meet their immediate needs. These differences were related to the historical development of the industrial relations system in each country.

In France the practice of collective bargaining is extremely weak, and the trade unions are politically fragmented. There has been a longer tradition of state intervention in industrial affairs, and employment relations have been subject to greater regulation because of the role of civil law. The result is that employers' use of labour flexibility has to correspond to formal conditions in the Labour Code. It has been easier for employers in the private sector, compared to the banks which have been under public control, to subvert these statutory requirements by implementing them in their mildest form, or by subcontracting to smaller companies, where these restrictions do not apply.

In Britain labour law has given employers considerable scope to contract around existing provisions. Despite a history of entrenched trade unionism, recognition has been one of the major problems for the unions in the banking sector, and the state has largely taken a laissez-faire attitude to industrial policy. As a result employers in the banks in Britain have had considerable capacity to introduce flexibility initiatives to meet changing requirements. Drawing attention to these differences takes the flexibility debates beyond the realm of individual employers actions and situates them within a wider social context. It also identifies how the capacity for employers to act is negotiated in relation to other social actors and that the nature of the resources and constraints these actors have access to also varies between countries.

4.3 Supply side influences

A third important aspect to consider is how the characteristics of available labour influence employers labour policies. The central assumption of the literature on labour flexibility is that employers are the key actors. As a result no account has been given of the influence of the attitudes and preferences of employees (an exception to this is the work of Lui 1990). This book redressed this bias, by interviewing a selection of closely matched full and part-time female employees in the banks in each country. French women doing the same jobs as British women had different attitudes to work. French women gave more importance to the wages they earned, and the social relations at work equally. British women were more likely to see themselves changing to part-time work than was the case for French women.

These differences in attitude were related to differences in the structural provision of education and training in the two countries. The education system in France encouraged more women to obtain higher qualification than was the case in Britain, and this affected their attachment to full-time paid employment. For example, French women were more interested in being promoted than their British counterparts.

The difference in child care provision in the two countries is often given as the main explanation for why British women are more willing to work part-time compared to French women. The system of child care clearly affects women's ability to work full-time. Although fewer women in France wanted to work part-time, approximately 18% of the French full-timers said they wanted part-time work . This fact suggests that explanations which correlate extensive child care provision with full-time employment are too deterministic. The demand for part-time employment in France could reflect the inadequacy of child care provision and the different aspirations of women employees. Bouillaguet-Bernard and Gauvin (1988b) argue that child care provision in France has greater inadequacies than is normally perceived. It is not enough to concentrate solely on one aspect of structural difference, i.e. child care to understand differences in working patterns in the two countries. Consideration of the influence of the system of education and training also has to be taken into account, to understand how this affects women's willingness to take up paid employment. This approach avoids explanations which focus on single deterministic variables, and it gives employees a more active role. It also shows how hidden conflicts exist, for example, between a minority of French women who wanted to work part-time in a society which encourages full-time employment.

Drawing attention to the differences in the attitudes and qualifications of a comparable group of employees, shows how employers have recourse to different categories of workers. This also shows how these employees are flexible in different ways: British women are more likely to want to work part-time, and French women, in general, are more likely to want to work full-time and be promoted. By identifying the differences in the organisation of banking, the nature of competition, the system of industrial relations and labour regulation, and the characteristics of the available supply of female workers in each country, we can see how an analysis of employers use of labour flexibility needs to be situated in a broader societal context.

5. Towards an integrated societal and gendered approach to cross-national employment research

This book has shown that there are significant differences in the use of labour flexibility in each country. The central argument presented here has been that the concepts of functional and numerical flexibility are too rigidly drawn to account for the way employers use different forms of labour in both countries. If we want to understand how labour markets are segmented by employers we need to have a clearer understanding of how employers develop their labour market policy. In order to avoid attributing employers with a monopoly on action we need to situate their behaviour within a specific social and economic context. This allows us to take account of the actions and influence of other social actors, and the way their behaviour shapes the context within which employers are capable of developing labour strategies.

The key factors which affect employers policy, and which have been discussed more fully in earlier chapters of this book, are outlined in diagram 1. Employers and the firm are located at the centre of this diagram because they have been our main focus of attention. The factors which are considered to have an important influence on the way employers develop their flexible labour policies are presented as operating outside the firm.

Looking first at the system of industrial relations and the nature of employment regulation, this includes both the role of the trade unions and the system of labour regulation which were discussed in Chapter 9. This diagram shows how there is a two-way relationship between employers and the industrial relations system. On one hand legal protection imposes constraints on the type of flexibility employers can have recourse to. Second, trade unions seek to exercise power over employers' control of the labour process. On the other hand employers also use the system of industrial relations to legitimise their actions (Sisson 1987).

The nature of the education and training system also has an influence on employers, in the way the labour force is skilled

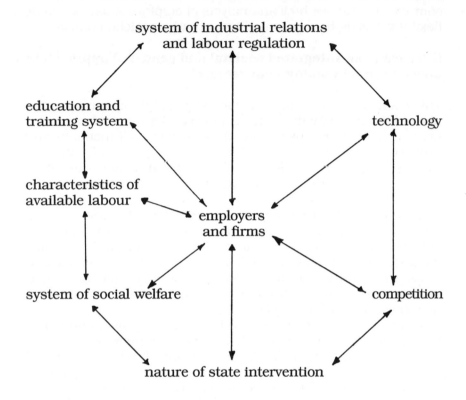

**Figure 1. An integrated societal and gendered approach
to cross-national employment research**

260

and the role employers play in this training process, i.e. how much they are prepared to invest collectively or individually. This system is influenced by the system of industrial relations, especially in craft industries where apprenticeship training has been controlled or influenced by the trade unions. The nature of the education and training system affects the characteristics of available labour. Who is skilled, and what skills do they have? This affects who employers can employ, and how they organise these jobs (Maurice et al. 1982; Prais and Wagner 1983). Where the available work force is highly skilled, employers are more likely to integrate a wider range of tasks for their staff. Where work force skills are low, either an employer needs to train these workers, or, alternatively employ them to perform low skilled tasks.

Who is available to take up paid employment is also affected by the way the system of tax, social welfare and child care provision are organised in a given country. Where there is extensive child care provision, as in France, women for example will find it easier to work full-time. Where this provision is only partial, as in Britain, the hours women are available to work in paid employment is dependent on how they can have their children cared for, either through partial state provision or, through informal child care usually provided by the family. The provision of these facilities is related to the way governments have enacted social welfare legislation.

The nature of state intervention in the provision of social welfare, and in the firm also establishes the environment in which employers labour market decisions are framed. For example, in Britain, the National Insurance threshold can encourage employers to offer low paid jobs, so that they are not eligible to pay employer contributions (O'Reilly 1994a). This can also have an effect on low paid workers, who have a disincentive to earn more if it means they cross the tax threshold. This is because they have to work considerably more hours to maintain their take home pay.

State intervention can also have an impact on the way competition is regulated. Certain institutions like the Building Societies in Britain, and the mutual banks in France, have benefited from government support allowing them to offer preferential loans to specific sectors of the economy. These privileges are related to the historic role these institutions have had in providing funds to specific sectors.[3] In Britain government deregulation of financial services has increased competition for the banks who now have to compete with the building societies. In France the government set up strict demarcations between the services offered by the nationalised banks after the war. These divisions were relaxed in 1967, which led to increased competition. This has an impact on how employers experience competition and how they look for labour flexibility.

Competition is also related to the extent and nature of technological change. Innovations in technology can be adopted by firms to temporarily give them a competitive edge. It can also change the nature of competition between firms, where firms are forced to co-operate on standards or investment in new collective projects. How a company decides to adopt a particular technology system is related to the nature of competition and the behaviour of their competitors. Finally, the extent to which employers can introduce a new automated system can be dependent on the system of industrial relations, the strength of the trade unions in collective bargaining, and the ability of workers to exercise job property rights.

The aim of this model is to highlight the inter-relationship between a diverse array of institutions in a given society. These institutions can be considered as relatively independent, in the sense that they have a separate sphere of autonomy from other institutions and agents in a given society. However, this autonomy is relative in the sense that their behaviour is constrained by the nature of their relationship with other institutions. In this way this model has the advantage of identifying specific areas which have a direct/indirect affect on employers decision making. It also shows how these different elements are related to each other. This model is not, however, static. Conflict is present in the recognition of a two-way direction of influence. The most obvious example of this is in the industrial relations system, but also in the nature of competition, the extent of technological change and the system of education and training. This approach acknowledges that the agents involved in each of these institutions are capable of forming their own rationales. The way they construct their own interests, and seek to achieve these, leads us to recognise that employers ability to act is based on a continuous process of negotiation with other social agents who may be weaker or stronger than the employers themselves. This avoids reducing employers behaviour to deterministic explanations. For example, attempts by trade unions, or the state, to effect a specific technological solution, or a new pattern of training interact with the way employers use labour, the basis on which they compete, and their vision of the future. The implications of change in one area can have a progressive, but not necessarily deterministic, influence on change in other areas (Connell 1987). The advantage of this model is to show how employers are not isolated decision makers, but that their behaviour is tied to the way other aspects in their society are organised. This perspective is more fruitful in explaining how employers behave, compared to the previous literature on flexibility which tends to see employers as atomistic decision makers. It also allows us to incorporate an more integrated conception of the relationship between social reproduction and economic production than has been the case in previous research. Further, in terms of cross-national comparisons it also establishes a framework in which the similarities and differences of specific societies can be acknowledged. This allows us to recognise how particular institutions are constituted in a given society, as well as permitting an analysis of the relationships between the various institutions and actors. Such a societal framework can be then be compared between different societies to identify similarities, differences and the development of convergence or divergence.

The central conclusion of this book is that in order to understand why employers use different forms of labour flexibility, we need to approach this from an integrated societal and gendered perspective. We need to understand how divisions in the labour market have been established over time, and how these have changed. We need to outline the relationship between employers, the state, trade unions, and employees in each society so as to avoid falling either into purely structuralist explanations, or, attributing too much influence to the role of one set of actors, which have usually been employers. Such an approach allows us to identify both the constraints and opportunities open to employers to deploy labour, and how these decisions are related to embedded, on-going social relations within a specific society. Such a perspective can provide a more fruitful framework of analysis for future labour market research.

Notes

1. There have been moves to a system of tiered entry for those with A-Levels, and those with degrees, but this latter category

represents only approximately 3% of the banks annual intake.

2. In the post-offices in France there was often a sign on the door warned customers of the busy periods, when they could expect more delays at the counter, and advised them to come at a different time. However no such signs were used in the banks.

3. For example, in France the Crédit Agricole was originally set up to provide subsidised loans the farming community; the Popular banks did the same for urban artisan; and in Britain the Building Societies were originally `friendly societies'.

Bibliography

Adam, G., Reynaud, J-D. and Verdier, M. (1972), *La Négociation Collective en France*, Les Editions Ouvrières, Paris.

Adams, G.R. and Schvaneveldt, J.D. (1985), *Understanding Research Methods*, Longmans, London.

AFB (1986), *La Banque: Le Système Bancaire Français*, Association Française des Banques, Paris.

AFB (1988), *Rapport sur l'evolution de l'emploi dans les banques AFB 1986-7*, Internal document of the AFB, Paris.

Aglietta, M. (1988), 'Structures Economiques et Innovations Financières', *Problèmes Economiques*, no.2,071, 20 avril.

Almond, G.A. and Verba, S. (1963), *Political Attitudes and Democracy in Five Nations* Princeton University Press, Princeton N.J.

Alwin, D., Braun, M. and Scott, J. (1992), 'The Seperation of Work and the Family: Attitudes Towards Women's Labour-Force Participation in Germany, Great-Britain, and the United States' *European Sociological Review*, vol.8, no.1 pp.13-37.

Anderman, S. (1986), 'Unfair Dismissals and Redundancy Legislation' in Lewis, R. (ed.), *Labour Law in Britain*, Basil Blackwell, Oxford.

Anderson, G. (ed.)(1988), *The white-blouse revolution: Female office workers since 1870*, Manchester University Press, Manchester.

Appert, M. (1977), *L'Emploi Féminin dans une Grande Banque*, Direction régionale du travail et de la main-d'oeuvre de la région d'Ile de France, Paris.

Armer, M. and Marsh, R. (1982), *Comparative Sociological Research in the 1960's and 1970's*, E.J. Brill, Leiden.

Armer, M. (1973), 'Methodological Problems and Possibilities in Comparative Research' in Armer, M. and Grimshaw, A.D.(eds.) *Comparative Social Research: Methodological Problems and Strategies*, John Wiley, New York.

Armer, M. and Grimshaw, A. (1973), *Comparative Social Research: Methodological Problems and Strategies*, John Wiley and Sons, NY.

Atkinson, J. (1984), 'Manpower strategies for flexible organizations', *Personnel Management*, August.

Atkinson, J. and Meager, N. (1986), *Changing Working Patterns: How Companies achieve flexibility to meet new needs*, NEDO, London.

Atkinson, J. (1986), 'Union and the Flexible Workforce: Ostriches or Opportunists?' *Manpower Policy and Practice* vol.2, no.4, Summer, IMS, Brighton.

Atkinson, J. and Gregory, D. (1986), 'A Flexible Future: Britain's Dual Labour Force' *Marxism Today*, April.

Atkinson, J. (1985), 'Flexibility: Planning for an Uncertain Future', *Manpower Policy and Practice*, Summer, IMS, Brighton.

Austrin, T. (1991), 'Flexibility, Surveillance and Hype in New Zealand Financial Retailing', *Work, Employment and Society* vol.5,no.2,pp. 201-221.

Autrand, A. (1987), *Les Syndicats et le Temps de Travail: Revendications confédérales et pratiques des acteurs dans trois secteurs industriels*, CRESST, Université de Paris Sud.

Azumi, K. and Hull, K. (1982), 'Comparative Organisations' in Armer, M. and Marsh, R. (eds.) *Comparative Sociological Research in the 1960's and 1970's*, E.J. Brill, Leiden.

Bailey, E. (1990), 'Banking on everything but money' *The Telegraph*, 23rd April.

Bain, G.S. (ed.)(1983), *Industrial Relations in Britain* Basil Blackwell, Oxford.

Banque de Règlements Internationaux et La Banque de France (1986 and 1989), *Systèmes de Paiement dans Onze Pays Developpes*, BIS, Paris.

Barchard, D. (1988), 'Technology in the front line', UK Banking Survey, *Financial Times*, 26th September.

Barchard, D. (1989), 'Raising the stakes in the high street' *Financial Times* 6th January.

Barchard, D. (1990), 'How Firstdirect aims to ring the changes' *Financial Times*, 14th September.

Baroin, D. and Loos, J. (1982), 'Protection juridique et couverture sociale du travail à temps partiel en Europe' *Droit Social* no.7-8 Juillet-Août.

Baron, J. and Bielby, W. (1984), 'The Organisation of Work in a Segmented Economy' *American Sociological Review*, vol. 49, August, pp. 454-473.

Barrat, S. and Grandclaude, J. (1983), *Le Travail à Temps Partiel en Lorraine*, Direction regionale du travail and de l'emploi de la region Lorraine, Paris.

Barrère-Maurisson, M-A., Daune-Richard, A-M. et Letablier, M-T. (1989), 'Le Travail à temps partiel plus développé au Royaume-Uni qu'en France.' *Economique et Statistique* no. 220 avril, Paris.

Barrère-Maurisson, M-A. (1992), *La Division Familiale du Travail: La vie en double* PUF, Paris

Barsoux, J-L. and Lawrence, P. (1990a), *The Challenge of British Management* Macmillan, London.

Barsoux, J-L. and Lawrence, P. (1990b), *Management in France* Cassell Education Limited, London.

Becker, G. (1975) *Human Capital* Washington DC: National Bureau of Economic Research.

Bedin, J-M. (1987), 'Les entreprises face aux fluctuations de la demande' *La Lettre d'information du Centre d'etude de l'emploi* no.6 December, Paris.

Beechey, V. and Perkins, T. (1985), 'Conceptualising part-time work' in Roberts C, Finnegan R, and Gallie D (eds.) *New Approaches to Economic Life* Manchester University Press, Manchester.

Beechey, V. (1989), 'Women's Employment in France and Britain: some problems of comparision' *Work Employment and Society* vol. 3, no. 3 pp.369-378.

Beechey, V. and Perkins, T. (1987), *A Matter of Hours: Women, Part-time work and Labour markets* Polity, Cambridge

Belloc, B. (1986), 'De plus en plus de salariés à temps partiel.' *Economie et Statistique* no.193-194, Nov-Dec, Paris.

Bennett, N. (1991), 'Banks face 30,000 job losses over 2 years' *The Times*, 22nd January.

Benoit-Guilbot, O. (1989), 'Quelques réflexions sur l'analyse sociétale: l'exemple des régulations des marchés du travail en France et en Grande-Bretagne' *Sociologie du Travail* no. 2-89.

Benoit-Guilbot, O. (1987), 'Les structures sociales du chômage en France et en Grande-Bretagne, influences sociétales.' *Sociologie du Travail* no.2-87, pp.219-236.

Berger, P. and Luckmann, T. (1971), *The Social Construction of Reality* Penguin, Harmondsworth.

Berger, S. and Piore, M. (1980), *Dualism and Discontinuity in Industrial Societies* Cambridge University Press, Mass. USA.

Berger, S. (1985), 'The Socialists and the patronat: the dilemmas of co-existence in a mixed economy' in Machin, H. and Wright, V. (eds.) *Economic Policy and Policy Making Under the Mitterrand Presidency 1981-4* Frances Pinter, London.

Bernard, M.P. (1987), 'L'ajustement des effectifs' in Meurs, D. (ed.), *La Flexibilité du Travail, Les Cahiers Français* no.231 mai-juin, pp.7-14, Paris.

Bernard Brunhes Consultants (1990), *Rapport Condensé sur la Gestion des Ressources Humaines dans les banques Europpéennes* Info CGT, Paris.

Bernoux, P., Cressey, P., Eldridge, J. and MacInnes, J. (1990), *New Technology and Employee Relations in a Scottish and a French Bank*, Summary report of a research project undertaken by the Department of Sociology and Social and Economic Research, University of Glasgow, and Groupe Lyonnaise de Sociologie Industrielle, Université de Lyon II, May.

Bernoux, P. (1985), *La sociologie des organisations* Editions du Seuil Points, Paris.

Bertrand, H. (1990), *La gestion des ressources humaines dans les Banques Europpeennes: Quelles strategies Aujourd'hui?* Paper presented at 'La journée 'Banque'' 1st December, Laboratoire d'Economie Sociale, Université de Paris I - Pantheon-Sorbonne.

Bertrand, O. and Noyelle, T. (1988), *Ressources Humaines et Stratégies des Entreprises - Changement technologique dans les Banques et Assurances: Allemagne, Etats-Unis, France, Japon et Suède* Centre pour la recherche et l'innovation dans l'enseignement, OECD, Paris.

Bertrand, O. and Noyelle, T. (1987), 'L'Emploi dans les Banques et Assurances: Comparaison Internationale et Perspectives d'Evolution' *Economie et Humanisme*, mai-juin.

Bibes, G. and Mouriaux, R. (1990), *Les Syndicats Européens à l'épreuve Presses de la Fondation Nationale des Sciences Politiques*, Paris.

Bichon, M. et al. (1981), *Le travail à temps partiel dans le secteur privé en Poitou-Charentes* Institut d'Administration des entreprises de l'Université de Poitiers, Paris.

BIFU (1993), *Job Losses, as at February 1993*, internal

document.

BIFU (1991), *Facing Redundancy: Current Practice in the Finance Sector*, BIFU Research, London.

BIFU (1990), *Temporary Working in the Finance Sector* BIFU Research, London.

BIFU (1988), *Survey of terms and conditions for part-time, temporary and casual staff* BIFU Research, London.

BIFU (1985), *Jobs for the Girls? The impact of automation on women's' jobs in the finance industry* BIFU Research, London.

Bisset, L. and Huws, U. (1984), *Sweated Labour: Homeworking in Britain Today* Low Pay Unit no. 33, London.

Blanchflower, D. and Corry, B. (1986), *Part-time Employment in Great Britain: An analysis using establishment data* Department of Employment, Research Paper no. 57, DE, London.

Blanden, M., Timewell, S. and Laurie, S. (1991), 'Times they are a-changin' *The Banker*, Jan.

Blanden, M. and Laurie, S. (1989), 'Hail to thee, great hero' *The Banker*, Jan.

Bloch-London, C. (1987), *Les aides au développement du travail à temps partiel et à l'aménagement du temps de travail.* Bilan de l'Emploi 1986, Service des Etudes et de la Statistique, Ministère des Affaires Sociales et de l'emploi, pub. Masson no. 34-35 Oct, Paris.

Blyton, P. and Turnbull, P. (eds.)(1992), *Reassessing Human Resource Management* Sage, London.

Bonin, H.(1985), 'La Banque, société de services tertiaires dans les années 1980.' in *Profile Economiques* no.18.

Bouillaguet-Bernard, P. and Gauvin, A. (1988a), 'Female labour reserves and the restructuring of employment in booms and slumps in France.' in Rubery, J. (ed.), *Women in Recession* Routledge and Kogan Paul Ltd, London.

Bouillaguet-Bernard, P. and Gauvin, A. (1988b), 'Women's employment, the state and the family in France: contradiction of state policy for women's employment.' in Rubery, J. (ed.), *Women in Recession* Routledge and Kogan Paul Ltd, London.

Boyer, R. (1990), *The Regulation School: A Critical Introduction* Columbia University Press, New York.

Boyer, R. (1987), 'Labour flexibilities: Many forms, uncertain effects.' *Labour and Society* vol.12, no. 1, January.

Boyer, R. (1986), *La flexibilité du travail en Europe* Editions La

Découverte, Paris. Translated in (1988), as *The Search for Labour Market Flexibility: The European Economies in Transition* Clarendon Press, Oxford.

Bradshaw, J., Ditch, J., Holmes, H. and Whiteford, P. (1993), *Support for Children: A comparison of arrangements in fifteen countries*, Department of Social Security, Research Report no. 21, HMSO, London.

Bradshaw, D. (1990), 'Dial M for Money' *Financial Times*, 8th March.

Bridgeford, J. (1990), 'French trade unions; crisis in the 1980's' in *Industrial Relations Journal* vol. 21 no. 2.

Brierley, D. (1991), 'Bad debts batter the banks' *Sunday Times*, 6th January.

Brizard, P. (1987), 'L'informatique au secours des banques' *Decision Informatique*, no. 132, 16 mars.

Bronstein, A.S. (1991), 'Temporary Work in Western Europe: Threat or complement to permanent employment?' *International Labour Review*, vol.130, no.3, pp.291-310.

Brown, R. (1990), 'A flexible future in Europe? : Changing patterns of employment in the United Kingdom' *British Journal of Sociology* vol. 41, no. 3, Sept.

Brown, A. and Behrens, M. (1990), *Comparative failures: Peripheral workers 'in the making' in England and Germany* Paper presented at the Work, Employment and European Society Conference, Newton Park, Bath 6-8th September.

Bruegel, I. (1979), 'Women as a reserve army of labour: a note on recent British experience' *Feminist Review* no. 3.

Brunhes, B. et al. (1989), *La flexibilité du marché du travail: Nouvelles tendances dans l'entreprise* OCDE, Paris.

Brunhes, B. (1989), 'Labour flexibility in Enterprises: A Comparison of firms in four European Countries' in *OECD Labour Market Flexibility: Trends in Enterprises* OECD, Paris.

Büchtemann, C. and Quack, S. (1989),'*Bridges' or 'Traps': Non-standard Forms of Employment in the Federal Republic of Germany. The case of part-time and temporary work.* WZB Discussion Paper, FSI 89-6, Berlin.

Büchtemann, C. and Quack, S. (1990), 'How precarious is non-standard employment?' *Cambridge Journal of Economics*, vol.14, pp.315-329.

Bue, J. and Cristofari, M-F. (1986), 'Constraintes et Rythme de travail des salaries à temps partiel.' *Travail et Emploi* no.27 mars.

Bullock, A. and Stallybrass, O. (1982), *The Fontana Dictionary of Modern Thought*, Fontana Books: London.

Burawoy, M. and Lukacs, J. (1987), 'Mythologies of Work: A Comparison of Firms in State Socialism and Advanced Captialism' *American Sociological Review*, vol.50, pp.723-37

Burawoy, M. (1979), *Manufacturing Consent*, University of Chicago Press, Chicago.

Burgard, J-J. (1988), *La Banque en France*, Presses de la Fondation Nationale des Sciences Politiques and Dalloz, Paris.

Burgess, B. (1982), *Field Research: A Sourcebook and Field Manual* George Allen Unwin, London.

Burgess, B. (ed.)(1988), *Studies in Qualitative Methodology* vol.1 JAI Press Ltd, London.

Butt Phillip, A. (1985), 'Comment' in Machin, H. and Wright, V. (eds.) *Economic Policy and Policy Making Under the Mitterrand Presidency 1981-4*, Frances Pinter, London.

Campinos-Dubernet, M., Grando, J-M., Möbus, M. and Margirier, G. (1988), *Europe et Chantiers: Le BTP en Europe: Structures Industrielles et Marche du travail*, Acts de Colloque, Ministere de l'Equipement, du Logement, des Transports et de l'Espace: Paris

Casassus, B. (1989), 'Getting Married' *The Banker*, May.

Cassasus, B. (1987), 'The Squirrel Branches Out' *The Banker*, October.

Casassus-Montero, C. (1989), 'Les différentes approches dans les comparaisons internationales du travail industriel' in *Sociologie du Travail* no.2-89.

Casey, B. (1988), *Temporary Employment: Practice and Policy in Britain* PSI, London.

Casey, B. (1987), *The Extent and Nature of Temporary Employment in Great Britain* Revised paper presented to the International Conference for the European Communities, "Transformations de l'Emploi: Nouvelles Formes, Nouveaux Domaines", Paris, Palais des Congres, 19-20th June.

Casey, B. (1991), 'Survey Evidence on Trends in 'Non-Standard' Employment' in Pollert (ed.), *Farewell to Flexibility?* Blackwells, Oxford.

Castro, A., Mehaut and Rubery, J. (1992), *International intergration and labour market organisation*, London: Academic Press.

CERC (1987), *Salaires et compléments de rémunération analyse des pratiques d'entreprises* Centre d'etude des revenues et des coûts, La Documentation Française no.87, Paris.

CEREQ (1975), *Repertoire Français de l'Emplois Cahier 2: les emplois types des banques.* Centre d'Etudes et de Recherches sur les Qualifications, Paris.

CFDT avec Faivert, J-Ph., Missika, J-L., Wolton, D. (1980), *Le Tertiaire Eclaté: Le travail sans modèle* Editions du Seuil, Paris.

Child, J. (1985), 'Managerial Strategies, New Technology, and the Labour Process' in Knights, D., Willmott, H. and Collinson, D. *Job Redesign: Critical Perspectives on the Labour Process* Gower, Aldershot.

Child J and Loveridge, R. (1990), *Information Technology in European Services: Towards a Microelectronic Future* ERSC/Basil Blackwell, Oxford.

Chouraqui, A. and Tchobanian, R. (1991), Le droit d'expression des salariés en France. Un séminaire international Institut International d'Etude Social, Genève.

CIC (1984), Enquête sur le temps partiel et le temps choisi Survey conducted by the Département du Personnel et des Affaires Sociales Crédit Industriel et Commercial de Paris, Paris; internal document.

Clarke, S. (1992) 'What in the F---'s Name is Fordism?' in Gilbert, N. et al. *Fordism and Flexibility*, Macmillan:London.

CNC (1989), *Modernisation et gestion sociale des établissements de crédit*, Rapport de mission Conseil National du Credit, Paris.

Cockburn, C. (1981), 'The Material of Male Power' *Feminist Review* no.9 October.

Collinson, D. and Knights, D. (1986), ''Men only': Theories and Practices of Job Segregation in Insurance' in Knights, D. and Willmott, H. *Gender and the Labour Process*, Gower, Aldershot

Combault, P., Peronnet, F. and Rocherieux, F. (1985), 'Temps partiel en hausse parmi les Femmes Salariées.' Bilan de l'emploi 1984, *Dossiers Statistiques du Travail et de l'emploi* no. 12-13, Sept.

Commission of European Communities (1981), *Proposal for Council Directive on voluntary Part-Time Work* Cmd (81), 7775 Brussels, 22 Dec.

Connell, R. W. (1987), *Gender and Power* Polity, Oxford.

Cooke, G. (1986), 'Technology and Clearing Banks creating New Paths' in *Manpower Policy and Practice* (IMS), Autumn.

Coope, N., Cooper, C. and Huges, R. *Banking* AGCAS 1987 Oct,

Central Service Unit.

Cornut, J. (1988), 'Réveil tardif' *Le Mois*, mai.

Cossalter, C. (1990), *Renouvellement des Qualifications et de la Gestion des Ressources Humaines dans les Banques et les Assurances*, Collection des Etudes no. 53 CEREQ, Paris

Cox, A. (ed.), (1986), *State, Finance and Industry: A Comparative Analysis of Post-War Trends in Six Advanced Industrial Economies* St. Martin's Press, New York.

Creigh, C. (1986), 'Self employment in Britain' *Employment Gazette*, June, London.

Creusat, J. and Richard, A. (1987), 'Une approche des systemes industriels régionaux le cas de l'Alsace et de la Haute-Normandie' *Economie et Statistique* no. 199-200 mai-juin.

Crompton, R., Hantrais, L. and Walters, P. (1990), 'Gender relations and employment', *The British Journal of Sociology*, vol.41, no.3, pp.329-349.

Crompton, R. (1990), *Professions and the 'Service Class'*, paper presented for the BSA Conference Social Divisions and Social Change; University of Surrey, Guilford, 2nd-5th April.

Crompton, R. and Sanderson, K. (1990), *Gendered Jobs and Social Change* Unwin Hyman, London.

Crompton, R. (1989), 'Women in Banking: Continuity and Change since the Second World War' *Work, Employment and Society* vol..3, no.2, pp.141-156.

Crompton, R. (1988), 'The feminisation of the clerical labour force since the Second World War' in Anderson, G. (ed.), *The white-blouse revolution: Female office work since 1870* Manchester University Press, Manchester and New York.

Crow, G. (1989), 'The use of the concept of 'strategy' in recent sociological literature' *Sociology* vol.23, no.1, pp. 1-24.

Crozier, M. (1963), *Le phénomène bureaucratique* Seuil, Paris

d'Arvisenet, P. (1978), 'Le Travail à temps partiel' *Droit Social* no.12 Décembre.

Dale, A. (1987), *The role of theories of labour market segmentation in understanding the position of women in the occupational structure.* Occasional Papers in Sociology and Social Policy, no. 4 University of Surrey

Dale, A. and Glover, J. (1990), *An Analysis of Women's Employment Patterns in the UK, France and the USA: The Value of Survey Based Comparisons.* Department of Employment Research Paper no. 75, DE, London.

Dale, A. and Bamford, C. (1988), 'Temporary Workers: Cause for concern or complacency?' *Work, Employment and Society*, vol.2, no.2, pp.191-209.

Dale, A. and Glover, J. (1987), 'Women's Work Patterns in the UK, France and the USA' in *Social Studies Review* vol.3 no.1.

Dale, A. and Glover, J. (1989), 'Women at Work in Europe: The potential and pitfalls of using published statistics.' in *Employment Gazette* June.

Daniel, W.W. (1987), *Workplace Industrial Relations and Technical Change* PSI, ESRC, ACAS, London.

Daune-Richard, A-M. (1993), 'Activité et emploi des femmes: des constructions sociétales différentes en France, au Royaume-Uni et en Suède', *Sociétés Contemporaines*, 3.

Davies, D. and Shackleton, V. (1982), *Psychology and Work* Menthuen and Co., London, first published 1975.

Dayan, J-L. (1987), 'Assouplir la législation pour créer des emplois?' in Meurs, D. (ed.), *La Flexibilité du Travail, Les Cahiers Français* no.231 mai-juin, Paris.

de Quillacq, L.M. (1987), 'Restructuring of French Banks' *Retail Banker*, 26th January.

De la Mothe, J.R. (1986), 'Financial Services' in Smith, de la Mothe and Brodie *Technological Trends and Employment 5, Commerical Services Industries*. Gower, Aldershot.

De Neubourg, C. (1985), 'Part-time work: an International Quantitative Comparison' *International Labour Review*, vol.124, no.5, pp.559-576.

Deakin, S. (1992), *Atypical Workers and the European Charter* paper given to the seminar series 'Current Developments in Labour Law and Labour Relations' Nuffield College, Oxford, 28th February.

Delarue, J-M. (1987), 'Temps partiel, intérim, contrats à durée déterminée: la progression du travail atypique.' *Regards sur l'actualité* no. 129, Mars.

Desplanques, G. (1985), 'Modes de garde et scolarisation des jeunes enfants' *Ecomomie et Statistiques* no.176 April, INSEE Paris.

Desplanques, G. and de Saboulin, M. (1986), 'Activité féminine carrières continues et discontinues.' *Economie et Statistique*, Dec., pp.51-62, INSEE, Paris.

Dex, S., Walters, P. and Alden, D.M., (1993), *French and British Mothers at Work* Macmillan, Basingstoke.

Dex, S. and Walters, P. (1989), 'Women's Occupational Status in

Britain, France and the USA: Explaining the Difference' *Industrial Relations Journal* vol.20, no.3, Autumn pp.203-212.

Dex, S. (1988a), 'Gender and the Labour Market' in Gallie, D. (ed.),. *Employment in Britain* Basil Blackwell, Oxford.

Dex, S. (1988), *Women's Attitudes Towards Work* Macmillan Press, London.

Dex, S. (1987), *Women's Occupational Mobility: A Lifetime Perspective* Macmillan Press, London.

Dex, S. (1985), *The Sexual Division of Work: Conceptual Revolutions in the Social Sciences* Wheatsheaf Books, Sussex.

Dickens, L. (1992) *Whose Flexibility? Discrimination and equality in atypical work* Institute of Employment Rights, London.

d'Iribarne, P. (1991), 'Culture et effet sociétal' *Revue Française de Sociologie*, vol.32, pp.599-614.

Disney, R. and Szyszczak, E. (1984), 'Protective Legislation and part-time employment in Britain' *British Journal of Industrial Relations*, vol xxii no.1 pp.78-100.

Dixon, H. (1987a), 'Midland races ahead in radical thinking' *Financial Times*, 8th January.

Dixon, H. (1987b), 'Penetrating the market segments' *Financial Times*, 21st September.

Doeringer, P. and Piore, M. (1971), *Internal Labor Market and Manpower Analysis* Heath Lexington Books, Massachusetts.

Dohrn, S. (1988), 'Pioneers in a dead-end profession: the first women clerks in banks and insurance companies' in Anderson, G. (ed.), *The white-blouse revolution: Female office workers since 1870* Manchester University Press, Manchester and New York.

Dore, R. (1973), *British Factory - Japanese Factory. The Origins of National Diversity in Industrial Relations* Allen and Unwin, London.

Doyle, B. (1986), 'Legal Regulation of Collective Bargaining' in Lewis, R. (ed.), *Labour Law in Britain* Blackwells, Oxford.

Dufloux, C. (1989), 'La déréglementation bancaire est-elle toujours d'actualité?' *Revue Politique et Parlementaire* 91e, no. 934, sept-oct.

Dupeyroux, J-J. (1985), *Droit de la Sécurité Sociale* Dixième édition, Précis Dalloz, Paris.

Durand-Prinborgne, C. (1991), 'L'enseignement préscolaire: la maternelle' *Le système éducatif, Les Cahiers Français*, La Documentation Française, Paris.

Easterday, L., Papademas, D., Schorr, L. and Valentine, C. (1982), 'The Making of a Female Researcher: Role problems in Fieldwork', in Burgess, B. (ed.), *Field Research: A Sourcebook and Field Manual* George Allen Unwin, London.

Economist Publications (1989), *European Financial Centres: no.1 France* Special Report no.1176 June, Sponsored by Samuel Montagu and Co. Ltd. London.

Edwards, R. (1979), *Contested Terrain: The Transformation of the Workplace in the Twentieth Century* Heinemann, London.

Edwards, R. and Ribbens, J. (1991), 'Meanderings Around Strategy; A Research Note on Strategic Discourse in the Lives of Women' *Sociology*, vol.25, no.3 August, pp.477-489.

EIRR (1993) 'A decade of the "Auroux" laws', *European Industrial Relations Review*, issue 233, June, pp.30-32.

EIRR (1991), 'Banking unions face the Single European Market' *European Industrial Relations Review*, no.205, February.

Elbaum, M. (1987), 'L'attitude des entreprises françaises.' *Economie et Statistique*, no. 197, mars.

Elger, T. and Fairbrother, P. (1990), *Inflexible Flexibility: case study evidence and theoretical considerations* Paper presented to the BSA Conference Social Divisions and Social Change; University of Surrey, Guilford, 2nd-5th April.

Elias, P. and Main, B. (1982), *Women's working lives: Evidence from the National Training Survey* University of Warwick Institute for Employment Research, Research Report.

Employment Gazette (1991), '1990 Labour Force Survey preliminary results' *Employment Gazette* April, pp.175-195.

EUROSTAT (1989), *Labour Force Survey Results* 3C Statistical Office of the European Community, Luxembourg.

Euvard, F. (1982), *L'indemnisation du chômage en France et à l'étranger* Document du CERC no.62.

Fabra, P. (1985), 'Banking Policy under the Socialists' in Machin, H. and Wright, V. (eds.) *Economic Policy and Policy Making Under the Mitterrand Presidency 1981-4* Frances Pinter, London.

Felstead, A. and Green, F. (1993), *Cycles of Training? Evidence from the British Recession of the Early 1990's* Discussion Papers in Economics, Faculty of Social Sciences Department of Economics, University of Leicester.

Ferguson, M. (1989), 'Male Perceptions of the division of family and employment roles in France and Britain' in Hantrais, L. (ed.), *Franco-British Comparisons of Family and*

Employment Careers Cross-National Research Papers, Special Issue, Aston, Birmingham.

Finegold, D. and Soskice, D. (1988), 'The Failure of Training in Britain' *Oxford Review of Economic Policy*, vol.4, no. 3, pp.21-53.

Frazer, P. and Vittas, D. (1982), *The Retail Banking Revolution an International Perspective* Michael Cafferty Publications, London.

Gallie, D. and White, M. (1991), *Employers Policies, Employee Contracts and Labour Market Structure*, Paper presented at the 2nd Nuffield/PSI Conference, 11th January, Nuffield College, Oxford.

Gallie, D. (1985), 'Les lois Auroux: the reform of French Industrial Relations?' in Machin, H. and Wright, V. (eds.) *Economic Policy and Policy Making Under the Mitterrand Presidency 1981-4* Frances Pinter, London.

Gallie, D. (1991), 'Patterns of Skill Change: Upskilling, Deskilling or the Polarisation of Skills?' *Work, Employment and Society* vol.5, no.3, pp.319-351.

Gallie, D. (1988), *Employment in Britain* Blackwells, Oxford: Blackwells.

Gallie, D. (1983), *Social Inequality and Class Radicalism in France and Britain.* Cambridge University Press, Cambridge.

Gallie, D. (1978), *In Search of the New Working Class: Automation and social integration within the capitalist enterprise* Cambridge University Press, Cambridge.

Gandillot, T. (1988), 'Votre banquier vous vole-t-il?' *Le Nouvel Observateur*, 30 septembre-6 octobre.

Gapper, J. (1991), 'Cold Comfort in the high street' *Financial Times*, 22nd February.

Gapper, J. (1987), 'Employers break ranks' *Financial Times*, 21st September.

Garnsey, E. (1984), *The Provision and Quality of Part-time Work: The Case of Great Britain and France.* A preliminary study carried out for the Director-General of Employment, Social Affairs and Education of the Commission of European Communities.

Garrahan, P. and Stewart, P. (1992), *The Nissan Enigma: Flexibility at Work in a Local Economy* Mansell, London

Gaspard, M., Loos, J. and Welcomme, D. (1985), 'Aménagement et réduction du temps de travail: Comparaisons internationales, expérience d'entreprises' *Travail et Emploi* no. 23 Mars.

Gazier, B. (1987), 'Bilan des politiques d'emploi menées en France 1973-1985' in Meurs, D. (ed.), *La Flexibilité du Travail, Les Cahiers Français* no.231 mai-juin, Paris.

Geledan, A. (1978), *Les Syndicats* Hatier, Paris.

Gershuny, J. (1983), *Social Innovation and the Divison of Labour* Oxford University Press, Oxford.

Gilbert, N., Burrows, R. and Pollert, A. (1992), *Fordism and Flexibility* Macmillan, London

Glover, E. (1985), 'Professional Education for Bankers' in Livy (ed.), *Management and People in Banking* 2nd Edition, The Institute of Bankers, London.

Glover, J. (1990), *Horizontal and vertical occupational segregation: part-time and full-time working amongst women in Britain and France.* Paper presented to the British Sociological Association Annual conference "Social Divisions and Social Change" 2-5th April, University of Surrey, Guilford.

Godet, M. and Plas, J-P. (1979), *Le Monde* 22 fév.

Gordon, D. M., Edwards, R. and Reich, M. (1982), *Segmented Work, Divided Workers: The historical transformation of labor in the United States* Cambridge University Press, Cambridge.

Graham, G. (1988), 'Stagnation on the plateau' *Financial Times*, 18th May.

Granovetter, M. and Swedberg, R. (eds.) (1992) *The Sociology of Economic Life,* San Fransico: West Press.

Granovetter, M. (1985), 'Economic Action and Social Structure: The Problem of Embeddedness' in *The American Journal of Sociology* vol.91, no.3, pp.481-510.

Granovetter, M. (1984), 'Small is bountiful: Labour markets and establishment size' *American Sociological Review,* vol. 49, no.2, pp.323-334.

Green, D. (1986), 'The State, Finance and Industry of France' in Cox, A. (ed.), *State, Finance and Industry: A Comparative Analysis of Post-War Trends in Six Advanced Industrial Economies,* St. Martin's Press, New York.

Gregory, A. (1991), 'Patterns of Working hours in Large-Scale Grocery Retailing in Britain and France: Convergence after 1992?' Work, Employment and Society, vol.5 no.4, pp.497-514.

Gregory, A. (1989), *A Franco-British comparison of the patterns of working hours in large-scale grocery retailing, with specific reference to part-time work* Ph.D thesis, Aston University,

September.

Gregory, A. (1987), 'Le Travail à temps partiel en France et en Grande-Bretagne: temps imposé ou temps choisi?' *Revue Française des Affaires Sociales*, no. 3.

Gregory, A. (1987a), *Flexibility for Whom? Part-Time Work in Food Retailing in Britain and France* Paper presented to the WYCROW Conference, September.

Gregory, D. (1985), 'Flexible Manning - Curse or Challenge for Trade Unions?' *Manpower Policy and Practice*, IMS Brighton, Summer.

Grimshaw, A. (1973), 'Comparative Sociology: In What Ways Different from Other Sociologies?' in Armer, M. and Grimshaw, A. (eds.) *Comparative Social Research* John Wiley, New York.

Guelsin, A. (1988), 'Les Salariés du Crédit Agricole' *Economie et Finances Agricoles* no. 234, Juillet-Août.

Guillemot, J. (1983), 'Le Travail à Temps Partiel' *Droit Ouvrier* juin.

Hague, H. (1987), 'Banking union to ballot staff on further disruption' *The Independent*, 10th August.

Hakim, C. (1991), 'Grateful Slaves and self-made women: fact and fantasy in women's work orientations' *European Sociological Review* , vol.7, no.2, pp.101-122.

Hakim, C. (1991), 'Cross-national Research Using the European Community Labour Force Surveys' in *Work, Employment and Society*, vol. 5 no. 1, pp. 101-117.

Hakim, C. (1988), 'Women at Work: Recent research on Women's Employment' *Work, Employment and Society*, vol.2 no.1.

Hakim, C. (1987), 'Trends in the Flexible Workforce' *Employment Gazette* vol. 95, no.11 November.

Hakim, C. (1985), *Employers use of Outwork* Department of Employment Research Paper no. 44.

Hakim, C. (1982), *Homeworking in Wages Council Industries* Department of Employment Research Paper no.37, DE, London.

Hall, P. (1986), *Governing the Economy: The Politics of State Intervention in Britain and France* Polity Press, Cambridge.

Hanson, D.G. (1982), *Service Banking, The Arrival of the All-Purpose Bank* The Institute of Bankers, London.

Hantrais, L. (1990), *Managing Professional and Family Life: A Comparative Study of British and French Mothers* Dartmouth, Aldershot/Vermont.

Hantrais, L. (1989), *Franco-British Comparisons of Family and Employment Careers* Cross-National Research Papers, Special Issue, Aston, Birmingham.

Hantrais, L. (1985), 'Leisure Lifestyles and the Synchronisation of Family Schedules: A Franco-British Comparative Perspective' *World Leisure and Recreation,* April, pp.18-24.

Hantrais, L. (1982), *Contemporary French Society* Contemporary Language Studies, Macmillan Press, London.

Haribson, F.H., Kochling, E., Cassell, F.H. and Ruebmann, H.C. (1955), 'Steel Management in Two Continents', *Management Science,* vol.2, pp.31-9.

Hayward, J. (1986), *The State and Market Economy: Industrial Patriotism and Economic Intervention in France* Wheatsheaf Books, Harvester Press, Brighton.

Henniquau, L. (1984), *Protection sociale et fiscalité: une législation sexiste!* Cahier no.8 du Club Flora Tristan, March.

Henriet, B., Harff, Y. and Bourdonnais, J. (1985), *Les Comités d'entreprise moyens d'action et intervention économiques* (C.R.E.S.S.T), Centre de recherche en Sciences Sociales du Travail, Paris.

Hepple, B. and Fredman, S. (1986), *Labour Law and Industrial Relations in Great Britain* Kluwer Law and Taxation Publishers, The Netherlands

Hickson, D.J., McMillan, C.J., Azumi, K. and Horvath, D. (1979), 'Grounds for Comparative Organisation Theory: Quicksands or Hard Core?' in Lammers, C.J. and Hickson, D.J. (eds.) *Organisations Alike and Unlike* Routledge and Kegan Paul, London

Hickson, D.J., Hinings, C.R., McMillan, C.J. and Schwitter, J.P. (1974), 'The Culture-Free Context of Organisation Structure: A Tri-National Comparison', *Sociology,* vol.8, pp.59-80.

Hill, R. (1973), 'In Retrospect: A brief analysis of the confessions of comparativists' in Armer, M. and Grimshaw, A. (eds.) *Comparative Social Research* John Wiley, New York

HMSO (1991), *Social Trends 21,* HMSO, London

HMSO (1991a), *Health and Personal Social Services Statistics for England 1991 edition* Department of Health, Government Statistical Service, London.

Hodson, R. and Kaufman, R. (1982), 'Economic Dualism: A Critical Review' *American Sociological Review,* vol. 47, December, pp.727-739.

Hofstede, G. (1980), *Culture's Consequences. International Differences in Work-Related Values* Sage, London

Hofstede, G. (1980a), 'Motivation, Leadership and Organisation: Do American Theories Apply Abroad?' in Pugh, D.S. (ed.), *Organisation Theory* (3rd Edition, 1990), Penguin Business, Harmondsworth

Hofstede, G. (1979), 'Hierarchical Power Distance in Forty Countries' in Lammers, C.J. and Hickson, D.J. (eds.) *Organisations Alike and Unlike: International and inter-institutional studies in the sociology of organisations* Routledge and Kegan Paul, London

Hoinville, G., Jowell, R. and Associates (1978), *Survey Research Practice* Heinemann Educational Books, London.

Horrell, S. and Rubery, J. (1991), 'Gender and working time: an analysis of employers' working-time policies' *Cambridge Journal of Economics*, vol.15, pp.373-391.

Hu, Y-S. (1975), *National Attitudes and the Financing of Industry* PEP vol. XLI Broadsheet no.559, London.

Huet, M. (1984), 'L'impact des politiques d'emploi menée depuis 1981 sur la situation socio-professionnelle des femmes.' *Travail et Emploi* Sept no. 21.

Hunter, L. McGregor, MacInnes, J. and Sproull, A. (1993), 'The 'Flexible Firm': Strategy and Segmentation' *British Journal of Industrial Relations* vol.31, no.3, pp.383-407.

Hunter, L. and MacInnes, J. (1992), 'Employers and Labour Flexibility: The evidence from case studies' *Employment Gazette*, June pp.307-315.

Hurstfield, J. (1988), 'Parenthood and part-time work: the Swedish approach' *Poverty* 68 pp.12-14.

Hurstfield J (1978), *The Part-time Trap* Low Pay Unit pamphlet no.9.

Huws, U. (1984), *The New Homeworkers: New Technology and the changing location of white collar work* Low Pay Unit no. 28.

Hyman, R. (1990), *European Unions: Towards 2000* Paper presented at the Work, Employment and European Society Conference, Newton Park, Bath 6-8th September.

IDS Study (1986), *Private Sector Part-timers* Study 374 Nov. Incomes Data Service.

ILO/ Thurman, J. and Trah, G. (1989), *Conditions of Work Digest: Part-time Work*, vol.8, no.1, ILO, Geneva.

Industrial Relations Review and Reports (1989), *Bridging the Career Break* no.431, 10th Jan, IRRR.

INSEE (1991), *Annuaire Statistiques de la France 1991* INSEE, Paris

INSEE (1985), *Le Travail temporaire en 1983: Enquête annuelle d'entreprise dans les services resultats detailles* Sept, Archives et Documents l'INSEE no.135.

INSEE (1989), *L'Enquête sur l'Emploi,* INSEE, Paris

Izarelewicz, E. (1988), 'Une priorité: la rentabilité' *Le Monde,* 12 mars.

Jacquier, J-P. (1986), *Les cow-boys ne meurent jamais: l'aventure syndicale continue* Syros, Paris.

Jallade, J-P. (1984), *Towards a Policy for Part-time Employment* European Centre for Work and Society, Maastricht.

Jenson, J. (1989), 'The talents of women, the skills of men: flexible specialisation and women' in Wood, S. (ed.), *The Transformation of Work?* Unwin Hyman, London.

Jenson, J., Hagen, E. and Reddy, C. (1988), *Feminization of the Labour Force: Paradoxes and Promises* Polity, Cambridge.

Jenson, J. (1988), 'The Limits of 'and the' Discourse: French women as Marginal Workers' in Jenson, J. et al. *Feminization of the Labour Force: Paradoxes and Promises* Polity, Cambridge.

Johnson, C. (1988), 'The Revolution in UK Banking' *Lloyds Bank Economic Bulletin,* no. 119, Nov.

Jones, D. (1987), 'The Last Wave?' *The Banker,* September.

Kenrick, J. (1981), 'The Politics and Construction of Women as second class workers' in Wilkinson F (ed.), *The Dynamics of labour market segmentation* Academic Press, London.

Kerfoot, D. and Knights, D. (1991), *Management, Masculinity, and Corporate Strategy: An Illustration from Contemporary Financial Services in Britain* paper presented to the 10th EGOS Colloquium `Societal Change between Market and Organisation' Vienna 15-17th July.

Kergoat, D. (1984), 'Les Femmes et le Travail à Temps Partiel: Une relation multiforme et complexe au temps travaillé.' *Travail et Emploi* Sept no. 21.

Kerr, C. (1983), *The Future of Industrial Societies: Convergence or Continuing Diversity?* Harvard University Press, Cambridge, Mass.

Kerr, C., Dunlop, J.T., Harbison, F.H. and Myers, C.A. (1960), *Industrialism and Industrial Man: The Problems of Labor and Management in Economic Growth* Heinemann, London

Khun, S. (1989), 'The limits to industrialisation: Computer software development in a large commercial bank' in

Woods, S. (ed.), *The Transformation of Work?* Unwin, Hyman.

King, S. (1988), 'Temporary Workers in Britain: Findings from the 1986 Labour Force Survey.' *Employment Gazette*, April, pp.238-247.

Knights, D. and Morgan, G. (1990a), 'Management Control of the Sales Force: A case study from the Labour Process of Life Insurance' *Work, Employment and Society* vol.4, no.3, September, pp.369-390.

Knights, D. and Morgan, G. (1990b), 'The concept of Strategy in Sociology: A Note of Dissent' *Sociology* vol.24, no.3, August, pp.475-483.

Knights, D. and Murray, F. (1990), *Information Technology and the Marketing-Driven Firm: Problems and Prospects* PICT Policy Research Papers, January, ESRC.

Knights, D., Morgan, G. and Murray, F. (1991), *Financial Systems, Consumers and the Production of Social Order* Paper presented for EGOS Colloquium Group 10 'Business Recipes' Vienna 15-17th July.

Knights, D. and Willmot, H. (1986), *Gender and the Labour Process* Gower, Aldershot.

Knights, D., Willmot, H. and Collinson, D. (1985), *Job Redesign: Critical Perspectives on the Labour Process* Gower, Aldershot.

Kohn, L. M. (ed.)(1989), *Cross-National Research in Sociology* Sage, London

Kumazawa, M. and Yamada, J. (1989), 'Jobs and skills under the lifelong nenkô employment practice' in Wood S (ed.), *The Transformation of Work?* Unwin Hyman, London.

Banque des Reglements Internationaux - La Banque de France (1985), (1986), and (1989), *Systèmes de Paiement dans Onze Pays Développés* La Documentation Française, Paris.

Labour Research and Review 15 *Privatisation and Contracting Out* Mid West Center for Labor Research, Chicago, Illinois, Spring, vol.IX, no.1.

Labourie-Racape, A., Grozelier, A-M., Chalude, M., De Jong, A., Povell, M. and Seear, N. (1982), 'L'emploi féminin dans le secteur bancaire: l'exemple de quatre banques Belgique, France, Pays-Bas et Royaume-Uni' in *Banque* no. 416 avril.

Lallem, M. (1987), 'Le Travail à domicile.' *Regards sur l'actualité* no. 129, Mars.

Lammers, C.J. and Hickson, D.J. (eds.)(1979), *Organisations Alike and Unlike: International and inter-institutional studies in the sociology of organisations* Routledge and Kegan Paul, London

Lane, C. (1993), Gender and the Labour Market in Europe: Britain, Germany and France compared *The Sociological Review* vol.41, no.2 pp.274-301.

Lane, C. (1990), *Industrial Re-organisation in Europe: Patterns of Convergence and Divergence in Germany, France and Britain* Paper presented at the Work, Employment and European Society Conference, Newton Park, Bath 6-8th September.

Lane, C. (1989), 'Management and Labour in Europe: The Industrial Enterprise in Germany, Britain and France' Edward Elgar Publishing, Hants.

Lane, C. (1988), 'Industrial Re-organisation in Europe: The pursuit of flexible specialisation in Britain and West Germany.' *Work, Employment and Society* vol.2, no.2, pp.141-168.

Lane, C. (1987), 'Capitalism or Culture? A Comparative Analysis of the Position in the Labour Process and Labour Market of Lower White-Collar Workers in the Financial Services Sector of Britain and the Federal Republic of Germany' *Work, Employment and Society* vol.1, no.1, pp.57-84.

Languepin, O. (1988), 'Des ordinateurs derrière les guichets' *Le Monde*, 10 mai.

Lascelles, D. (1989), 'Golden era is withdrawn from the banks' *Financial Times*, 6th March.

Lascelles, D. (1988), 'Less like a father-figure', UK Banking Survey, *Financial Times*, 26th September.

Lascelles, D. (1990), 'Banking battles swings to the home front' *Financial Times*, 6th March.

Lasfargues, R. (1980), 'La compensation départementale des chèques: nouveau régime applicable à partir du 1er octobre 1980' in *Banque* no.399, Oct., pp.1103-1106

Laurie, S. (1989a), 'Decision Time' *The Banker*, Jan.

Laurie, S. (1989b), 'Questions of Strategy' *The Banker*, September.

Lawrence, P.R. and Lorsch, J.W. (1967), *Organisation and Environment* Harvard University Press, Cambridge, Mass.

Legge, K. (1988), 'Personnel Management in recession and recovery: a comparative analysis of what the surveys say' *Personnel Review* vol.17, no.2.

Lehmann, A. (1985), 'Le Travail à temps partiel de 1978 à 1983: Pratiques des employeurs et conditions d'emploi des salariés.' *Travail et Emploi* no. 26 Déc.

Letablier, M-T. (1986), 'Les Dynamiques de diffusion du travail à temps partiel aux Etats-Unis et en France' *Travail et Emploi* no.26, December.

Lewis, R. (ed.)(1986), *Labour Law in Britain*, Basil Blackwells, Oxford.

Lewis, V. (1987), 'French banks face further reforms' *The Banker*, May.

Liasons Sociales Mensuel (1990), *Tour de vis sur l'intérim* pp.53-72, Liaisons Sociales, no.50, 13th juin, Paris.

Liasons Sociales (1990a), 'Les Régimes Sociaux des Etats Membres' *Liaisons Sociales* no. 10775, 30th août, Paris.

Liasons Sociales (1990b), 'Travail précaire et à temps partiel' *Legislation Sociale* no. 5229, Paris.

Liasons Sociales (1989), 'Droit aux prestations familiales' *Liaisons Sociales* 30 mars, Paris.

Liasons Sociales (1989a), 'Le Statut juridique des syndicats' *Liaisons Sociales* 2 fév, Paris.

Liasons Sociales (1988), 'Le travail à temps partiel et le travail intermittant' *Liaisons Sociales* 3 déc, Paris.

Liasons Sociales (1988a), 'La Durée du Travail' *Liaisons Sociales* 7 avril, Paris.

Liasons Sociales (1988b), 'Les seuils d'effectif en droit social' *Liaisons Sociales* 3 mars, Paris.

Liasons Sociales (1987), 'Travail à durée déterminée, Travail temporaire' *Liaisons Sociales* 4 juin, Paris.

Liasons Sociales (1987a), 'Syndicats II' *Liaisons Sociales* 15 oct, Paris.

Liasons Sociales (1986), 'Travail différencié, Contrat à durée déterminée, travail temporaire, temps partiel' *Legislation Sociale* no. 5839 du 20 août, Liaisons Sociales, Paris.

Liasons Sociales (1985), *Le Contrat de Travail* Numéro spécial diffusé dans le cadre de l'abonnement aux liaisons sociales. Dec no. 9632. Paris.

Littler, C. (1985), 'Taylorism, Fordism and Job Design' in Knights, D., Willmott, H. and Collinson, D. (1985), *Job Redesign: Critical Perspectives on the Labour Process* Gower, Aldershot.

Livy, B.L. (ed.)(1985), *Management and People in Banking* 2nd Edition, The Institute of Bankers, London.

Lockwood, D. (1989), *The Blackcoated Worker: A Study in Class Consciousness 2nd Edition* Clarendon Press, Oxford. (First published in 1958 by George Allen and Unwin),

Loetsch, M. (1982), 'How to Achieve Comparability' in Nießen, M. and Peschar, J. *International Comparative Research* Pergamon Press, Oxford

Lolliver, S. (1984), 'Revenu offert, prétentions salariales et activitié des femmes mariée un modèle d'analyse' *Ecomomie et Statistiques* no. 167 june.

Loveridge, R. and Mok, A.L. (1979) *Theories of Labour Market Segmentation: A Critique*, Martinus Nijhoff Social Sciences Division: The Hague.

Lui, T.L. (1990), *The Social Organisation of Outwork: The Case of Hong Kong* A Thesis presented for the Degree of Doctor of Philosophy at the University of Oxford.

Machin, H. and Wright, V. (eds.) (1985), *Economic Policy and Policy Making Under the Mitterrand Presidency 1981-4* Frances Pinter, London.

MacInnes, J. and Hunter, L. (1991), *ELUS Case Studies: Segmentation and Strategy* Paper presented to the Department of Employment 26th April, London.

MacInnes, J. (1988), 'New technology in Scotbank: Gender, Class and Work.' in Hyman, R. and Streeck, W. (eds.), *New Technology and Industrial Relations* Blackwells, Oxford.

MacInnes, J. (1987), *The Question of Flexibility* Research Paper no.5, Department of Social and Economic Research University of Glasgow.

Maier, F. (1991), *The Regulation of Part-time work: A Comparative Study of Six EC-Countries* Discussion paper FS I 91-9, WZB, Berlin.

Manpower Policy and Practice (1987), 'School Leavers: Here Today, Gone Tomorrow?' *Manpower Policy and Practice*, Autumn, IMS, Brighton.

Manwaring, T. (1984), 'The extended internal labour market' *Cambridge Journal of Economics*, vol.8, pp.161-187.

Marsh, D. (1985), 'Winds of Change: French Banking and Finance' *The Banker*, April.

Martin, J. and Roberts, C. (1984), *Women and Employment Survey: A Lifetime Perspective* HMSO.

Maruani, M. and Nicole, C. (1989), *Au labeur des dames: Métiers masculins, emplois féminins*, Syros Alternatives, Paris.

Maruani, M. and Nicole, C. (1988a), *La Flexibilité dans le Commerce: Temps de travail ou mode d'emploi?* Paper presented to the Colloque International sur les formes d'Emploi, Paris 3-4 Nov 1988.

Maruani, M and Nicole, C (1988b), *Au carrefour de la flexibilité, conditions d'emploi et politiques de gestion de la main-d'oeuvre dans le commerce* Rapport AIRESSE/CNAM june.

Maurice, M., Sellier, F. and Silvestre, J-J. (1992), 'Analyse sociétal et cultures nationales: Réponse à Philippe d'Iribarne' *Revue Française de Sociologie*, vol.33, pp.75-86.

Maurice, M. (1990), *Convergence and/or Societal effect for the Europe of the future?* Paper presented at the Work, Employment and European Society Conference, Newton Park, Bath 6-8th September.

Maurice, M. (1989), 'Méthode comparative et analyse sociétale: Les implications théoriques des comparisons internationales' *Sociologie du Travail*, no.2.

Maurice, M., Sellier, F. and Silvestre, J-J. (1984), 'The Search for a Societal Effect in the Production of Company Hierarchy: A Comparison of France and Germany' in Osterman, P. (ed.) *Internal Labour Markets*, The MIT Press, Massachusetts.

Maurice, M., Sellier, F. and Silvestre, J-J. (1982), *Politique d'éducation et organisation industrielle en France et en Allemagne*, Presses Universitaires de France, Paris. Translated in (1986), as *The Social Foundations of Industrial power: A Comparison of France and Germany*, The MIT Press, Massachusetts.

McDougall, R. (1987), 'Balzac's Kitchen' *The Banker*, July.

McMillan, C.J., Hickson, D.J., Hinings, C.R. and Schneck, R.E. (1973), 'The Structure of Work Organizations across Societies' *Academy of Managment Journal*, vol. 16, pp.555-69.

Meade-King (1987), 'Wouldn't you like to go to work like this?' *Sunday Times* October 1987.

Meager, N. (1993), *Self Employment and Labour Market Policy in the European Community* Discussion paper, FS I 93-201, WZB, Berlin.

Meager, N. (1986), 'Temporary Work in Britain' *Employment Gazette* January vol.94, no.1, pp.7-15.

Meurs, D. (ed.)(1987), *La Flexibilité du Travail, Les Cahiers Français* no.231 mai-juin, Paris.

Michon, F. (1987) 'Segmentation, Employment Structures and Productive Structures', in Tarling, R. *Flexibility in the Labour Markets*, London: Academic Press.

Michon, F. (1981), 'Dualism and the French Labour Market: Business Strategy, Non-Standard Job Forms and Secondary Jobs' in Wilkinson, F. (ed.), *The Dynamics of* labour market segmentation, Academic Press, London.

Miller, D. C. (1967), *Handbook of Research Design and Social Measurement* McKay Social Science Series, New York.

Millward, N. and Stevens, M. (1986), *British Workplace Industrial Relations 1980-84* Gower, Aldershot.

Ministere des affaires sociales et de l'emploi (1987), 'Aménagement du temps de travail, travail en équipes en 1984.' *Dossiers statistiques du travail et de l'emploi.* no. 36 Octobre.

MISEP (1993), 'Employment in Europe' *Employment Observatory Policies,* 42 Summer.

Mitter, S. (1986), 'Industrial Restructuring and Manufacturing Homework: immigrant women in thc UK clothing industry' *Capital and Class,* Winter pp.37-80.

Möbus, M. (1990), *Les politiques actuelles de recrutement et de promotion: concurrence entre fillères de formation générale, place des femmes et importance accrue de la formation continue, secteur financier en RFA* Paper presented at "La journée 'Banque'" 1st December, Laboratoire d'Economie Sociale, Université de Paris I - Pantheon-Sorbonne.

Moorhouse, H. F. (1989), 'No Mean City? The Financial Sector and the Decline of Manufacturing in Britain' Review article in *Work, Employment and Society,* vol.3 no.1, pp.105-118.

Morgan, G. (1990), *Organisations in Society* Macmillan, London.

Morgan, G. and Knights, D. (1991), 'Gendering Jobs: Corporate Strategies, Managerial Control and Dynamics of Job Segregation' in *Work, Employment and Society,* vol.5, no.2, pp.181-200.

Morgan, D. (1989), 'Strategies and Sociologists: A Comment on Crow' *Sociology* vol.23, no.1, pp.25-30.

Morris, T. (1986), *Innovations in Banking: Business Strategies and Employee Relations* Croom Helm.

Morris, L. (1990), *The Workings of the Household: A US-UK Comparison* Polity, Oxford.

Morton, L. (1987), *A Part-Time Predicament* West Midlands Low Pay Unit.

Mosley, H. and Kruppe, T. (1993), *Employment Protection and Labor Force Adjustment: A Comparative Evaluation* WZB Discussion paper FS I 92-9, WZB, Berlin.

Moss, P.(1990), *Childcare in the European Community 1985-1990* Commission of the European Communities `Women of Europe Supplements, no.31', Brussels, August.

Mouriaux, R. (1982), *La CGT* Editions du Seuil, Paris.

Moussy, J-P. (1989), 'L'emploi au coeur de la mutation bancaire' *Banque et Emploi, Revue d'Economie Financière* no.7

Mumford, K. (1989), *Women Working: Economics and Reality* Unwin Hyman, Australia.

Murphy, P. (1989), 'Hello, Mister Chips' *The Banker*, May.

Murray, F. (1983), 'The Decentralisation of Production - the decline of the mass-collective worker?' *Capital and Class*, no.19, Spring.

Murray, R. (1985), 'Benetton Britain: The New Economic Order' *Marxism Today*, London.

Myrdal, G. (1973), 'The Beam in Our Eyes' in Warwick and Osherson *Comparative Research Methods* Prentice-Hall, Englewood Cliffs, N.J.

Nicole, C. (1984), 'Les femmes et le travail à temps partiel: tentations et perversions.' *Revue Française des Affaires Sociales* Oct-Déc.

Nicole, C. (1989), 'Conceptual equivalence: female strategies, trajectories and part-time work' in Hantrais L (ed.), *Franco-British Comparisons of Family and Employment Careers* Cross-National Research Papers, Special Issue, Aston, Birmingham.

Niessen, M. (1982), 'Qualitative Aspects in Cross-National Comparative Research and the Problem of Functional Equivalence' in Nießen, M. and Peschar, J. *International Comparative Research* Pergamon Press, Oxford.

Niessen, M. and Peschar, J. (eds.)(1982), *International Comparative Research: Problems of Theory, Methodology and Organisation in Eastern and Western Europe* Pergamon Press, Oxford.

Nishida, J. M. and Redding, S. G. (1992),'Firm Develpoment and Diversification Strategies as Products of Economic Cultures: The Japanese and Hong Kong Textile Industry', in Whitley, R. (ed.) *European Business Systems*, Sage, London.

Nishiguchi, T. (1989), *Strategic Dualism: An Alternative in Industrial Societies* D.Phil, Social Studies Faculty, Oxford University.

Noblecourt, M. (1989), 'Une exigence de qualification' *Le Monde*, 11 juillet.

Noblecourt, M. (1990), *Les Syndicats en Questions*, Collection Portes Ouvertes, Les Editions Ouvrières, Paris.

Nolan, P. (1983), 'The Firm and Labour Market Behaviour' in G.S. Bain (ed.), *Industrial Relations in Britain* Basil Blackwell, Oxford.

Nolan, P. and Edwards, P.K. (1984), 'Homogenise, divide and rule: an essay on Segmented Work, Divided Workers' in *Cambridge Journal of Economics*, vol.8, pp.197-215.

Nowak, S. (1989), 'Comparative Studies and Social Theory' in Kohn, L.M.(ed.) *Cross-National Research in Sociology* Sage, London

O'Reilly, J. (1994) "What flexibility do women offer? Comparing the use of, and attitudes to, part-time work in Britain and France in Retail banking" *Gender, Work and Organisation*, vol.1, no.3, pp.138-150.

O'Reilly, J. (1994a) *Part-time work and Employment Regulation: Britain and France in the context of Europe* Wissenschaftszentrum Berlin, Discussion Paper Series (forthcoming).

O'Reilly, J. (1992), *Banking on Flexibility: A Comparison of Employers' Flexible Labour Strategies in the Retail Banking Sector in Britain and France* D.Phil Thesis, Nuffield College, Social Studies Faculty, Oxford University, April.

O'Reilly, J. (1992a), 'Where do you draw the line? Functional Flexibility, Training and Skill in Britain and France' *Work, Employment and Society*, vol.6, no.3, pp.369-396.

O'Reilly, J. (1992b), 'Subcontracting in Banking: Some evidence from Britain and France' *New Technology, Work and Employment* vol.7 no.2, pp.107-115.

O'Reilly, J. (1992c), 'The Societal Construction of Labour Flexibility' in Whitley, R. (ed.), *European Business Systems*, Sage, London.

O'Reilly, J. (1992d), 'Banking on Flexibility: A Comparison of Employment Strategies in the British and French Retail Banking system' *The International Journal of Human Resource Management*, vol.3 no.1, pp.35-58.

O'Reilly, J. (1992e), 'Comparaison des stratégies d'emploi flexible dans le secteur bancaire en Grande-Bretagne et en France' *Sociologie du Travail*, no.3/92, pp.293-313.

OECD (1984), *The Employment and Unemployment of Women in OECD Countries*, OECD, Paris.

OECD (1986), *Labour Market Flexibility: Report by a High Level Group of Experts to the Secretary General*, OECD, Paris.

Oliver, N. and Wilkinson, B. (1988), *The Japanisation of British Industry* Basil Blackwell, Oxford.

Osterman, P. (ed.)(1984), *Internal Labor Markets* MIT Massachusetts.

Ouchi, W. (1981), *Theory Z: How American Business Can Meet the Japanese Challenge* Addison-Wesley, Reading, Mass.

Parker-Jervis, G. (1991), 'Big Five in Crisis' *Sunday Observer*, 6th January.

Parsons, D. (1990), 'Winning Workers: Rising to the demographic challenge.' in *Employment Gazette*, February.

Payne, S. L. (1980), *The Art of Asking Questions* Princeton, New Jersey.

Penn, R. (1992) 'Flexibility in Britain during the 1980s: Recent Empirical Evidence', in Gilbert, N. et al. *Fordism and Flexibility*, London: Macmillan.

Pépin, M. and Berges, S. (1984), *Le Temps Partiel*, ANACT lettre d'information no.85, avril.

Pernet, F. (1988), 'La Place Financière de Paris' in *Le Mois* 3/88

Peschar, J. (1982), 'Quantitative Aspects in Cross-National Comparative Research: Problems and Issues' in Nießen, M. and Peschar, J. *International Comparative Research* Pergamon Press, Oxford

Peters, T. (1992), *Liberation Management* KNOPF, California

Pfau-Effinger, B. (1993), 'Modernisation, Culture and Part-time Employment: the Example of Finland and West Germany' *Work, Employment and Society* vol.7, no.3 pp.383-410.

Piore, M. and Sabel, C. (1984), *The Second Industrial Divide: Possibilities for Prosperity* Basic Books, New York.

Platt, J. (1988), 'What can case-studies do?' in Burgess, B. (ed.) *Studies in Qualitative Methodology* vol.1 JAI Press Ltd, London, Connecticut.

Plenk, H. (1987), 'Evolution des Postes de Travail Bancaires' *Bancatique*, no.32, Nov.

Pollert, A. (ed.)(1991), *Farewell to Flexibility?* Oxford, Blackwells.

Pollert, A. (1990) Book Review of Boyer, R. (ed.) The Search for Labour Market Flexibility: The European Economies in Transition. in *British Journal of Industrial Relations* 28,1, pp.129-131.

Pollert, A. (1989), 'L'entreprise flexible: réalité ou obsession?' *Sociologie du Travail* vol. 31, no.1.

Pollert, A. (1987), 'The Flexible Firm: A Model in Search of Reality or a Policy in Search of a Practice?' *Warwick Papers in Industrial Relations*, no. 19, IRRU, Warwick.

Potel, J-Y. (1990), 'France: La Lutte Fratricide' in Bibes, G. and Mouriaux, R. (eds.) *Les Syndicats Européens à l'épreuve* Presses de la Fondation Nationale des Sciences Politiques, Paris.

Prais, S.J. and Wagner, K. (1983), 'Some Practical Aspects of

Human Capital Investment: Training Standards in Five Occupations in Britain and Germany' *National Institute Economic Review*, no.105, August, pp.46-65.

Prandy, K., Stewart, A. and Blackburn, R. (1982), *White Collar Work* Macmillan, London.

Przeworski, A. and Tuene, H. (1973), 'Equivalence in Cross-National Research' in Warwick, D. and Osherson, S. *Comparative Research Methods* Prentice-Hall, Englewood Cliffs, N.J.

Purcell, J. and Sisson, K. (1983), 'Strategies and Practices in the Management of Industrial Relations' in Bain, G.S. (ed.) *Industrial Relations in Britain* Basil Blackwell, Oxford.

Quack, S. (1992), *Dynamik der Teilzeitarbeit: Implikationen für die sozial Sicherung von Frauen* Sigma, Berlin

Quack, S., O'Reilly, J. and Hilderbrandt, S. (1993), *From national to sectoral production regimes: the case of training in banking in Britain, Germany and France* paper presented to conference on "National Production Regimes" WZB, Berlin July.

Queme, P. (1989), 'Banque-SSII: Quelle Sous-traitance?' *Technologies Bancaires Magazine*, no. 113, mars-avril.

Rajan, A. (1984), *New Technology and Employment in Insurance, Banking and Building Societies: Recent Experience and Future Impact* IMS, Brighton.

Räsänen, K. and Whipp, R. (1992), 'National Business Recipes: A Sector Perspective' in Whitley, R. (ed.) *European Business Systems*, Sage, London.

Reed, B. (1988), 'Banker or Retailer?' Ernest Sykes Memorial Lecture, *Banking World*, June.

Reissert, B. (1993), 'National Unemployment-Support Schemes in the EC' *Employment Observatory* inforMISEP no.43 Autumn pp. 19-27.

Reynaud, J-D. (1989), *Les Régles du Jeux: L'action collective et la régulation sociale* Armand Colin, Paris.

Roberts, K.H. (1970), 'On looking at an Elephant: An Evaluation of Cross-Cultural Research Related to Organisations' *Psychological Bulletin*, 74, pp.327-50.

Roberts, C., Finnegan, R. and Gallie, D. (eds.)(1985), *New Approaches to Economic Life* MUP, Manchester.

Robinson, O. and Wallace, J. (1984), *Part-time Employment and Sex Discrimination Legislation In Great Britain* Department of Employment Research Paper, no. 43, DE, London.

Robinson, O. (1979), 'Part-time Employment in the European

Community.' *International Labour Review* vol. 118, no.3 May-June.

Rose, M. (1985), 'Universalism, culturalism and the Aix group: promise and problems of the societal approach to economic institutions' in *European Sociological Review*, vol.1, no.1.

Rosenberg, S. (1989), 'From Segmentation to Flexibility' *Labour and Society*, vol.14, no.4.

Rosser, M. and Mallier, T. (1983), 'Part-Time Working: Employment Conditions and the Trade union response' *Employee relations* vol. 5, no. 2.

Rubery, J. (1993), *The UK Production Regime in Comparative Perspective* Paper presented to the International Conference on Production Regimes in an Integrating Europe, WZB, Berlin, July.

Rubery, J. and Fagan, C. (1992) 'Occupational Segregation and Part-time work: some evidence from the European Community', UMIST: mimeo.

Rubery, J. (1992), 'Productive systems, international integration and the single European market' in Castro, A., Méhaut, P. and Rubery, J. (eds.) *International Integration and Labour Market Organisation* Academic Press, London.

Rubery, J. (1989), 'Precarious Forms of Work in the UK' in Rodgers, G. and Rodgers, J.(eds.) *Precarious Jobs in Labour Market Regulation: The Growth of Atypical Employment in Western Europe* International Institute for Labour Studies, Geneva.

Rubery, J. (ed.)(1988), *Women and Recession* Routledge and Kegan Paul, London.

Rubery, J. (1988a), 'Employers and the Labour Market' in Gallie, D. (ed.) *Employment in Britain* Basil Blackwell, Oxford.

Rubery, J. and Wilkinson, F. (1981), 'Outwork and Segmented Labour Markets' in Wilkinson, F. (ed.) *Dynamics of Labour Market Segmentation* Academic Press, London.

Rubery, J. (1978), 'Structured Labour Markets, Worker Organization and Low Pay' *Cambridge Journal of Economics*, vol. 2, pp.17-36.

Ryan, P. (1981), 'Segmentation, duality and the internal labour market' in Wilkinson F (ed.) *The Dynamics of labour market segmentation* Academic Press, London.

Sarrazin, B. (1987), 'L'évolution des concepts d'architecture informatique dans les grands réseaux bancaires' *Analyse Financière* -2e trimestre.

Savage, M. (1989), *Career Structures and Managerial*

Hierarchies: *The case of Lloyds Bank 1870-1950* mimeo University Surrey (july).

Schecter, D. (1994) *Radical Theories: Paths Beyond State Socialism and Social Democracy*, Manchester University Press: Manchester.

Schmid, G., Reissert, B. and Bruche, G. (1992) *Unemployment Insurance and Active Labor Market Policy: An International Comparison of Financing Systems*, Wayne State University Press: Detroit.

Schmid, G. (1993), Equality and Efficiency in the Labour Market: Towards a Socio-Economic Theory of Cooperation in the Globalizing Economy *The Journal of Socio-Economics* vol.22, no.1, pp.31-67.

Schoer, K. (1987), 'Part-Time Employment: Britain and W. Germany' *Cambridge Journal of Economics*, vol 11.

Schömann, K. and Kruppe, T. (1993), *Fixed-Term Employment and Labour Market Flexibility - Theory and Longitudinal Evidence for East and West Germany* WZB Discussion Paper FS I 90-204, WZB, Berlin.

Segrestin, D. (1985), 'Trade unions versus power: the French socialist experience after 1981.' in Spyropoulos G (ed.) *Trade unions Today and Tomorrow: Trade Unions in a Changing Europe* vol. 1, Presses Interuniversitaires Européennes, Maastricht.

Sengenberger, W. (1981), 'Labour Market Segmentation and the Business cycle' in Wilkinson, F. (ed.) *Dynamics of Labour Market Segmentation* Academic Press, London.

Shreeve, G. and Alexander, J. (1991), 'My heart belongs to Daddy' *The Banker*, February.

Silverman, D. (1987), *The Theory of Organisations: A Sociological Approach* Gower, Hants. First published in 1970 by Heinemann Educational Books.

Sisson, K. (1987), *The Management of Collective Bargaining: An International Comparison* Basil Blackwell, Oxford.

Smelser, N.J. (1973), 'The Methodology of Comparative Analysis' in Warwick, D. and Osherson, S. (eds.) *Comparative Research Methods* Prentice-Hall, Englewood Cliffs, N.J.

Société pour le Developpement des Techniques Bancaires (1988), *La Banque en Chiffres* AFB, Paris.

Sorge, A. (1994) 'Actors, systems, societal effects and culture: Conceptualising variations in cross-national personnel and organisations', paper presented to the EMOT Group 1 workshop, Humbolt University, Berlin 22-24th March.

Sorge, A. and Warner, M. (1986), *Comparative Factory Organisation: An Anglo-German Comparison of Manufacturing, Management and Manpower* Gower, Aldershot.

Sorge, A. (1982-3), 'Cultured Organisation' *International Studies in Management and Organisation*, vol.12, pp.106-38

Springer, B. (1991), 'Changing patterns of employment for women in banks: case studies of the UK, France and the USA' in Brewster, C. and Tyson, S. (ed.) *International Comparisons in Human Resource Management* Pitman, London

Spyropoulos, G. (ed.)(1985), *Trade unions Today and Tomorrow: Trade Unions in a Changing Europe* vol. 1, Presses Interuniversitaires Européennes, Maastricht.

Steedman, H. and Hawkins, J. (1993), *Mathematics in Vocational Youth Training for the Building Trades in Britain and Germany* NIESR mimeo.

Storey, J. (ed.)(1991), *New Perspectives on Human Resource Management* Routledge, London

Strober, M. and Arnold, C. (1987), 'The Dynamics of Occupational Segregation amongst Bank Tellers.' in Brown, C. and Pechman, J. (eds.) *Gender in the Workplace*, The Brookings Institution, Washington.

Sullerot, E. (1973), *Les Françaises au Travail* Hachette, Paris

Tainio, R. and Santalainen, T. (1984), 'Some Evidence for the Cultural Relativity of Organisational Development Programs', *The Journal of Behavioural Science*, vol.20, no.2, pp.93-111.

Tarling, R. (1987) *Flexibility in the Labour Markets*, London: Academic Press.

Tajan, M. (1990), *Les Entreprises de Travail Temporaire en 1988* INSEE, Paris

Tayeb, M. (1988), *Organisations and National Culture: A Comparative Analysis* Sage, London.

Teague, P. (1990), *The Emergence of A European Industrial Relations Structure?* Paper presented at the Work, Employment and European Society Conference, Newton Park, Bath 6-8th September.

Teyssié, B. (1982), 'Le travail à temps partiel (ordonnance no. 82-271 du 26 mars 1982),' *Droit Social*, no. 5, Mai.

Thurley, K. (1989), 'La 'recherche-action' dans les comparisons internationales' *Sociologie du Travail*, no.2-89.

Tillet, P. (1988), '1992 and All That: A Common Market for

Banks' *Banking World,* June.

Tilly, L. and Scott, J. (1987), *Les femmes, le travail et la famille* Editions Rivages, Marseilles.

Torriani, M. (1988), 'L'économie française se transforme' in *Le Mois,* 3/88.

Truman, C. and Keating, J. (1988), 'Technology, Markets and the design of women's jobs the case of the clothing industry.' in *New Technology, Work and Employment,* vol. 3, no. 1 Spring.

TUC (1983), *Where are the new jobs coming from?* NECD (83), 59 24th November.

Upton, R. (1984), 'The 'home office' and new homeworkers' *Personnel Management,* September.

Vaughan, L. (1990), 'Branchless banking poised to bear fruit' *The Independent,* 12th September.

Vielcanet, F. (1983), 'J. Borel: temps partiel et polyvalence "tirés" par la modernisation.' *Intersocial* no. 94, Août.

Wainwright, H. (1987), 'The Friendly Mask of Flexibility' *New Statesman,* Dec.

Walby, S. (1986), *Patriarchy at Work* Polity Press, Cambridge.

Walby, S. (1989), 'Flexibility and the changing sexual division of labour' in Wood, S. (ed.) *The Transformation of Work?* Unwin Hyman, London.

Walton, J. (1973), 'Standardized Case Comparison: Observations on Methods in Comparative Sociology' in Armer, M. and Grimshaw, A.D. (eds.) *Comparative Social Research* John Wiley, New York.

Warwick, D.P. and Osherson, S. (eds.)(1973), *Comparative Research Methods* Prentice Hall, Englewood Cliffs, N.J.

Watson, G. and Fothergil, B. (1993), 'Part-time employment and attitudes to part-time work' *Employment Gazette,* May, pp.213-220.

Whitehill, A.M. (1991), *Japanese Management: Tradition and Transition* Routledge, London.

Whiteman, J. (1981), *The Service Sector - a poor relation? A Review of its role, performance and prospects in the UK.* NEDO Discussion Paper no.8, NEDO, London.

Whitley, R.(ed.)(1992), *European Business Systems: Firms and Markets in their National Contexts* Sage, London.

Whitley, R. (1992a), *Business Systems in East Asia: Firms, Markets and Societies* Sage, London.

Wilkinson, F. (ed.)(1981), *The Dynamics of Labour Market Segmentation,* Academic Press, London.

Wilks, S. and Wright, M. (1987), *Comparative Government-Industry Relations: Western Europe, the United States, and Japan* Claredon Press, Oxford.

Willcock, J. (1991), 'A recession the big four did not bank upon' *Guardian*, 19th February.

Wilson, D. (1992), *A Strategy of Change* London, Routledge.

Wilson, F. L. (1985), 'Trade Unions and Economic Policy' in Machin and Wright, V. and Machin, H. (eds.) *Economic Policy and Policy Making Under the Mitterrand Presidency 1981-4* Frances Pinter, London.

Wood, L. (1991), 'Banking's age of uncertainty' *Financial Times*, 22nd February.

Wood, S. (ed.)(1989), *The Transformation of Work* Unwin Hyman, London.

Wood, D. and Smith, P. (1992), *Employers' labour use strategies: First Report on the 1987 Survey* Social and Community Planning Research, Department of Employment Research Paper no.63, DE, London.

Woodward, J. (1970), *Industrial Organisation: Behaviour and Control* OUP, Oxford.

Woodward, J. (1965), *Industrial Organisation: Theory and Practice* OUP, Oxford.

Wright, D. and Valentine, W. (1988), *Business of Banking* Second Edition, Northcote House, Plymouth

Wright, V. (1983), *The Government and Politics of France* second edition, Hutchinson, London.

Yeandle, S. (1984), *Women's Working Lives: Patterns and Strategies* Tavistock Publications, London.

Zeldin, T. (1983), *Les Français* Librairie Arthème Fayard, Paris.

Zysman, J. (1983), *Governments, Markets and Growth: Financial Systems and the Politics of Industrial Change* Martin Robertson, Oxford.